PACIFIC

OCEAN

Equator

INDIAN

OCEAN

THE
PINOT NOIR
GRAPE

VIKING

375 HUDSON STREET, NEW YORK, N.Y. 10014

Review Copy

TITLE: PINOT NOIR

AUTHOR: Andrew Barr

PRICE: $20.00

PUBLICATION DATE: January 4, 1993

Kindly send two copies of your review to the Viking Publicity Department.

ERRATA

The third sentence in the last paragraph on p. 67 should read:

'Maybe the Pinot Noir-based sparkling wine which they are proposing to release as "Leighton" in 1994 will silence those who argue that Pinot Noir grown under English conditions is not the ideal grape variety for making sparkling wine...'

In the entry for Domaine de la Pousse d'Or on p. 155, the fourth sentence in the third paragraph should read:

'(The estate used to be named Domaine de la Bousse d'Or, after the vineyard, but this was changed in 1967 after a decree was passed forbidding an estate from calling itself after one vineyard if it also included other vineyards...'

GUIDES TO GRAPE VARIETIES

PINOT NOIR

Andrew Barr

Series editor: Harry Eyres

VIKING

VIKING

Published by the Penguin Group
Penguin Books Ltd, 27 Wrights Lane, London W8 5TZ, England
Penguin Books USA Inc., 375 Hudson Street, New York, New York 10014, USA
Penguin Books Australia Ltd, Ringwood, Victoria, Australia
Penguin Books Canada Ltd, 10 Alcorn Avenue, Toronto, Ontario, Canada M4V 3B2
Penguin Books (NZ) Ltd, 182–190 Wairau Road, Auckland 10, New Zealand

Penguin Books Ltd, Registered Offices: Harmondsworth, Middlesex, England

First published 1992
1 3 5 7 9 10 8 6 4 2

Set in 9/12 pt Linotron Janson Text 55 by Wyvern Typesetting Ltd, Bristol
Printed in Great Britain by Butler & Tanner Ltd, Frome and London

A CIP catalogue record for this book is available from the British Library

ISBN 0-670-82514-X

CONTENTS

MAPS

FOREWORD

For many wine-makers, especially in the New World, Pinot Noir is what space was for the Americans in the 1960s: the Final Frontier, the ultimate challenge, the Holy Grail. It is not difficult to see what makes Pinot Noir so desirable. This grape produces simply the most delicious, sensuous, overwhelming red wines in the world. Claret may be the ultimate intellectual challenge, but even claret-lovers usually admit that the wine which most excited their senses was a great burgundy. The appeal of burgundy is shamelessly physical. Those inimitable scents of rooty decay, graced with fleeting suggestions of violets or strawberries, called forth perhaps the most scandalous tasting note of all time: Anthony Hanson's 'great burgundy smells of shit'. The trouble is, great burgundy is damnably difficult to find. Neither has the quality–price ratio improved since James Thurber drew the cartoon in which a host told his guests, 'It's a naive domestic burgundy, with no great breeding, but I think you'll be amused by its presumption', and a newspaper wit changed the last four words to 'astonished by its price'. As for imitations of burgundy, the success rate among makers of New World Pinot Noir has been vastly lower than that achieved with Cabernet Sauvignon and Chardonnay. Perhaps its rarity gives Pinot Noir added cachet.

So what is it that makes Pinot Noir so problematic? The grape is a tricky one to grow. The vine itself is so prone to mutation that it can start producing grapes which are not red but white or pinkish-grey. The ripening process is very delicately poised, much more so than that of Cabernet Sauvignon. Pinot Noir grapes are never very rich in colour: pick them under-ripe and the wine will have barely enough hue to be called *rosé*; pick them over-ripe (hardly ever a problem in Burgundy) and the flavours turn to mushy jam.

But it is in the winery that Pinot Noir poses the most demanding questions. This is not a grape that needs to be mauled about, like Cabernet Sauvignon. Just as its skin is thinner, its flavours are more delicate. Too much maceration and the wine turns stewy; too little and it lacks the substance to qualify as a red wine. Too hot or too cool a temperature can ruin everything. Oak must be used with the utmost care: whereas great Cabernet Sauvignon can be made and matured in American oak barrels, Pinot Noir demands the finest-grained oaks from France.

Pinot Noir is the most controversial of all wine grapes, and Andrew Barr, a born controversialist, leaps into the questions of massal versus clonal selection, of the benefits and dangers of pre-fermentation maceration, of the importance or irrelevance of soil, with infectious relish. Though Burgundy can often seem the most closed and traditional of wine regions, Barr reveals that intense debates and daring experiments are being conducted behind the solid stone walls of Vosne-Romanée, Beaune and Nuits-St-Georges. He provides what is surely the most up-to-date, fearlessly critical and penetrating guide to the best red burgundies.

This is not just a guide to Burgundy, however. Pinot Noir may not have travelled as successfully as Cabernet Sauvignon or Chardonnay, but there are signs that its secrets are being cracked outside its homeland. The New World region which has made the most news with Pinot Noir is Oregon, on roughly the same latitude as Burgundy and with a not dissimilar climate. Barr shares my suspicion that Oregon Pinot Noirs may not always have lived up to the hype which greeted them in the mid-1980s, but he gives comprehensive coverage of a region far removed from the glitter of the Napa Valley. For years the fashion was to decry California Pinot Noirs: the climate was too hot, the soil wrong, the wine-making insensitive. All that has now changed: even Oregonian wine-makers now admit that the best Pinot Noirs coming out of America are Californian. Andrew Barr charts an extraordinary change in the Golden State, where as recently as the late 1970s wineries sold Pinot Noir as Gamay Beaujolais; now the touchstone Robert

Mondavi Winery is as proud of its Pinot Noir Reserve as of its Cabernet Sauvignon.

In Australia Pinot Noir has shone fitfully: the success of Tyrrells in the 1979 Gault-Millau Wine Olympiad seemed a flash in the pan. But the efforts of James Halliday, both as wine-maker and wine-writer, have established the Yarra Valley outside Melbourne as a serious Pinot Noir stronghold. In Andrew Barr's view Tasmania has the most exciting potential for the grape of any Australian region. However, if cool climate really is essential for Pinot Noir, then New Zealand must be the Shangri-La – but so far achievement is a long way behind promise.

Amid all this talk of the New World the few European regions outside Burgundy where good Pinot Noir is produced are in danger of being forgotten. In Champagne, of course, Pinot Noir is arguably the most important of the three grapes which go to produce the world's finest sparkling wines – now being imitated, with increasing confidence, in California, Australia and New Zealand. Returning from fizzy white to still red wine, the most significant and surprising European Pinot Noir producer outside France is Germany, where skilled vine-growing wine-makers such as Rainer Lingenfelder and August Kesseler have had striking success. Spain, at the other extreme of Europe, is an equally unexpected source of good Pinot Noir, but the ingenious Miguel Torres is making excellent wine from high-altitude vineyards in the Upper Penedès, and Raimat richer, riper Pinot from the hotter flatlands outside Lérida. Burgundy may still be inimitable, but the Pinot Noir is perhaps undergoing yet another of its mutations, and turning into a cosmopolite.

Harry Eyres

PREFACE

The greater part of this book has been given over to gazetteer entries for the main regions and vineyards producing wines from the grape variety in question.

The selection of entries is dependent to a certain extent on my travels. I have been to California and Oregon but not to Australia and New Zealand. This is one reason why America has been given more attention – although, equally, the reason why I have visited America but not Australasia is that the production of Pinot Noir in the former is currently at a more rarefied level.

I have, however, met wine-makers from Australia and New Zealand when they have visited Britain. One of the strengths of this book, as of others in the series, is that I have either visited the estates or met the producers personally or – in most cases – both. There are five exceptions. If anyone would like to guess which ones they are and send his or her suggestions to Viking, I should be happy to reward a correct answer with a good bottle of Pinot Noir.

I have visited many more estates and tasted many more wines made from Pinot Noir than I have been able to discuss here. I have tried to include as many of the world's serious Pinot Noirs as possible. Where it has been necessary to eliminate countries, regions or individual producers this has been done either because they are not good, or because they are not interesting, or because they are new and have as yet no track record. The exception is Austria, which I have omitted for reasons of morality. Unlike South Africa, I believe that there is no evidence that Austria is making efforts to reject its racist past.

Andrew Barr

ACKNOWLEDGEMENTS

I have mostly travelled alone and at my own expense. I am therefore especially grateful to:

Denis Burger, owner of Yamhill Valley Vineyards, for the loan of his house and dog, and his marketing manager, David Rice, for helping to arrange my appointments in Oregon;

the barrel-broker Mel Knox, who accompanied me during my first few days in California and has kept up a constant stream of information and criticism ever since; Dick Ward of Saintsbury; and the Wine Institute of California, which paid for my flight from London to San Francisco and for the hire of a very large automobile;

Rainer Lingenfelder, for organizing my trip to Germany and acting as my translator;

the famously hospitable wine-brokers Becky Wasserman and Russell Hone, with whom I stayed in Burgundy for two weeks one winter; the normally grey wine-broker Roy Richards, for his brief emergence from the shadows; Karen Freeman, who accompanied me on two of my trips to Burgundy although she had no interest in the wines; and Catherine Manac'h of Food and Wine from France, for putting me in touch with Jean-Charles Servant of the Comité Interprofessionnel des Vins de Bourgogne and his secretary Claudine, who organized my schedule on several visits to the region.

I should also like to thank Tony Aspler, Garry Crittenden, Michael Fridjhon, James and Suzanne Halliday and Johanna Ryan, for their advice.

This book is dedicated to Randolph and Bettina, who have provided me with constant companionship and stimulation back home.

INTRODUCTION

The Pinot Noir grape variety is native to Burgundy and is single-handedly responsible for the red wines produced there. At its best, red burgundy is the finest wine in the world.

'Let there be no doubt about it, burgundy at its best overtops claret at *its* best,' wrote the Irish barrister and wine connoisseur Maurice Healey in *Stay Me With Flagons*, published during the Second World War. 'You can drink claret of the highest class several times in the year. You will be lucky to drink four or five bottles of truly first-class burgundy in your whole life. But I, a devotee of Bordeaux, solemnly declare that the three greatest bottles I have ever tasted were all from Burgundy.'

Claret – red Bordeaux – and red burgundy appeal in very different ways. Claret, especially when it is made principally from the Cabernet Sauvignon grape, is more tannic and austere in its youth; it has a better backbone and a more rigorous structure. It appeals to the intellect. Burgundy is softer, lusher, more exuberant, more exciting. It appeals to the senses.

This distinction explains why claret has been better appreciated in Britain. British wine connoisseurs have sought to justify their avoidance of red burgundy by pointing to its inconsistency. They say that you have to spend £500 (about $800) to buy a good bottle of burgundy – because only one in twenty is worth the money.

They are right. It is easy to waste a large sum of money on a dreadful, defective bottle of red burgundy bearing the prestigious label of a *premier* or *grand cru* vineyard. The inconsistency of red burgundy can be attributed partly to the climate, which is much less reliable even than that of Bordeaux, and partly to the varying degrees of competence of the producers: whereas most clarets are made by trained wine-makers on big professional estates, the majority of red burgundy is still produced by small peasant farmers, using methods which have been passed down from father to son.

The main reason for the inconsistency of red burgundy, however, is the grape variety used. If the climate and the wine-making abilities of the producers were really such a problem, then white burgundies would be as unreliable as red ones, but they are not.

The challenge of growing Pinot Noir has led many vine-growers in California, Oregon, Australia, New Zealand and South Africa to try to make it into fine wine. Most of them have failed. The region outside Burgundy which has so far achieved greatest success with the variety is probably Oregon, where the first Pinot Noir vines were planted only in the 1960s. Already Oregon has established a reputation for copying the incon-sistency of red burgundy as well as, in a few instances, its greatness.

The reason why Pinot Noir is so difficult to make is that it requires a completely different approach from other varieties. For trained wine-makers it is simple enough to make a good, complex Chardonnay. Complexity can be built in by ferment-ing it in cask, keeping it on its lees and ageing it in oak. For the same trained wine-makers, however, it is much harder to make a serious Pinot Noir – because they will have to forget all their wine-making techniques.

The point about Pinot Noir is that it makes itself. The repu-tation of Oregon for Pinot Noir has been created principally by David Lett of the Eyrie Vineyards. Lett is a perfectionist who sleeps in the winery while the grapes are fermenting so that he can punch the cap of grape skins down into the juice every two hours round the clock. Yet he claims no credit for his wines. 'I'm the caretaker here,' he said. 'My philosophy is to keep my hands off the wine so that I don't screw it up.' He describes this method as 'the lazy man's method to make wine'. He is wrong, of course. Every little detail matters, much more than with Chardonnay – or Cabernet Sauvignon.

Tony Soter makes a great Cabernet Sauvignon at Spotts-woode, a fine nineteenth-century country house and garden in St Helena in the Napa Valley in California. His success with

Cabernet Sauvignon has been made possible by his experiences with Pinot Noir. In 1980 he started making Pinot Noir as a 'vehicle to study red wine characteristics'. He sold the wine under the name *Étude* – which means 'study' in French. By the end of the decade he had concluded that good Pinot Noir is more difficult to make than good Cabernet Sauvignon. He believes that 'Cabernet survives successfully on the exuberance of its fruit – it forgives a lot of sins. What are small distractions with Cabernet become serious flaws with Pinot Noir.'

Unless the right clone of Pinot Noir is grown on the right training system in exactly the right climate and picked at precisely the right time, the wine that is made from it will not be successful. The margin for error is very small. If the grape is wrong, then the wine will be wrong – regardless of the skills of the wine-maker. 'All you do in wine-making,' says Frédéric Mugnier, the owner of Château de Chambolle-Musigny in Burgundy, 'is transform the grape. In fact, you can't do that – you can only take part of what is in the grape. You can't add anything to the grape – you can only take away as little as possible.'

Pinot Noir: A Cool-Climate Grape?

Pinot Noir is the fine-wine variety that has been grown with the least success in the New World. The principal reason for this is that it has been grown in excessively warm climates.

In order to produce fine wine vines need to enjoy as long a growing season as possible. Plants produce their best, most complex fruit at their cultivable limits – that is why Spanish oranges tend to be better than North African ones, French olives better than Spanish ones and English apples better than French ones.

It is pretty obvious where Pinot Noir's cultivable limit lies. It makes excellent red wine in Burgundy but, 150 miles to the north in Champagne, it very rarely ripens sufficiently to produce red wine and is turned into a sparkling one. The ideal climate for Pinot Noir is therefore one that is similar to Burgundy's.

To people living in Britain Burgundy may seem warm, but in vine-growing terms it has a cool climate. A cool climate can best be defined as one in which wine-makers usually have to warm up the grapes if they want them to begin fermenting at once and in which a heat-exchange mechanism to keep the fermentation temperature below the safety level of 35°C is not generally needed. A warm climate is one in which temperature control is almost always necessary.

In the 1950s and 1960s vine-growers in California and Australia planted Pinot Noir, a grape which produces its finest wine in a cool climate, in decidedly warm regions – such as the Hunter Valley in New South Wales in Australia, where Pinot Noir ripens in January (the equivalent of harvesting in July in the Northern Hemisphere).

They did this because they did not think the climate mattered. Both the American and Australian wine industries have been founded upon a belief in the ability of technology to override all other considerations. They have made perfectly good Chardonnays from grapes grown in excessively warm climates, so why not perfectly good Pinot Noirs?

They have been supported in their views by the very good Pinot Noirs that have been made in warm climates – by Tyrrell in the Hunter Valley and by Calera and Chalone in the Gavilan Mountains in California. In these three cases, however, another important factor is at work. The climate may not resemble Burgundy but the soil – which is limestone – does. (See the following section.)

They have also effectively been prevented from choosing climates as cool as Burgundy by the law against chaptalization (the addition of sugar to the grapes before fermentation in order to increase the wine's eventual alcohol content, named after Jean-Antoine Chaptal, Napoleon's industry minister, who was the first man to explain the method in print). In Burgundy the grapes very rarely ripen fully: chaptalization has been necessary in all but half a dozen vintages in the last generation. In Australia and California, however, vine-growers who wish to obey the law have to choose climates warm enough to ripen the grapes fully each year. If the grapes are not ripe enough, their only option is to turn them into sparkling wines – as is done, for example, by Ted Bennett at Navarro in the relatively cool Anderson Valley in California.

In Oregon and New Zealand chaptalization is permitted – one reason why growers there can plant grapes in cooler climates and why, as a result, they have better potential to produce top-class Pinot Noir. Oregon certainly has a cool climate. In 1966, when David Lett planted the first Pinot Noir vines at the Eyrie Vineyards in the Dundee Hills in the Willamette Valley, it was in the face of advice that the grapes would not ripen. Lett proved that advice wrong – with such success that many later arrivals to Oregon have paid him the ultimate compliment of buying land as close to his as possible.

When Lincoln and Joan Wolverton planted Salishan Vineyard, however, they sited it fifty miles away from Lett, at the cooler, northern end of the Willamette Valley, just over the border in Washington. The reason why they did so was that Lincoln Wolverton had compared the temperatures of the Dundee Hills in Oregon and the Côte d'Or in Burgundy and concluded that Oregon was warmer, with maximum daytime temperatures 3°C or 4°C higher.

Oregon is cool, but it is not that cool: it is not as cool as Burgundy, which is not necessarily a bad thing. The example of Burgundy is hardly capable of inspiring vine-growers who have to make saleable wines every year in order to meet the interest payments on their bank loans. During the 1960s and 1970s in Burgundy one vintage in three was a complete disaster.

Tony Smith, one of the owners of Plantagenet Wines in Mount Barker, Western Australia, grows Pinot Noir in a climate that is warmer than that of Burgundy, and more like that of Bordeaux. 'If the French were more open-minded,' he says, 'you would find that Pinot Noir would probably grow just as well in Bordeaux as in Burgundy.'

It can be argued that the reputation of Burgundy is more a

product of political geography than of soil or climate. This thesis was propounded by Roger Dion in a history of vine-growing in France which he published at the end of the 1950s.

The reputation of Burgundy was essentially a creation of the late fourteenth and early fifteenth centuries. The Valois Dukes of Burgundy employed what were then called the wines of Beaune in order to enhance their prestige, first in their rivalry with the Dukes of Bourbon and then – when they had thoughts of acquiring a kingdom of their own – against the King of France himself.

They ensured that their wines were served in copious quantities at the most brilliant festivals as well as at the King's table. They may never have won a kingdom of their own but it was, says Dion, 'the propaganda triumph of the Valois Dukes of Burgundy that the wines of Beaune were established as the finest in the world'.

The Importance of Soil

The importance that wine-makers attribute to the soil in which their vines grow depends upon the side of the Atlantic on which they are standing.

Most American wine-makers attribute greater influence on the taste of a wine to the climate than to the soil. This is because they are pragmatists. They consider that everything in life is measurable. They believe that the climate can be measured, whereas the soil cannot. French wine-makers, on the other hand, have a tendency to believe that only those elements that cannot be measured are important. They uphold the supremacy of soil over climate. They are romantics who believe in their birthright, in the quasi-mystical qualities of their soil. Who is right?

Dick Graff, the owner of Chalone Vineyards, is an exception who proves the rule, a Californian who thinks like a Frenchman, which is why he bought Chalone, where the vines are planted on limestone – a rarity in California.

Pinot Noir is grown in Burgundy on limestone subsoil – the result of its having been covered for eighty million years by shallow seas. Limestone rock was formed from petrified shell-fish and from the precipitation of carbonate of lime from sea-water. By contrast, the main vine-growing area of Oregon – the Willamette Valley in the north-west of the state – was lifted out of the sea twenty million years ago by the tectonic action of the earth's plates. The soil is young and volcanic. There is no limestone at all.

Some marvellous Pinot Noirs have been produced in Oregon, but, when I asked Graff what he thought of them, he replied, 'They have not made Burgundian Pinot Noirs in Oregon.' 'The point of having limestone,' he added, 'is that you can make Burgundian wines. The Burgundian quality comes from the soil.'

Most other vine-growers, not just in California but in the New World generally, disagree with Graff. 'I don't believe the soil argument for one second,' says James Halliday, Australia's leading wine-writer and a producer of Pinot Noir at Coldstream Hills in the Yarra Valley in Victoria. 'Coonawarra is warmer than the Yarra Valley but it is not a hot region. There is a solid bed of chalk – the famous terra rosa – limestone stained with iron. It is very good for sparkling wine but the Pinot Noir has been bad there ever since 1893. The Yarra Valley has limestone but not where the vineyards are. It produces the best Pinot Noir in Australia. Climate is infinitely more important than soil type.'

One would have thought that the difference of opinion between Graff and Halliday could easily be answered by asking a soil scientist. So I wrote to Bailey Carrodus, who produces perhaps the finest Pinot Noir in Australia at Yarra Yering, also in the Yarra Valley, and who used to work for the government as a plant physiologist. I asked him how soil types affect wine flavour. He replied that he had no idea. 'Soil science,' he explained, 'is not well advanced. We do not yet understand the underlying principles.'

This said, it is possible to understand the advantage in planting vines on limestone subsoil, as it stops the plant from growing too vigorously and producing too many leaves and grapes. The calcium in the limestone sequestrates the magnesium needed for photosynthesis, so the plant struggles and produces a small crop. This explains the difference between red burgundies and many New World Pinot Noirs. The soil in Burgundy is infertile. It was only planted with vines because rich soils were reserved for food production, as was historically the custom in Europe.

The same is not generally true in the New World. 'Nothing does well when it is struggling,' said Mark Rattray, then the wine-maker at St Helena in Canterbury on the South Island of New Zealand, in an interview with the British *Wine & Spirit* magazine. 'The best fruit will always come from well-nourished, good soil. Nothing is better for being starved of moisture or nutrients.'

It was the 1982 vintage from St Helena – only the second crop from the vineyard – that put New Zealand Pinot Noir on the map. As they have matured, however, the wines have got worse – when usually one would expect them to get better. The vines have been allowed to grow too vigorously, to develop large canopies of foliage and to produce correspondingly excessive quantities of fruit. These problems may be connected with the fact that the estate is only 150 feet above sea level and there is a high water table underneath. It is possible that as the roots have grown they have reached the subterranean water supply and that the vines grow too easily as a result.

On the other hand, some of the vine-growers outside Burgundy who have chosen to plant their Pinot Noir vines on limestone subsoil have done so not because it encourages the drainage of water but for precisely the opposite reason. Limestone can be compared to a sponge: it both drains well *and* retains water, releasing it slowly during the growing season. It has therefore been favoured by vine-growers such as Miguel Torres in Spain, Gary Farr at Bannockburn Vineyards in Australia and Danny Schuster at Omihi Hills in New Zealand over the alternative of irrigating their vines. The water-retaining properties of limestone have enabled Farr to close-plant a proportion of his vineyard on the Burgundian model, forcing the vines to dig deeper and thus to take up more flavouring elements from the soil. It would not be possible to do this in an irrigated vineyard. (For more on this topic see the introduction to Australia.)

What is clear is that, whatever Dick Graff may say, the part played by limestone has nothing to do with the taste of the soil – *le goût de terroir* – that is found in red burgundies. This characteristic is a product, not of the soil, but of the grape variety.

When I met Aubert de Villaine, the co-owner of the Domaine de la Romanée-Conti, and told him that I was writing a book about Pinot Noir, he said that he was shocked. 'It is the opposite of what burgundy is all about.' What matters in Burgundy, he explained, is the taste of the soil and growing conditions – the *terroir* – of each particular vineyard. Vine-growers in Burgundy have found in Pinot Noir the perfect vehicle to convey this taste. 'Pinot Noir shows the *terroir* more than any other variety because it has no taste of its own. It is a sort of ghost. It is like Rosebud [the sleigh] in the film *Citizen Kane*. It is everywhere and yet it is nowhere. Pinot Noir does not exist.'

His colleague, Lalou Bize-Leroy, appears at first to disagree. 'Pinot Noir does have a taste,' she says. 'But I don't want it. For a wine to taste of Pinot Noir in Burgundy is a mistake. It should express the *terroir*. Only small wines from lesser regions – such as Oregon – taste of Pinot Noir. We have a term for this, *pinotter*. It is pejorative.'

In the spring of 1991 I visited Bize-Leroy's new estate in Vosne-Romanée (Domaine Leroy) and tasted the wines. They were quite outstanding. Comparing two wines from different *premier cru* vineyards, I said that one had more tannin than the other. 'No,' she said, 'it is not tannin that you taste – it is the *terroir*.'

Burgundians can be so obsessed with *terroir* that they leave their reason and judgement behind. Jean-François Bouchard, who runs the merchant company Bouchard Père et Fils, told a journalist from *Wine* magazine a story about one elderly grower who assured Bouchard that his wines had a *goût de terroir*. In fact, they tasted of rot. 'He didn't know any better,' explained Bouchard, 'because he had never tasted his neighbours' wines.'

Clonal Selection

The variety of vine from which wine is made (*vitis vinifera*) is quite different from the wild vine (*vitis labrusca*), which grows naturally in Europe and America. It is not known when or how the wild vine was first transformed into the wine vine. It is known, however, that vines in northern Europe are closer to their wild prototypes than those of southern Europe, where the warmer climate has allowed them to evolve more. Pinot Noir has been described as an 'archaic variety' whose grapes taste similar to those of the wild vine.

Its closeness to the wild vine may help explain why Pinot Noir is unstable – that is to say, its chromosomes are not properly fixed and therefore it has a tendency to mutate. The half-white grape variety Pinot Gris and the white grape variety Pinot Blanc are simply mutations of Pinot Noir – selected from vines that one year, out of the blue, produced white grapes.

This tendency to mutate has its advantages as well as its disadvantages. It has encouraged growers to select and propagate the best mutations – the strongest, healthiest members of the race. The Pinot Noir that we know today is a mutation of what used in Burgundy to be called the Noirien. It is believed that in the fourteenth century a spontaneous mutation – a superior type of the Noirien, with small, tight bunches – was noticed and propagated by a grower. (It is thought that it was given the name Pinot because the bunch is shaped like a pine cone.)

The Pinot Noir that we know today is therefore the product of what is called massal selection. This term describes the process according to which cuttings are taken from a whole mass of plants in a particular vineyard and then propagated. Massal selection reproduces a range of the best plants in a particular vineyard, rather than the single best plant.

In Burgundy today massal selection is increasingly being replaced by clonal selection, in which the plants that are propagated are the children of a single mother and are therefore identical in all important respects. The best-known of the clones available – numbers 113, 114, 115, 667 and 777 – are all descended from individual plants that grew in vineyards belonging to Jean-Marie Ponsot in Morey-St-Denis. The region is converting from massal to clonal selection because many of the vines are diseased. With massal selection, the plants that look the healthiest are chosen – but there is no guarantee that they are free from disease. In the case of clonal selection, tests are carried out in a laboratory on a single plant to ensure that it is healthy.

Clonal selection started at the beginning of the 1960s because of the spread of disease among Chardonnay vines in Côte de Beaune. As a result of the activities of a microscopic root-sucking worm, the plants started to degenerate – to produce fewer and smaller grapes – when they were about fifteen years old, just when they should have been producing their biggest and best harvests. But although the purpose of clonal selection is laudable, it is not clear that it does its job. Today the degeneration of Pinot Noir vines is just as grave a problem as that of Chardonnay. Much of the blame must be laid, not on the vines themselves, but on the rootstock on to which they are grafted to protect them from the appetite of the phylloxera louse.

Since the 1960s the most popular rootstock has been one called SO 4. It has many advantages: it resists disease well, it ripens fruit early and it produces a heavy crop. Unfortunately, it became evident in the mid-1980s that it degenerates after fifteen years: it has lots of small roots, which don't go very deep; it has no real roots; it doesn't grow. Clones planted on SO 4 degenerate like anything else.

If clones do not prevent degeneration, what use are they? Do they in fact perform a negative rather than a positive function?

Many growers fear that if you plant the same clones throughout the Côte d'Or, the wines will taste more similar than they otherwise would. Burgundy will be homogenized. When I met Lalou Bize-Leroy and told her that I was writing a book about Pinot Noir, the first thing she said was, 'I hope you will criticize clonal selection. It is a grave error.' 'What needs to be done,' she explained, 'is a clonal selection of the best vines in every vineyard in Burgundy – not in just one.'

Another advantage of doing a massal selection is that you have a mixture of different plants in your vineyard, some bringing acidity and others fruit, some bringing colour and others tannin. In order to have the same effect with clones, it would be necessary to plant a large number of different clones – all of them selected, in theory, from the same vineyard. In other words, the best type of clonal selection would be almost exactly the same as the massal selection it was meant to replace.

It is even more important to have a clonal mix in a new region than in an old one because it will not yet be evident which clones are best suited to the particular combination of microclimate and soil. Moreover, a clonal mix builds in instant complexity to the wine – which is particularly necessary if a wine is likely to be drunk young, before it has developed secondary aromas because of physical and chemical reactions during ageing in bottle.

In the New World of vine-growing – California, Oregon, Australia, New Zealand and South Africa – however, a clonal mix is difficult to achieve because only a limited number of clones are available. Most of the Pinot Noirs so far produced in New Zealand and South Africa have been made from single clones – called 10/5 and BK 5 respectively – both of which were originally selected for producing sparkling wines. It is remarkable in the circumstances that New Zealand has managed to produce such good, fruity, decently coloured Pinot Noirs.

In Australia roughly a dozen clones are available, but most of them have been imported, not from Burgundy but from the University of California at Davis. Clones are only released for commercial plantation after they have been tested for their health and productivity. The quality of the wine that is made from them is not a consideration. Mediocre but healthy clones have been released; good but slightly virus-infected ones have not.

In theory the new Burgundy clones are virus-free, but the reason why they have not yet been released in Australia is that they are considered to be infected. In the late 1980s the government did appoint an official who said that he would not oppose the entry of some clones with low-level virus infection. One company, Seppelt, managed to get a consignment of Pinot Noir clones as far as the port of Melbourne. But then (according to James Halliday) there was a palace revolution and the official was shunted aside. His replacement accused the French of not knowing how to test for the presence of virus. This led to a diplomatic row, and Seppelt's vines died in quarantine.

In the circumstances it is hardly surprising that the more enterprising vine-growers have smuggled cuttings back from Burgundy in a suitcase. It is probably not coincidental that the vineyard which produces the best Pinot Noir in Tasmania, Moorilla Estate, also happens to be the only one on the island to make wine from Burgundy clones. It was sent ten parcels in 1982, of which three got through Customs successfully. In the opinion of Julian Alcorso, the wine-maker at Moorilla, the wines made from these clones have 'exciting flavours', although they need to be blended with other material to show of their best.

In California, one of the leading producers of Pinot Noir planted part of his vineyard some years ago with cuttings brought over from Romanée-Conti. Unexpectedly, he says that this selection makes very similar wine to the local nursery clone he also grows. David Lett, who was responsible for introducing Pinot Noir into Oregon at the Eyrie Vineyards in 1966, also planted at one point a selection from Romanée-Conti that had been brought into California. 'It made lousy wine,' he says.

Quality versus Quantity

The new Burgundy clones of Pinot Noir were imported into Oregon in 1984 but were not released for five years because they were judged to be slightly infected with virus – an absurd decision as many of the vines growing in Oregon were already infected.

The Abbey Ridge vineyard was planted in 1985 by John Paul of Cameron winery with several types of Pinot Noir including Coury – so called because it had been brought by Chuck Coury, one of the two pioneers of Pinot Noir production in Oregon, from California in the 1960s.

Coury is virused – yet it produces the best fruit at Abbey Ridge and constitutes the dominant part of Cameron's Reserve blend. 'Virus is necessary,' says Paul, 'because it reduces yield.' Coury is the product not of a clonal but of a massal selection: some of the vines are healthier than others; some crop heavily, others lightly and others not at all.

On the other hand, the yield from a plantation of clonally selected vines is generally larger than from a plantation of massally selected ones. 'A clone guarantees us 50 hectolitres per hectare,' explains Maurice Chapuis, a grower in Burgundy with vineyards in the *grand cru* Corton, 'when the legal limit is 35. It is absurd that we are allowed to plant something which produces more than we are allowed. It is a situation that I cannot understand.'

Growers in Burgundy who have planted clones are at liberty to overcrop if they wish, but they will have to send the excess away to be distilled – and what they are allowed to sell as red burgundy will be watery. It makes sense, then, for them to take measures to reduce the crop to its legal limit.

There are two means of doing so. Grapes can be cut out in summer. That is what Chapuis did in 1983. 'The 1982 vintage,' he explains, 'was a very big harvest. In 1983 there were just as many bunches on the plant so I cut out at least two or three bunches in July. In September there was a great deal of rot and I ended up with half the quantity of 1982. It was a huge mistake to have cut out grapes. What I should have done in 1982 was to draw off some juice before fermentation.'

The technique of bleeding juice from the vat before fermentation – the *saignée* – was invented by Max Léglise, the director of the Station Oenologique in Beaune, at the end of the 1960s. Léglise believed that the quality of the wine depends on the ratio of solid to liquid in the fermentation vat. He said that the ratio ought to be one-third solid to two-thirds liquid – and that, if there was too much liquid, then it should be removed from the vat before fermentation begins.

This technique has its critics, however. Bernard Serveau, a vine-grower in Morey-St-Denis, says that it unbalances the wine by accentuating the tannin. In his book on Burgundy Robert Parker cites the great Vosne-Romanée producer Henri Jayer as saying that a *saignée* is nothing but a gimmick whose shortcomings become apparent after the wine has spent five or six years in bottle.

The *saignée* is a desperate measure which is necessary partly because the legal restrictions on production in Burgundy were in force before the new clones were introduced. These restrictions were introduced on the grounds that the soil in Burgundy is so poor that it can only feed a limited quantity of grapes. The maximum crop that is compatible with quality is probably about 40–45 hectolitres per hectare. As we have seen, in Europe wine grapes were only grown on soils that were too poor to produce food crops. The situation is quite different in the New World, however. In the Umpqua Valley in Oregon Scott Henry grows his vines on fertile soil on the valley floor. After carrying out trials with various different yields, he concluded that the plants were balanced at 100 hectolitres per hectare. The vines were so vigorous that if he tried to reduce the yield they would simply send off lateral shoots which would set a second crop.

With traditional methods of vine-training it would not be possible to put enough fruit on each plant to crop 100 hecto-litres per hectare. The grapes would be crowded together and would rot. In the early 1980s Henry developed a training system which he compares to parting hair: he trains the grapes high on wires, with an open space halfway up which allows air to pass through, drying out the fruit and thus preventing rot. What is called the Scott Henry training system has become very popular in New Zealand, where many vineyards have been planted on over-fertile soil.

Crops in the New World have to be higher than in Burgundy – even if the wines suffer from dilution as a result. As vine-growers in the New World never tire of pointing out, most growers in Burgundy have either owned the land they work for generations, or else rent it through an ancient system called *métayage* – sharecropping – in which they give the owner of the land half their crop in lieu of rent.

In the New World vine-growers have purchased and planted the land themselves. The price of their wine must reflect the cost of their investment (including the interest charges they pay to the bank). On poorer soils this may not be possible. At the Santa Cruz Mountain Vineyards in California the vines suffer from drought conditions in summer and the crop averages only 10–15 hectolitres per hectare. A few years ago the owner, Ken Burnap, calculated that it cost him between $50 and $60 a bottle to make Pinot Noir which he was selling for $15. With the sole exception of the much-hyped single-vineyard Rochioli bottling of Williams Selyem, it is not possible to sell a California Pinot Noir at $50 a bottle.

For a *premier cru* or *grand cru* red burgundy, on the other hand, this is a perfectly normal price. It is not strictly true to say that vine-growers in Burgundy have no land costs to pay – these are reflected in death duties. The reason why they can afford to concentrate their wines by reducing their yields is that they can sell them for high prices. These do not reflect the present quality of the wines but rather their historic reputation. Only when wine-makers in the New World have been producing top-quality Pinot Noirs for a hundred years or more will they be able to sell their wines quite so expensively.

Harvesting Pinot Noir

In 1989 Claude Bouchard and his son Jean-François, the directors of Bouchard Père et Fils, one of the most respected merchant companies in Burgundy, were arrested and charged with
two offences: adding an excessive amount of sugar to some of
their 1987s, and adding acidity at the same time. They were
released on a bail of four million francs, which was said to have
been the value of the wine in question. At the time of writing,
the case has not yet come to court. It may well never do so.

What the Bouchards were accused of doing was common
practice in Burgundy: chaptalizing grapes so as to increase the
eventual alcohol content of the wine by 2.5 per cent. (The
maximum increase that is allowed in Burgundy is 2 per cent.)

It is understandable that grapes in Burgundy should need to
be chaptalized. The region is a cool one and the grapes do not
always ripen properly. Vine-growers say that in three vintages
out of four they need to chaptalize the grapes in order that they
should reach the 12.5 per cent or 13 per cent alcohol that is
considered to be the minimum necessary for their preservation.
Light wines, they say, do not keep. The evidence does not
necessarily support them, however. Virgile Pothier in Pommard and Hubert de Montille in Volnay make low-alcohol,
high-acid wines that mature superbly. The problem is that they
taste rather lean and austere in their youth. Alcoholic wines, on
the other hand, taste rich and ripe, but can decline rapidly.

When Comte Odart, an ampelographer (an expert on vine
varieties), visited Burgundy in 1845, he was very surprised to
find that the wine there was less good than the burgundy he had
drunk in Paris. He discovered that the difference was due to the
work of chemists – manufacturers of glucose or of potato sugar,
who had persuaded the Burgundians to add their product to the
must. 'This mixture,' Odart observed, 'gave the wine strength
and colour – so that it might suit common drinkers – but it took
away those qualities which had created the reputation of red

burgundies, denaturing them to such an extent that they were no longer recognizable.'

One reason for picking the grapes early and chaptalizing is to preserve the acidity: grapes lose acidity as they ripen, so early-picked grapes should have higher levels of acidity than late-picked ones. This is why wine-makers in Burgundy are not allowed to add acid at the same time as they add sugar. In theory they should not need to, but, as the Bouchard affair showed, they do.

Pinot Noir in Burgundy can be low in acidity even when it is not ripe. This is related to the fertilization of the soil. In the 1960s representatives of the Alsatian potassium mines – which had been set up by the French government after the Second World War – descended upon Burgundy, carried out soil analyses and told growers that they were suffering from a lack of potassium. Had they read Comte Odart's book, they would have known to beware the unsolicited advice of men of science. But they had no means of knowing that their advisers were wrong. They took their advice, added too much potassium, and the grapes grown in Burgundy are suffering the consequences – a lack of acidity – to this day.

It may also be that a low level of acidity is inherent in the nature of the Pinot Noir grape. It is not an exclusively Burgundian problem. It has led, for example, to the early senescence of some of the vintages of Pinot Noir made in Canterbury in New Zealand by the pioneering St Helena winery.

Pinot Noir relies on acidity for its stability because it has very little tannin, which is the principal preservative of other red wines. In this respect Pinot Noir is more like a white wine than a red one. Adding acidity, however, is just as bad as adding too much sugar. There are naturally several different acids in the grapes, so adding just one type – growers in Burgundy add tartaric, although what they are supposed to use is citric acid – is not going to give the wine the balance it would otherwise have had.

Pinot Noir can be ruined by over-enthusiastic acidification. At the David Bruce winery in the Santa Cruz Mountains in

California I tasted all the Pinot Noirs they had produced between 1982 and 1989. I told the wine-maker, Keith Hohlfeldt, that they were all too acidic. He said that the 3,000-mile journey to the East Coast was enough to soften them up. Well, I took the opened bottles and drove them up to Oregon (600 miles), around Oregon and back in the boot of my car. They were still green and aggressive on my return.

In theory the grapes should simply be picked when they are ripe. But they do not all ripen at the same time. The ones on the top of the bunch ripen before the ones in the middle. 'One should not wait until all the grapes have reached the same degree of maturity,' wrote Abbé Tainturier in the eighteenth century. 'Cooked, roasted and green grapes are all necessary – the green ones bring liveliness to the wine. Experience has taught us that complete maturity produces fat, heavy wines that ooze like oil.'

Some vine-growers in the New World pick Pinot Noir grapes when they are over-ripe because they do not know what ripe grapes taste like. They associate fruit tastes with jelly or jam, which are made from crushed fruit. Pinot Noir grapes may have a taste of raspberries or strawberries – but not the rich, sweet taste of raspberry or strawberry jam. Ripe, uncrushed Pinot Noir grapes taste slightly green.

It may well be, in fact, that Pinot Noir grapes produce their best flavours before they are fully ripe. They may well produce their best wine if they are picked at about 11.5 or 12 per cent potential alcohol – the level they normally achieve in Burgundy – rather than the 13 per cent at which they are generally picked in warmer climates. If so, that is a huge problem for vine-growers in Australia and California because they are not allowed to chaptalize their wines.

One of the most famous sources of Pinot Noir grapes in California is the Rochioli vineyard in Sonoma County, from which only two people are allowed to buy the grapes, Gary Farrell and Burt Williams of Williams Selyem. Gary Farrell takes care to pick the grapes before the acidity level starts to fall. 'I pick the grapes less ripe than Williams Selyem,' he says. 'I pick up to two weeks before they do. I'm looking for ageability. I question the ability of their wines to age.' When I visited Williams Selyem in the spring of 1990 I challenged Burt Williams with Farrell's assertion that his wines did not age. He replied, 'It is deliberately my style to make accessible wines – for people to enjoy in a restaurant. Pinot Noir should be drinkable young.' But then he brought out a bottle of 1982, half of it made from fruit from the Rochioli vineyard. It was delicious.

Colour – A Red Herring

The late André Noblet, who was almost as well known for his sexist comments as for having been manager of the Domaine de la Romanée-Conti, once declared: 'Colour in a beautiful wine is no more important than clothes on a beautiful woman.'

Most wine-drinkers would disagree with him. One reason why wines made from Pinot Noir are difficult to sell in America and Australia is that they are light-coloured. Most wine-drinkers think that the deeper the colour, the better the wine. The Pinot Noir grape does not normally produce a deep-coloured wine because it has a thin skin and thus a relatively low ratio of colouring skin to colourless juice. Moreover, of the two types of colouring pigments (anthocyanins) normally found in grape skins, it has only one.

In the 1980s, however, there appeared in Burgundy a man who was able to produce deep-coloured wines from Pinot Noir – the consultant oenologist, Guy Accad. In order to produce deep-coloured wines Accad advises a cold maceration of the mash of skins and juice for a long period before fermentation. When the grapes come into the winery, some of them are crushed to extract some juice, then they are poured into the fermentation vat. They are cooled, and sulphur dioxide is added. They are allowed to macerate for a week or so before they are warmed up and fermentation begins.

Other growers in Burgundy practise cold maceration – among them Henri Jayer, the most famous small grower of all

– but Accad does so for longer, at a lower temperature, and adds more sulphur dioxide. His wines are much deeper-coloured than those of other people. This may well be attributed to the sulphur dioxide, which acts as an acid to extract the colour.

The sulphur dioxide causes several problems. In particular it blocks the links between tannins so that they do not precipitate out of the wine during fermentation, and therefore the wine is harsher and more tannic. Although much of the sulphur dioxide is dispelled during fermentation, some of it has bound itself on to other molecules and so remains in the wine.

Despite this drawback, many wine-makers in Oregon took up cold maceration in 1989 – after Philippe Senard, one of the growers advised by Accad, came to the annual Pinot Noir conference at Steamboat and talked about it. However, Carol Adams did not try it. 'In Burgundy they need cold maceration to extract fruit,' she explained. 'In Oregon we already have fruit.' (In this respect cold maceration before fermentation resembles warm maceration afterwards, which is discussed in the next section. It is an extraction technique which is useful in Burgundy because the grapes are not fully ripe, but is probably not necessary in America.)

Wines made by Accadian methods taste rather like Beaujolais in their youth – they have aromas of bubblegum and bananas – although they are certainly vastly more concentrated. This character is generally blamed on the cold maceration – but I wonder if it is not the product of low-temperature fermentation. Accad's growers boast that they keep their fermentation temperatures down to about 26°C, compared with a peak of 32°C or more which is normal in Burgundy. They say that by fermenting the grapes at a low temperature they ensure that the aromas stay in the wine and are not blown off.

The problem is, the yeasts suffer too much – and produce aromas which are more typical of Beaujolais than of Burgundy. It is low-temperature fermentation which explains why Oregon Pinot Noirs are not as complex as red burgundies. Most Oregon Pinot Noirs are fermented in small (four by four feet) fruit bins with plastic liners, which were originally developed for picking cherries. Fermentation temperatures in these bins –

which are called totes – do not go above 30°C because there is only a small volume of juice in which the temperature can build up. They produce a lighter, less complex style of wine than do the larger vats (about three times the size) used in Burgundy.

The elegant, approachable style of Oregon Pinot Noir which was established at the beginning of the 1970s by David Lett of the Eyrie Vineyards was a direct consequence of the small size of his fermentation vats. Dick Erath of Knudsen Erath and John Paul of Cameron are two producers who have converted to larger tanks in order to have a hotter fermentation. It may not be a coincidence that they produce two of the most profound and long-lived wines in Oregon. It is not so much heat itself that is important as the fact that the wine ferments at the whole range of temperatures between 25°C – when colour starts to be extracted – and 35°C – when the yeasts are asphyxiated and the wine is in danger of turning to vinegar. Different aromas are produced at each temperature.

The problem with fermenting at above 30°C, however, is that the wine can finish fermenting very quickly, after only four or five days. Some wine-makers do not believe that it is possible to extract enough flavour from the grapes in so short a period. They could, of course, extend the fermentation by keeping the temperature down – but wine-makers who do not want their wines to have the aromas of those produced by the Accadian method have resorted to other means in order to extend either the fermentation period itself or the length of time the wine spends in contact with the grape skins.

Individual entries have been given to the following Accadians:

René Bourgeon
Georges Chicotot
Domaine Clos Noir
Domaine Confuron-Cotetidot
Domaine Grivot
Domaine Pernin-Rossin
Domaine Daniel Senard
Château de la Tour de Vougeot

The Length of Fermentation

The flagship of the Margaret River region in Western Australia is Leeuwin Estate, which was set up at great expense in 1974 by the Perth-based industrialist Denis Horgan. Its Chardonnay has been widely acclaimed and has been sold at an extremely high price. So has the Pinot Noir – although the quality does not justify it.

The wine-maker Bob Cartwright is aware of the problem, which he ascribes to the fact that the grapes ferment too fast. The first vintage in 1980 fermented out to dryness in three to four days and was sold off as a barbecue wine because 'that was all it was good for'. Since then Cartwright has managed to extend the fermentation period to five to six days. That is not enough. The wine lacks extract and backbone, and tastes rather confected.

The problem for producers of Pinot Noir in Australia (and, indeed, in California) is that they are prohibited from extending their fermentation periods the way the Burgundians do. The wine-makers must therefore resort to other methods in order to extend the fermentation period. They could reduce the fermentation temperature, but the defects of this method have been discussed in the previous section.

One option is simply to put whole bunches of grapes – uncrushed – in the fermentation vat. This is, in fact, the historic way of making wine in Burgundy, before crushing machines were invented. André Mussy, an old vine-grower in Pommard who was born at the beginning of the First World War, remembers that his grandfather used to put whole bunches of grapes in the vat, climb in, and tread on them. This broke some of the grapes and got fermentation going, but the majority of grapes remained unbroken during much of the fermentation. So the juice fermented inside the grapes. This type of fermentation – that of the juice inside the grapes – is the standard method by which wine is made today in the Beaujolais, where it is called *macération carbonique*.

Needless to say, burgundies that were traditionally made by whole-bunch fermentation – and still are, at the Domaine de la Romanée-Conti in Vosne-Romanée, at Clos de Tart in Morey-St-Denis, and in the winery of the merchant company Pierre Bourée – did not, and do not, taste like Beaujolais. There is a basic difference between the two methods. With the system of *macération carbonique* practised in Beaujolais, the vat is covered. The fermenting grapes produce carbon dioxide, which is trapped by the top of the vat and sits like a blanket on top of the wine. So the fruit does not come into contact with oxygen. It is the absence of oxygen – plus the low fermentation temperature – which produces the aromas of bubblegum and bananas which are typical of Beaujolais. In Burgundy the vat is not covered, so there is no blanket of carbon dioxide. Any taste of bubblegum or bananas that may have been produced as a result of the juice fermenting inside the grapes is soon dispelled on contact with the air.

The highest-profile proponent of whole-bunch fermentation in Burgundy today is Jacques Seysses of Domaine Dujac in Morey-St-Denis. He bought his estate in 1968, so he does not use this method for reasons of tradition. He says that by putting whole bunches into the vat he has a slower fermentation and more complex wines. 'I try to interfere as little as possible,' he explains. 'You should let nature do its work.'

This is the sort of comment that is made by Burgundian peasants – which is not the class to which Seysses belongs. He is a wine-lover who decided to indulge his hobby by moving to Burgundy and making wines there. An outsider himself, he is open to other outsiders. He has an American wife and speaks English, which is rare among Burgundians. Indeed, he believes that his reputation started because he had the advantage of speaking English.

New World wine-makers who want to learn how Pinot Noir is made in Burgundy tend to go and visit Seysses, and perhaps help with a vintage or two. Seysses's acolytes include Josh Jensen at Calera, the late Joseph Swan in California, James Halliday at Coldstream Hills and Gary Farr at Bannockburn in Australia. Of the four it is Farr who has most directly copied

Seysses's methods. By putting whole bunches into the vat and breaking them up gradually he is able to keep on releasing more sugar and thus to extend the fermentation period to two weeks or more. He produces one of the finest Pinot Noirs in Australia.

In general, however, there is a major drawback with using whole bunches in the New World: the stalks. In Burgundy, at least in good vintages, the stalks are brown and mature; in most vineyards in the New World, in all vintages, the stalks are green and immature. The difference can be explained by the vigour of the vines. In Burgundy, where there are 4,000 vines to the acre, the plants are much more stressed than in vineyards in the New World, where there are 700 or 800. In order to produce the same yield each vine in the New World has to be capable of carrying five times as many grapes as a vine in Burgundy, so it has to be much more vigorous. It may be able to produce riper grapes, but the stalks will still be green.

There are exceptions – such low-yielding, low-vigour vineyards as Bannockburn in Australia (of which one-third is close-spaced on the Burgundian model), Calera and Chalone in California and Seven Springs in Oregon (from which Adelsheim and Drouhin buy grapes) – but on the whole it is not a good idea to ferment whole bunches in the New World because the wines take on a herbaceous taste from the green stalks. The solution which has been found, above all in California but also to a large extent in Oregon, is not to try and extend the fermentation itself but simply to leave the grape skins in the wine after the end of fermentation.

Wine-makers who use this method say that macerating the grape skins in the wine for between one and two weeks after the end of the alcoholic fermentation makes wines taste softer and rounder. No one knows why. The standard theory is that the tannins link up in large chains – polymerize – and therefore taste sweeter. However, Bill Dyer, the wine-maker at Sterling Vineyards in the Napa Valley, who researched this theory while he was studying at the University of California at Davis, could not find any evidence of polymerization. Dyer does not believe that wines get softer. He says that the effect of an extended maceration is simply to extract more from the grapes. It is, he says, useful in France where the grapes are picked less ripe but not in the warmer climate of California.

It is important to avoid extracting too much from Pinot Noir grapes. In 1990 I tasted an experimental wine made by a grower in Nuits-St-Georges who wishes to remain nameless. He heated the wine to 35°C for two days at the end of the maceration in order, he said, to see if he could not extract something extra. This method of hot post-fermentation maceration is one which is used in Bordeaux. The wine had the tannin and structure of a Bordeaux and the fruit of a burgundy: it tasted like a bizarre cross between the two.

Pinot Noir and New Oak

The wines which are sold at the Hospices de Beaune auction in November each year are taken away by their purchasers in the spring. In the spring of 1977, however, it was found that one barrel in five of the 1976 vintage had turned vinegary. The defective wines were repurchased by the Hospices and sent to Dijon for use in mustard manufacture. The problem was that some of the wines had been put into old casks which had not been properly sterilized. In 1977 the Hospices hired a new wine-maker, André Porcheret, who took to maturing the wines entirely in new casks. In order to prevent the wine from being dominated by the flavour of the oak, he developed a technique of washing out the casks with hot water and salt before use. In 1988 Porcheret left the Hospices for Lalou Bize-Leroy's new domaine in Vosne-Romanée, taking his cask-washing technique with him. The wines that are now made at the Hospices are spoilt by an excessive taste of new oak.

The experience of the Hospices demonstrates the difficulty of maintaining a traditional practice in altered circumstances. At the beginning of the century the wines of the Hospices, like those of other growers, were stored in new oak. There were two reasons for this: hygiene and the system by which growers sold wines to merchants. It was standard practice for a merchant to buy both the wine and the cask in which it was stored from the grower. A grower never had any old casks, so had to use new ones each year. (This is precisely what happens today with the Hospices wines.)

Before the Second World War there was no problem in maturing wines in new oak casks because the wines had been made from low-yielding vines and were therefore sufficiently concentrated to cope with the flavours that the oak added to the wine. But yields have increased dramatically since. The historic yield in Burgundy was 20 hectolitres per hectare. In the 1950s it reached 30, in the 1960s it got to 40, and today it is closer to 50. Many of the wines that were made in the 1960s and 1970s were simply not capable of standing up to new oak. This was fortunate, because the growers who started bottling their own wines during the economic crisis in the early 1970s – when the merchants refused to buy their wines – certainly had no money to spare for new casks. New oak fell out of use.

During the 1980s new oak came back into fashion again. This is related to the increasing wealth of producers, who can now afford to pay 2,500 francs for a cask capable of holding 300 bottles' worth of wine. But it is also related to the changing demands of the market. People want wines that they can drink young – and new oak produces wines that are tremendously appealing in their youth. It gives them not only a toasty, spicy character and a taste of vanilla but actual sweetness – unfermentable sugar is extracted from the oak by the solvent action of alcohol. This is why the American importer Robert Kacher encourages growers from whom he buys – Henri Girardin in Pommard, Christian Serafin in Gevrey-Chambertin and Robert Jayer in the Hautes Côtes de Nuits – to mature their wines in new oak. Most American wine-drinkers like to buy wines that they can enjoy immediately.

Many growers criticize the excessive use of new oak. 'You lose the individuality of a wine – its *goût de terroir* – if you mature it in 100 per cent new oak,' says Arnaud Machard de Gramont, a vine-grower in Nuits-St-Georges. 'You don't get

Nuits-St-Georges Les Argillières, you get Nuits-St-Georges Chêne d'Allier [from the Allier forest].' There are producers who age their wines entirely in new oak with complete success – but they are the exceptions that prove the rule because they make, by modern standards, concentrated wines from low-yielding vines. It is no coincidence that the majority of them are in Vosne-Romanée, the village that produces the richest and best wines in Burgundy. They are Henri Jayer and the associated Domaine Méo-Camuzet, Domaine Jean Gros, Domaine Leroy and the Domaine de la Romanée-Conti.

Because Pinot Noir generally produces a delicate, subtle wine, the same rule applies the world over – only the most concentrated wines should be matured in new oak. That explains why new oak works for Williams Selyem in Sonoma County in California (their Rochioli bottling), but not for Joachim Heger in Baden in Germany. This said, most serious producers of Pinot Noir do use some new oak. Many of them renew their casks on a three-year cycle, so that they have a third new oak, a third one year old and a third two years old.

People who use a certain proportion of new oak do not necessarily do so in order to add flavours from the oak to the wine. 'You do not add anything with oak,' says Jacques Lardière, the brilliant wine-maker for the merchant company Louis Jadot. 'You only enhance the aromas. If the oak gives something, it is because the oak is bad.' The pores of new casks are much more open than those of old ones, so there is more exchange between the wine inside and the air outside. This is very important if wine is kept in contact with its lees – as Pinot Noir usually is. The exchange with the outside helps to prevent the development of unpleasant sulphury smells (mercaptans) and to stabilize the colour.

If a wine-maker is cunning, he can achieve a similar effect with old casks. Rainer Lingenfelder, a grower in the Rheinpfalz in Germany, matures his Pinot Noir in casks which he bought second-hand in 1983 from Château Grand Puy Lacoste in Bordeaux. They were mostly made in 1979. Lingenfelder explains, 'We are not interested in oak flavours as such. What matters is that the barrels bring slow oxidation.' The cask-ageing transforms the wine so dramatically that Lingenfelder's 1985 Pinot Noir, the first vintage he made entirely in this way, was rejected by the official tasting board on the grounds that it was not typical of German Pinot Noir. (For further discussion of this question, see the section on Germany.) Lingenfelder achieves this dramatic effect with old casks because he introduces a certain amount of extra oxidation: he replaces the wine that has evaporated only once a month, compared with the once a week that is common in Burgundy. The members of the official tasting board were shocked because they were used to wines that had been matured only in large old casks – in which the exchange with the outside air is minimal.

With Pinot Noir what matters is not so much whether you use a new or an old cask but whether you use a small or a large one. The size of the Burgundy *barrique* may have been established at 225 litres because that was the ideal size for transportation but equally because it was the ideal size for exchange with the outside air. The issue of small versus large oak casks remains a vexed one in Germany. But Karl-Heinz Johner in Baden, who produced his first Pinot Noir in 1985, has no doubts about the necessity of using small ones. 'The Frogs have one up on us,' he says. 'We can avoid thirty years of trying.'

Pinot Noir's 'Barnyard' Aromas

'There is something animal, often something erotic about great burgundy,' wrote Anthony Hanson in his book on the region. He added, in a phrase that will live for ever, 'great burgundy smells of shit.'

Is this 'animal' character a product of the Pinot Noir grape, or of wine-making methods that are practised in Burgundy? These differ in several important respects from those used in the New World. In Burgundy, most producers still ferment their grapes in open wooden vats, about six feet high and eight feet in diameter. During fermentation the grape skins tend to settle and form a cap on the top of the juice. The cap needs to be mixed back into the juice in order to maximize the extraction of colour and tannins and to stop vinegar from developing. The operation of punching down the cap is called *pigeage*. Traditionally it was performed by the wine-maker climbing into the vat.

According to a story told by Edward Ott in *A Tread of Grapes* the monks who used to make the wine at Clos de Vougeot climbed naked into the vats on three occasions during vinification. 'It was the only occasion in the year when the monks had a bath, and for many years after this unhygienic stirring was abandoned it was said that a real burgundy expert could declare by taste whether a wine was pre- or post-*pigeage*.'

There are still many growers in Burgundy who climb naked or semi-naked into the vat, although it is now more common to punch down the cap by hand, with a plunger. The latter method is common in Oregon, where the grapes are normally fermented in small cherry boxes, but in California most producers ferment their Pinot Noir grapes in closed stainless-steel tanks. In this case the cap of grape skins is kept wet by pumping juice taken from the bottom of the vat back over the top.

Fermentation in open wooden vats has survived in Burgundy partly for aesthetic reasons. Maurice Chapuis in Aloxe-Corton is one of the most enlightened of Burgundian wine-makers. When I visited him in 1989 he was complaining about a shortage of space and said that he would have to get rid of his wooden vats and replace them with cement ones. 'I don't want to do so. I find it industrial. It may seem a stupid idea to you but industrial things are for industry.'

Chapuis is not being at all ridiculous. The marketing of the wines of Burgundy depends on the preservation of its antique image – be it the open wooden vats or the cobbled streets of Beaune. There is also a technical reason for fermenting the grapes in open vats (although for this purpose cement vats are just as appropriate as wooden ones). Pinot Noir has lots of big pips. Because they are heavy, they fall to the bottom of the fermentation vat. There is much less alcohol at the bottom of the vat. It is alcohol that extracts the bitter tannin from the pips. If the grapes are fermented in an open vat and the cap is trodden or punched down, the grape pips fall to the bottom of the tank and stay there. Very little tannin is extracted. If the grapes are fermented in a closed stainless-steel vat and juice at the bottom of the vat is pumped back over the cap – or else (in what is called a roto-tank) there is a screw inside the vat which rotates at regular intervals – then too much tannin is extracted from the pips.

The Burgundian merchants Louis Jadot have been experimenting with roto-tanks since 1982. According to their wine-maker, Jacques Lardière, 'In many vintages you get much more extraction and colour from the roto-tanks; traditional open vats only work very well in top vintages but perhaps wine made in them has more aroma.'

This aroma may well have less to do with the different treat-ment of the cap on the top and the pips at the bottom than with the fact that the fermenting juice is exposed to the air. If a grower wants his grapes to be fermented by their natural yeasts, rather than control the fermentation by adding a yeast culture, then he chooses an open tank, so that the yeasts present in the cellar can get to work.

It is possible that much of the character and aroma of red burgundy can be attributed to fermentation with natural yeast strains. Russ Raney corresponded with Henri Jayer in Vosne-Romanée before setting up his winery at Evesham Wood in Oregon. He regards Jayer as his mentor. In 1989 he paid him the ultimate compliment by fermenting a batch of his grapes with yeast which he had taken from the sediment in a bottle of Jayer's burgundy. When I tasted this wine in 1990 I found it to be softer, richer and better knit than wine from the same vineyard fermented with a selected, commercially available yeast strain called Montrachet. In Raney's opinion, 'It has, compared with the other yeast types, a definite Burgundy "barnyard" character.'

Growers in Burgundy describe this 'barnyard character' as being *le goût de terroir*. If it has come into the wine as a result of fermentation with the natural vineyard yeasts, then this description is probably appropriate. There are other means, however, by which red burgundy can develop animal, not to say faecal, aromas. It seems likely that, on the whole, bacteria are responsible. John Middleton, the owner of Mount Mary Vineyard in the Yarra Valley in Victoria, makes some of the most Burgundian Pinot Noirs in Australia yet condemns many of the wines made in Burgundy as 'rubbish'. The problem, he believes, is that they go through their malolactic fermentation when they are already very low in acidity. In these conditions, a bacterium called *Pediococcus* often gets to work on the malic acid, producing unpleasant 'barnyard' aromas.

Jean-Pierre de Smet, the wine-maker at Domaine de l'Arlot in Nuits-St-Georges, recognizes that there is a problem, but believes that it has less to do with the bacteria that involve themselves in the malolactic fermentation than with the bacteria that are present in the lees. 'Burgundies,' he says, 'acquire a gamey taste from spending too long in contact with their lees in cask. It is a defect. I do not want it in my wine.'

De Smet's theory answers several questions. It explains why wines made from Pinot Noir become gamey but those made from Cabernet Sauvignon do not. Pinot Noir is generally kept longer on its lees in cask than, say, Cabernet Sauvignon. Most red wines need oxygenation – to be racked regularly from one cask to another – to develop and soften their tannins. Pinot Noir is quite different. It is a delicate thing, and naturally low in tannin. It does not like oxygen.

De Smet's theory also helps explain why red burgundies taste more gamey than most New World Pinot Noirs. The majority of producers of Pinot Noir in the New World put the wine through its malolactic fermentation immediately after its alcoholic one; red burgundies often do not go through their malolactic fermentation until the next summer. New World producers of Pinot Noir then generally rack the wine immediately after the malolactic fermentation; producers of red burgundies do not always do this. So red burgundies generally spend much longer on their lees than New World Pinot Noirs.

If bacteria are the cause of faecal aromas and gamey tastes, then it is simple enough to explain why these characteristics become more pronounced during ageing in bottle. The bacteria attack the acids and other constituents of the wine and break them down. But these characteristics can be avoided if the wine is either given a sterile filtration or pasteurized before bottling. The first removes, and the second destroys, the bacteria. Unfortunately, these processes denature the wine in other respects. Moreover, it is likely that bacteria perform a positive, as well as a negative, function in the ageing of wine. It has been suggested that large bacteria are harmful, but small ones are beneficial. If so, a light filtration is ideal, as the small bacteria pass through the filters but the large ones do not.

Admittedly, it has not been proven that bacteria play an important rôle during ageing in bottle – but it would certainly explain the effect of cellar temperatures on the ageing of red burgundies. At under 10°C a wine ages too slowly; at 15°C or over it ages too fast. This may well be related to the speed at which the bacteria work. It is, says Gérard Potel of the Domaine de la Pousse d'Or in Volnay, the reason why a cellar should be between 10°C and 14°C.

When to Drink Pinot Noir

It is popularly imagined that red burgundy has always been a full-bodied, long-lived wine. In fact, from its beginnings in Roman times, through its period of greatest glory in the Middle Ages, right up until the end of the eighteenth century, red burgundy was a light wine for drinking young. It only started to become a full-bodied wine at the end of the eighteenth century, in order to suit the vitiated taste of consumers in export markets, particularly in the Low Countries.

Wine-making methods changed. Growers picked the grapes later and therefore riper; if they were still not ripe enough, they chaptalized them. They fermented the wine for longer in contact with its skins, so as to extract more tannin. Often the merchants who bought wines from the growers beefed them up by adding alcohol and full-bodied wines from the Rhône Valley and the South of France. By the end of the nineteenth century red burgundies were big, tannic wines which were at their best at between fifteen and twenty years of age. They were, said the wine-writer P. Morton Shand, 'rather hot, rough and heady if drunk much earlier'.

The style of red burgundy did not change again until after the Second World War. Jean-Marie Ponsot, a vine-grower in Morey-St-Denis, was a young man at the time. 'People were infatuated with modernization,' he explains. 'Growers took to fermenting the wine for a shorter period because that way it could be sold younger. They macerated the skins in the juice for only four days. The wines were a bit like Beaujolais.' In the 1960s and 1970s the fashion for making lighter wines swept across much of Burgundy. 'People talked about money,' says Frédéric Mugnier, the owner of the Château de Chambolle-Musigny. 'They wanted to rationalize the work and to increase the crop. So they planted Pinot Droits – high-yielding vines which were easy to work, but which were not very good.' It was not until the 1982 vintage – when naturally very high yields produced red wines with no more colour than a *rosé* and considerably less taste – that many growers realized that they had gone too far and started to make wines with a little more stuffing. (Ironically, many 1982s have taken on colour and body in bottle and are good to drink now.)

The fuller-bodied red burgundies of today do not resemble the 'hot, rough and heady' wines of the early twentieth century. In general, the grapes are larger, with a higher ratio of juice to skin, so the wine made from them is less tannic. The best modern red burgundies are capable of ageing but can, in most cases, be drunk quite young.

The production of red wine which can equally well be drunk young or old is the Holy Grail for which wine-makers in all countries have been searching. Pinot Noir offers more potential in this respect than many other varieties. Because it is low in tannin, there is nothing to stop you from drinking it young.

Moreover, it often contains a lot of glycerol, which gives an impression of sweetness. On the other hand, Pinot Noir can be rather one-dimensional in its youth. It sometimes seems to be a doughnut wine – fragrant at the start and very long at the finish, but with a hole in the middle. This hole is filled up as a result of chemical and physical reactions during ageing.

It is well worth the wait. Wines made from Pinot Noir can be really pretty in their youth – but so can ones made from such lesser grape varieties as Gamay and Dolcetto. The only justification for paying what are generally very high prices lies in the complexity, finesse and length on the palate that is offered by a mature bottle. Moreover, the wait for a bottle of Pinot Noir to develop is not usually a long one. Because it is naturally low in both tannin and acidity, it matures much sooner than a wine made from Syrah or Cabernet Sauvignon. Pinot Noir is usually mature at between five and ten years of age. This is true even of top wines, such as Vosne-Romanées from Henri Jayer. The best analogy of the difference between young and old Pinot Noir has been offered by Régis Surrel, the wine-maker for the merchant house Faiveley in Nuits-St-Georges. He admits that he makes wines for keeping (*vins de garde*) which people drink young. This, he says, is like building Ferraris which can travel at 200 m.p.h. when on most roads there is a speed limit.

Pinot Noir and Food

'Before the First World War people had no refrigerators,' points out Gérard Potel, the manager of the Domaine de la Pousse d'Or in Volnay in Burgundy. 'People ate game that was high and fish that was not fresh. They cooked heavy sauces to hide the taste of decay. So people drank solid, tannic, acid wines.'

Today, most food is fresher and lighter – and so are the wines. One of the reasons for the development of a lighter style of red burgundy in the 1960s and 1970s was the advent of *nouvelle cuisine*. Most modern red burgundy is too delicate to be drunk with dishes with which burgundy was traditionally associated – essentially peasant cooking such as *boeuf bourguignon* and *coq au vin*. Nor does it stand up to strong Burgundian cheeses such as Époisses and Cîteaux. The same is true of Pinot Noirs from elsewhere in the world.

Pinot Noirs may be too light to cope with rich foods, but they are surprisingly successful with spicy ones. I have found Thai cuisine, for example, to bring out hidden depths in apparently delicate Pinot Noirs, whilst making bigger wines seem awkward and unsatisfying. Because they are intense in flavour, yet light in body and low in tannin, Pinot Noirs are generally more versatile than other red wines. It is the tannins in those which react badly with fish, producing a metallic taste, and which taste very aggressive when they are drunk with duck – but duck brings out the sweetness in wines made from Pinot Noir.

Because it is low in both tannin and acidity, young Pinot Noir can, and should, be drunk relatively cool, at about 15°C. When mature, Pinot Noir – and particularly red burgundy – develops a taste of decomposition. That is why it is thought of as the perfect partner for game, for entrails, and for meat served with mushroom-based sauces. It is best served a little warmer, at 18°C.

When tasting wine in cellars in Burgundy you will occasionally be offered *gougère*, a choux paste made with cheese. This can be served instead of the cheese course at a dinner party. A recipe is given by Elizabeth David in the Penguin edition of *French Provincial Cooking* (pp. 203f).

A Note on the Gazetteer

Production and Vineyard Figures

At the beginning of most of the entries figures are given for the number of acres of Pinot Noir cultivated by the estate, and for the number of bottles of wine made from Pinot Noir it produces in an average year. Where neither figure is given, it is because the estate has been unwilling to disclose them. Where no acreage is given, it is generally because most or all of the grapes are bought in. The production figures can serve only as an approximate guide, because many Burgundians underestimate their production in order to reduce their tax liability, whilst many of their more successful counterparts in America and Australia are in the course of expansion.

In this book yields are given in hectolitres per hectare (2.5 acres). This is the system used in Burgundy. Vine-growers in America and Australasia often talk about tons per acre. It is impossible precisely to correlate the two systems, because the quantity of juice extracted from a given amount of grapes depends on how hard they are pressed but, as a general rule, a conscientious wine-maker produces roughly 3 tons per acre, which is the equivalent of 45–50 hectolitres per hectare, or 2,400–2,700 bottles from each acre of vines.

Vintages

Pinot Noir differs from the other books in the same series in that a list of the best recent vintages is not given at the beginning of the gazetteer entry for each producer. In a few instances I have given details of individual vintages in the text, but by and large I have avoided doing so because it would be meaningless and sometimes misleading. Burgundy has enjoyed three successive outstanding vintages, 1988, 1989 and 1990, and in almost all cases these are the years that would be named. Outside France, the quality of Pinot Noir is improving so fast that a winery's most recent vintage is likely to be its best so far. Instead of concentrating on individual vintages, therefore, I have given an overview of the quality and style of the wines produced by each estate, observations which should prove relevant for every vintage, good, bad or indifferent. However, I have given general vintage charts for Burgundy on pp. 88–90 and for Oregon on p. 239.

GAZETTEER

KEY TO RATING SYSTEM

Quality

🍇 indifferent

🍇🍇 average

🍇🍇🍇 good

🍇🍇🍇🍇 very good

🍇🍇🍇🍇🍇 outstanding

Price

★ cheap

★★ average

★★★ expensive

★★★★ very expensive

★★★★★ luxury

Lists of the leading producers are provided at the end of the introduction to each country and/or region. An asterisk after the producer's name indicates that a separate entry follows.

AUSTRALIA

Why is Australia Not Known for Its Pinot Noirs?

Pinot Noir has been grown in Australia since the 1830s, much longer than in other parts of the New World. Yet, after a century and a half, Australian wine-makers have, on the whole, had little success with the variety. The most obvious reason for this relative failure is that it has generally been cultivated in inappropriately warm climates, such as the Hunter Valley in New South Wales. This explanation is an excessively simplistic one, however. The Hunter Valley may not be ideal for Pinot Noir but some good wines have been made there, particularly by Tyrrell. Indeed, it was the 1976 vintage from Tyrrell which put Australian Pinot Noir on the map when it came first in the Pinot Noir class at the 1979 Gault-Millau Wine Olympiad.

The Tyrrells have made a success of their Pinot Noir because they understand the variety. Unusually for Australia, they allow the wine to be fermented by its own natural yeasts. They are able to do this because they have a 130-year-old winery which they do not clean too scrupulously. This may produce some volatile acidity, but they do not mind. 'Volatility makes a wine exciting,' says Bruce Tyrrell. 'Australians don't like red burgundies,' he adds. 'They condemn them as volatile. We have been buying burgundies for years. We must account for 5 per cent of total Australian consumption.'

Garry Crittenden, the owner of Dromana Estate in the Mornington Peninsula in Victoria, is more typical of Australian wine-makers. When I asked him what he thought of the burgundies of Domaine Ponsot in Morey-St-Denis, he said that they were fabulous wines, but that he would be ashamed to

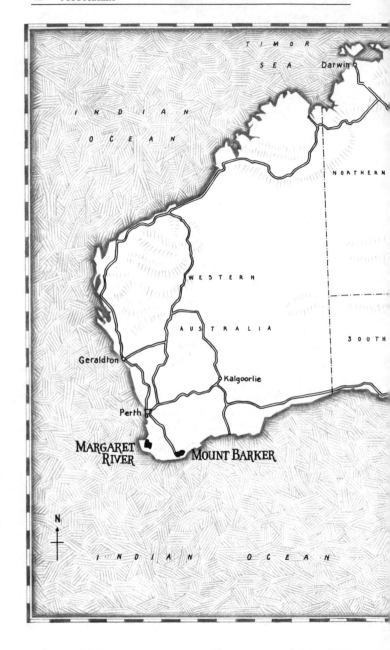

GULF OF CARPENTARIA

CORAL SEA

RRITORY

QUEENSLAND

USTRALIA

▲ Brisbane

PACIFIC OCEAN

Darling

NEW SOUTH WALES

ADELAIDE HILLS

Adelaide

HUNTER VALLEY

Newcastle

Sydney

Wollongong

VICTORIA

GEELONG

YARRA VALLEY

Melbourne

MORNINGTON PENINSULA

TASMAN SEA

PIPERS RIVER

TAYMAR VALLEY

TASMANIA

Hobart

DERWENT VALLEY

make them. Australian wine-makers were once memorably described by Adam Wynn, the wine-maker at Mountadam in the Adelaide Hills in South Australia, as 'a nation of phobic hand-washers'. It is possible to make good Cabernet Sauvignon and even good Chardonnay if you are excessively cautious but, to make good Pinot Noir, you have to be prepared to live dangerously.

The principal explanation for the relative failure of Australian Pinot Noir lies in the attitude of the people who produce it. The 1970s and 1980s saw a movement to cooler climates on the mainland, which were much more appropriate than the Hunter Valley for growing Pinot Noir. Vineyards were planted in Geelong, the Mornington Peninsula and the Yarra Valley in Victoria, in the Adelaide Hills in South Australia, and in the Margaret River and Mount Barker regions of Western Australia. This coincided with a movement to cooler climates within California and with the opening up of Oregon. So far, however, Australia has not produced as many convincing Pinot Noirs as California or Oregon. But attitudes can, and will, be changed. The first commercial Pinot Noir produced in the Mornington Peninsula was the 1980 vintage of Main Ridge. 'I was trained to be an "Australian" wine-maker,' says Nat White, the owner. 'I was taught to ferment the grapes cool and to preserve the fruit at all costs. It has taken me several years to overcome my training and make my wines in the French manner.'

The main problem facing producers on the mainland, however, will never go away. Australia is not merely a dry continent, it is an arid one. It has a phenomenal evaporation rate by European standards. Even in a relatively cool climate such as the Mornington Peninsula water evaporates from the soil three times as fast as in Burgundy. According to Garry Crittenden, a master viticulturalist who advises other vineyards on their vine-growing techniques, 'The fundamental issue of viticulture is how you manage vine stress – whether irrigation is easy to manage or whether the soil dries out very fast.'

Whereas vineyards in Burgundy are dry-farmed – the only water they receive is from rainfall – vines in Australia are generally irrigated. If a grower does not irrigate, his vines will stop growing. At Yeringberg in the Yarra Valley, although the vines shut off in the summer at 2 p.m. and the leaves droop, Guill de Pury, the owner, does not irrigate them. Irrigation promotes the development of a superficial root system which exacerbates water stress even more, thus tying the vineyard into a vicious circle. Vines in an irrigated vineyard will never dig the deep root system which is essential, not only for survival in the absence of water, but in order to produce the flavours of a fine wine.

John Middleton, the owner of Mount Mary, also in the Yarra Valley, opposes irrigation. 'It takes you a whole damn year to wait for those berries,' he says. 'Why stuff them up because you have some anthropomorphic hang-up about their being thirsty? Watering does relieve the stress but you can get three inches of rain the next day and you have to wait for another year to make a good Pinot Noir. I know my crop level suffers, but at least the wine tastes good. I am absolutely convinced that water regime is *the* critical factor in aroma, flavour and all the other aspects that make wine great.'

New South Wales

The Hunter Valley

The Hunter Valley was planted with vines because it was the closest possible area to Sydney. The Sydney metropolitan area itself was much too wet and humid. In theory at least the Hunter is far too hot for most fine-wine varieties, let alone Pinot Noir. It has only managed to produce good wines because the heat is mitigated by hazy cloud in the afternoon. But rain comes, too – particularly during the harvest, which is hardly what you want when you are growing a grape variety that is naturally susceptible to rot.

The fact that Tyrrell's Wines* have managed to produce a top-class Pinot Noir demonstrates either the triumph of mankind over nature or the superiority of soil – the Tyrrells have limestone, as in Burgundy – over climate.

South Australia

Although South Australia accounts for the majority of wine produced in Australia, most of it comes from warm regions which are quite unsuitable for Pinot Noir. The failure of Pinot Noir in the relatively mild district of Coonawarra only serves to support the argument that you cannot make great Pinot Noir, even from vines growing on limestone subsoil (as in Burgundy), if the climate is not cool enough. The greatest possibilities for Pinot Noir in South Australia are to be found in the high ground of the Adelaide Hills, where warm days are mitigated by cool nights. Unfortunately, these dramatic swings of temperature have caused Brian Croser of Petaluma great problems with pollination. Greater success has been achieved by Mountadam,* also in the Adelaide Hills, but in a warmer microclimate above the Barossa Valley, where only the cooler vintages are appropriate for the variety.

Tasmania

Tasmania ought to be producing the finest Pinot Noir in Australia. Its climate is similar to that of Burgundy, only drier in the autumn, so growers can wait until the grapes are fully ripe. It has nearly as many hours of daylight as Burgundy: it extends from 40 to 44°S, compared with the Yarra Valley in

Victoria at 37°S. (Burgundy is at 47°N.) Moreover, it is much greener and more humid than the mainland, with evaporation rates closer to that of Burgundy, so the vines do not have to be irrigated.

Tasmania enjoys a longer history of viticulture than Victoria, the state which currently produces the most successful Pinot Noirs. The first vines were planted in 1823; it was vineyards in Tasmania that provided cuttings for the first plantings in the Yarra Valley fifteen years later. Viticulture fell into decline in the 1860s but was revived in 1956, a decade before the Yarra Valley. Pinot Noir vines were planted at Lalla in the north-east of the island by a Frenchman, Jean Miguet, who had come to Tasmania to work on a civil engineering project. He called it La Provence. Miguet lasted eighteen years. He was forced to give up, not because of the difficulty of growing grapes – by all accounts, he made very good wine – but because of the puritanism of his neighbours. They prevented him from obtaining the licence he needed to sell his wines openly, so he sold them over the back fence. When his neighbours found out about that they tried burning his vines. In 1974 Miguet sold out, returned to France and died soon afterwards.

The oldest surviving – and best – producer of Pinot Noir in Tasmania is Claudio Alcorso, an Italian businessman, who planted vines at Moorilla Estate at Berriedale just north of Hobart in 1958. Yet, after more than thirty years of vine-growing, the only reputation which Tasmania as a whole has established is that of being *potentially* the best region for Pinot Noir. Many of the Pinot Noirs so far produced there have been disappointing. If you ask mainland producers, they are liable to say that they do not taste like Pinot Noir at all. James Halliday criticizes them for tasting minty. Andrew Pirie, the owner of Pipers Brook and the president of the Vineyards Association of Tasmania, says that this is 'a *terroir* flavour'. Certainly it is very marked in his wine.

Pirie does accept, however, that Tasmania has lagged behind the mainland in the introduction of appropriate techniques for making Pinot Noir. He points out that wine-makers in Victoria, especially Halliday at Coldstream Hills and Gary Farr at

Bannockburn, have received a great deal of information directly from Burgundy, not least from Jacques Seysses of Domaine Dujac in Morey-St-Denis. Pirie says that wine-makers in Tasmania only started generally to try out Burgundian techniques in 1986 and 1987, and only started to apply them correctly in the 1990 vintage. He believes that the 1990 Pinot Noirs from Heemskerk, Pipers Brook and Moorilla will make the reputation of the island.

To a certain extent the Tasmanian experience with Pinot Noir can be compared to that of Oregon. Both regions enjoy an an ideal climate for growing Pinot Noir grapes but, as Julian Alcorso, Claudio's son, points out, many of the vine-growers, having harvested good fruit, ruin it by their incompetence in the winery. Both regions have also suffered from inconsistencies from one vintage to the next. The same is true of Burgundy, but the situation is better understood by European consumers of French wines than it is by wine-drinkers in America and Australia who have been spoilt by the consistency of Californian and Victorian produce respectively. This said, Alcorso has no doubt that Tasmania is more suitable than even the cooler regions of the Australian mainland for growing Pinot Noir. He points out that the Mornington Peninsula and the Yarra Valley do best in cool years such as 1985, 1986 and 1987, whereas Tasmania is more successful in vintages such as 1990, which was generally too hot on the mainland.

Until now, wine-drinkers outside Tasmania have seen very little of its Pinot Noirs. This is hardly surprising, given that as late as 1990 there were only 90 acres of Pinot Noir vines in production – less than the size of the single *grand cru* vineyard Clos de Vougeot in Burgundy. Tasmania will succeed in establishing a reputation for its Pinot Noir – but it will take time.

The best Tasmanian producers of Pinot Noir include: Heemskerk, Moorilla Estate* and Pipers Brook Vineyard,* as well as a number of smaller estates, such as Delamere, Freycinet, Rotherhythe and Stoney. La Provence was revived in the 1980s and the wine is now made at Heemskerk.

Victoria

Geelong

This was the most important vine-growing region in Victoria in the 1860s and the 1870s but, when the phylloxera louse started attacking the vines, the government ordered that they should all be uprooted. This did not stop phylloxera from spreading but it did ensure that the area was kept free of vineyards until 1966. Whilst most of Australian viticulture was committed to producing big, full-bodied red wines, no one was interested in a region that was refreshed by Antarctic winds, requiring its inhabitants to wear a sweater on summer evenings.

Geelong is situated on the coast south of Melbourne, facing the Mornington Peninsula across Port Phillip Bay. Its climate is similar to that of the Mornington Peninsula: mild and maritime, cooler than the Yarra Valley but warmer than Tasmania. The relative successes in different vintages of the wines made from the four varieties Chardonnay, Pinot Noir, Cabernet Sauvignon and Shiraz by Gary Farr at Bannockburn Vineyards, the most important estate in the area, suggest that the warm-climate varieties, Cabernet Sauvignon and Shiraz, perform better in warm years such as 1986 and 1988 and that the cool-climate varieties Chardonnay and Pinot Noir are more successful in cool vintages such as 1987 and 1989.

The Bannockburn* Pinot Noir is certainly one of the finest, and probably the most Burgundian, in Australia. The other significant Pinot Noir vineyard in the area is Prince Albert, which was, like Bannockburn, planted in the mid-1970s on limestone subsoil. Although it was replanted on the site of one of the most famous nineteenth-century vineyards, Prince Albert does not enjoy quite as stellar a reputation as its neighbour.

*

Mornington Peninsula

The Mornington Peninsula is situated opposite Geelong, on the other side of Port Phillip Bay. It is the summer holiday playground of the inhabitants of Melbourne and the site of weekend and retirement homes. Land is very expensive and the vineyards are generally small ones. Vine-growers concentrate on wines which can be sold at high prices – such as Pinot Noir. The first commercial estate was Main Ridge, which was planted in 1975. Several others followed in the early 1980s.

The area has produced good Cabernet Sauvignon as well as good Pinot Noir. When I asked Nat White, the owner of Main Ridge, how a climate could be suitable for the one if it was suitable for the other, he answered, 'The climates of Bordeaux and Burgundy are in fact no further apart than the variation that occurs from year to year in the Mornington Peninsula.' He believes that the Mornington Peninsula is, with Tasmania, the best region for Pinot Noir in Australia.

This said, there are two distinctly different climates in the area: the higher altitudes, where Main Ridge is situated, are ideal for Pinot Noir, but Cabernet Sauvignon does not always ripen; the lower-lying vineyards, which include the well-known Dromana Estate, enjoy a slightly warmer climate, more like that of the Yarra Valley.

Dromana Estate* and Main Ridge are the best producers. Stonier's Merricks is also good.

Yarra Valley

The first vineyard in Victoria was planted in 1836 at Yering (the old Aboriginal name for the region) on the Yarra River. In the second half of the nineteenth century the Yarra Valley was famous for producing the closest wine in Australia to the European model. The wines suffered, however, from competition from the more productive vineyards of South Australia. Consumers lost interest in the Yarra Valley's elegant style of table wine, preferring fortified wine. The region organized itself for export but after the First World War the English started buying from South Africa instead. By the 1920s all the vineyards in the Yarra had gone bankrupt.

The region was revived at the beginning of the 1970s by three scientists (none of them qualified wine-makers): Guill de Pury at Yeringberg, Bailey Carrodus at Yarra Yering and John Middleton at Mount Mary. Today, all three make outstanding Pinot Noirs – not least because their vines have reached maturity. In this respect they can be compared to David Lett, Dick Erath and Dick Ponzi, who pioneered the cultivation of Pinot Noir in Oregon at much the same time. The Yarra Valley was not hyped until a little later than Oregon, however. It had to wait for James Halliday, the most powerful wine-writer in Australia, to establish his own vineyard there in 1985. 'Just as the Hunter Valley [where Halliday used to own part of the Brokenwood vineyard] has transformed itself between 1970 and 1985, so will the Yarra Valley between 1985 and the turn of the century,' he wrote in his *Australian Wine Compendium*.

If vine-growers in the Yarra Valley win their fight against urban expansion – the area is only ten miles outside Melbourne – then it could grow as big as the Napa Valley in California. What is as yet unclear is whether, like the Napa Valley, it will base its reputation on Cabernet Sauvignon – or whether it will become better known for Pinot Noir. 'All the objective evidence,' says Halliday, 'suggests that the Yarra Valley is the best area in Australia for Pinot Noir.' He points out that, although it is a small area, in 1987 it produced fifteen out of eighteen wines to receive gold medals on the National Wine Show circuit in the Pinot Noir Classes. Others disagree. Guill de Pury, the owner of Yeringberg, points out that Pinot Noir ripens in the first half of March, up to six weeks before Cabernet. 'We're obviously growing Pinot Noir in the wrong place,' he says. 'The Yarra Valley is ideal for Cabernet and too hot for Pinot Noir. Yet it still produces the best Pinot Noir in Australia.'

It is precisely because it is warmer than Tasmania, Geelong or the Mornington Peninsula that the Yarra Valley has rapidly established a reputation for Pinot Noir. The vines do not need quite as long to establish themselves, and produce a riper style of wine that is more accessible in its youth. In the long term the Yarra Valley may well be better-known for producing good, drinkable Pinot Noirs than for producing great ones. A lot of the noise that has been made about the potential of the region for Pinot Noir should be linked to the fact that – according to one of its more self-effacing producers – there are more prima donnas per acre in the Yarra than anywhere else in Australia.

The best producers include: Halliday's Coldstream Hills,* Diamond Valley Vineyards, Mount Mary Vineyard,* Tarrawarra, Yarra Ridge, Yarra Yering Vineyard,* Yeringberg.*

Western Australia

From 1829 until 1965 the only part of Western Australia where vines were planted was the Swan Valley, which was close to the centre of population in Perth. It was much too hot for fine-wine production but it was ideal for producing fortified and cheap table wines, which was what most people wanted. Then, in 1965, Dr John Gladstones, a government agronomist, published a paper in which he stated that the Margaret River and Mount Barker districts at the south-western tip of Australia, 200 miles south of Perth, were ideal for grape-growing.

The first vines were planted soon afterwards. Margaret River, which used to be known for surfing, has now established a reputation for Chardonnay and Cabernet Sauvignon. It is too warm for Pinot Noir. Moss Wood Vignerons* makes a good version, but the Pinot Noir from Leeuwin Estate, which enjoys a wholly undeserved reputation, is more representative of the region's lack of success. Mount Barker, 150 miles to the east, is cooler and wetter than Margaret River, and growers pick the grapes three or four weeks later. It ought to be more suitable for Pinot Noir – although there is as yet no firm evidence to prove this theory. Plantagenet is the best so far. Tony Smith, one of the owners of this vineyard (and a member of the family that owns the W.H. Smith chain of newsagents in Britain), says, 'I don't think I'll see the best wines in this area in my lifetime.'

Two of the most promising Pinot Noirs in Western Australia have been produced from vineyards in undervalued but undoubtedly cool regions: by Wignalls King River, near the port of Albany, thirty miles south of Mount Barker, and Lefroy Brook, near Manjimup, which lies between Mount Barker and Margaret River. Both vineyards benefit from the cooling influence of a maritime climate. Both wines are made under contract elsewhere: the Wignalls Pinot Noir is vinified by Tony Wade, the wine-maker at Plantagenet; it seems rather light and leafy when young but stands up well to food and may well have the capacity to improve with age. 'I don't worry about the demands of people for wines to drink at once,' says Wade. The Lefroy Brook Pinot Noir, which is vinified by Peter Fimmel, the wine-market Hainault, near Perth, may well offer even greater potential, as the vines have been close-planted on Burgundian principles. As yet, however, they are very young.

*   *   *

BANNOCKBURN VINEYARDS

Midland Highway, Bannockburn, Victoria 3331
Vineyard: 10 acres
Production: 20,000 bottles
Quality: 🍇🍇🍇🍇   Price: ★★★★

This vineyard in Geelong was established by the wealthy Melburnian businessman Stuart Hooper in 1974. The wine-maker Gary Farr produces Pinot Noir by methods that are more overtly Burgundian than anywhere else in Australia. Having worked five harvests with Jacques Seysses of Domaine Dujac in Morey-St-Denis, he makes his wine in the same simple manner. He puts whole bunches of grapes in the vats and leaves them till they start fermenting. Applying French methods to Australian fruit does not produce a hybridized style of wine but a quintessentially Australian one. 'The French say that we have more sunshine in our wine,' Farr points out. 'They also say that our wine lacks the finesse and elegance of theirs.'

Bannockburn Pinot Noir is rich, exciting and, by Australian standards, quite volatile. It can sometimes take a while to settle down after bottling and is at its best at between five and ten years of age.

COLDSTREAM HILLS

Maddens Lane, Coldstream, Victoria 3770

Vineyard: 14 acres

Production: 20,000 bottles

Quality: 🍇🍇🍇   Price: ★★★

In the 1970s James Halliday made mostly Shiraz and other warm-climate varieties at Brokenwood in the Hunter Valley – whilst establishing himself as a lawyer, a wine-show judge, and the most celebrated wine-writer in Australia. His involvement with Brokenwood came to an end when his law practice moved from Sydney to Melbourne. In 1985 he purchased the Coldstream Hills estate in the Yarra Valley, which was near enough to Melbourne to enable him to commute. Within three years, however, he had made such a success of Coldstream Hills that he was able to resign from his law practice.

Halliday builds complexity into his wine by combining a variety of wine-making methods, some of which, like cold-maceration of the grapes before fermentation, and fermenting whole bunches, he learnt from Jacques Seysses of Domaine Dujac in Burgundy, where he helped with the harvest in 1983. 'The problem with most Yarra Valley Pinot Noirs,' says Halliday, 'is that they have very pretty fruit but tend to be a bit evanescent.' The problem with the Coldstream Hills Pinot Noir, however, is not evanescence – it is drinkable in its youth yet sufficiently concentrated to be capable of maturing for a few years in bottle – but a lack of finesse.

DROMANA ESTATE

Harrisons Road, Dromana, Victoria 3936

Vineyard: 3 acres

Production: 9,000 bottles

Quality: 🍇🍇🍇   Price: ★★★

Second label: Schinus Molle (25,000 bottles)

Dromana Estate in the Mornington Peninsula was established in 1982 by Garry Crittenden, who advises a number of other producers on their vineyards. 'My role as a viticultural consultant is to build in economy,' he explains. He does this on his own estate by cropping Pinot Noir at between 80 and 90 hectolitres per hectare – twice the yield achieved in Burgundy. 'When we tell people this they get scared and start marking the wine down,' he says. 'That says a lot about the myths surrounding Pinot Noir. We have done comparative tests of wines made from different yields. Invariably the best wines are from higher yields. Pinot Noir is our heaviest-cropping variety. It has more bunches per shoot, greater shoot viability and heavier bunches and berries than Cabernet Sauvignon.' This is hardly surprising as Crittenden planted two high-yielding clones, which had been selected by the University of California at Davis.

The Dromana Estate Pinot Noir is a light wine, but it does not taste overcropped. It is long, clean, and by Australian standards very elegant. The second wine, Schinus Molle, is made by Crittenden from grapes he has bought in from other regions. It is pretty but lacks substance. Neither of these wines is designed for ageing. This is an issue that can make Crittenden angry. 'One of the first questions I am always asked is, "How will your wines age?"' he told me when I met him in the spring of 1990. 'What is wrong with drinking my 1989 Pinot Noir now? Many French wines age to a point of amalgamation at which I find them boring.'

*

MOORILLA ESTATE

655 Main Road, Berriedale, Tasmania 7011
Vineyard: 35 acres
Production: 100,000 bottles
Quality: 🍇🍇🍇–🍇🍇🍇🍇   Price: ★★★

Although the first Pinot Noir at Moorilla Estate were planted in the mid-1960s, it was not until the early 1980s that Moorilla acquired a reputation for the variety. Progress was prevented by the authorities, who forbade viticultural officials to visit the island, arguing that Tasmanian farmers should not have ideas above their station but should stick to growing apples. Even today, Julian Alcorso, who makes the wines admits, 'We haven't made the definitive Pinot Noir, not by a long chalk. I know bugger all about it, really.'

Modesty aside, in successful vintages such as 1989 and 1990 the Moorilla Estate Pinot Noir is the finest in Tasmania. It is long, clean and elegant, very Tasmanian in terms of its balance and harmony, but not affected by any of the minty or vegetal tastes that spoil several other Tasmanian Pinot Noirs. Alcorso attributes the quality of his wine to the fact that 'no one else in Tasmania has spent the care necessary in the vineyards in order to get the right fruit'. Unlike some of their rivals on the island, such as Pipers Brook, Moorilla net all their vineyards so that they can decide on the ideal date for picking rather than being forced to do so precipitously by the depredations of birds. Alcorso explains that by preventing bird damage he is able to avoid the development of acetic acid in the grapes while they are still on the vines, and so needs to add relatively little sulphur dioxide when the grapes are brought into the winery.

Good as it is, the Moorilla Estate Pinot Noir might be even better if Alcorso made it wholly by the traditional Burgundian method of punching down the cap of skins into the juice in an open vat rather than predominantly in mechanical rotary tanks which resemble cement mixers. Alcorso's choice of method may well help to explain why his wine shows in its youth more of the reserve of a claret than the excitement of a burgundy, and needs to be matured for several years before it is ready to drink.

MOSS WOOD VIGNERONS

P.O. Box 52, Busselton, Western Australia 6280

Vineyard: 3 acres

Production: 6,000 bottles

Quality. 🍇🍇🍇   Price: ★★★

This was the second vineyard to be established in the Margaret River region in 1969. The wine was originally made by the owner, Dr Bill Pannell, during his annual holidays, but his wife and children rebelled, forcing him to employ Keith Mugford as his assistant. Mugford has now taken over, allowing Pannell to spend more time in Burgundy (where he is one of several owners of the Domaine de la Pousse d'Or in Volnay).

Mugford makes a wonderful Cabernet Sauvignon. He also made a famous Pinot Noir in 1981, but since then it has not been in quite the same class. His Pinot Noir can seem rather sweet in its youth – the result of fermenting 50 per cent uncrushed bunches, which extends the fermentation period but gives the wine (he admits) an 'unusual maceration character'. As it matures, it becomes more complex and serious. It is by a long distance the best Pinot Noir made in Margaret River.

MOUNTADAM

High Eden Road, High Eden Ridge, South Australia 5235

Vineyard: 13 acres

Production: 20–30,000 bottles

Quality: 🍇🍇🍇   Price: ★★★

Samuel Wynn, born Solomon Weintraub, emigrated to Australia from Poland in 1913. He started by buying a wine-shop in Melbourne, then he bought a restaurant, then vineyards in South Australia. His son David was responsible for the development of Coonawarra after the Second World War. By 1972, however, Wynns Coonawarra had grown too large, and he sold it to the Penfolds Group.

He looked all over Australia for the ideal site to grow cool-climate grapes, principally Chardonnay. The choice was between going south (to Tasmania) and going up into the mountains. He chose the High Eden Ridge, 1,900 feet above sea level in the Mount Lofty Ranges which separate the Eden and Barossa Valleys. The advantage of a mountain climate is that it combines warm days with cool nights. The grapes can be relied upon to ripen fully whilst preserving their natural acidity. It is necessary to add acidity to most Australian wines, but not to the ones made at Mountadam.

The vineyard was planted in 1972 with all the nine clones that were then available in Australia. David Wynn's son Adam, who makes the wine, explains, 'Each clone tastes and behaves slightly differently and, if you are seeking to make a truly symphonic Pinot Noir, it makes sense to have as many clones as possible.'

The Mountadam Pinot Noir is a concentrated, slightly jammy wine, which even in a top vintage such as 1988 is more of a sonata than a symphony. Adam Wynn's best wine is his Chardonnay – the variety for which his father selected the site in the first place.

MOUNT MARY VINEYARD

Coldstream West Road, Lilydale, Victoria 3140

Vineyard: 4 acres

Production: 3,500 bottles

Quality: 🍇🍇🍇🍇   Price: ★★★★

Although John Middleton did not plant Mount Mary Vineyard at Lilydale in the Yarra Valley until 1972, he has been making

Pinot Noir on an experimental basis since 1964, so he knows a thing or two about the variety. He knows, for example, that it is not really suited to the Yarra Valley, which is too warm. Middleton says that the vintages from 1979 to 1984 were much too hot – although that does not stop him from claiming, with characteristic Australian understatement, that his 1984 'would make a Chambertin or a Musigny look like an L-plate wine'. Pinot Noir has been much more successful during the sequence of unusually mild summers which started in 1985. Middleton describes the wines he has made in this period as being comparable to wines from the Côte de Beaune – but even his 1985 is a big, explosive wine that was clearly produced in a warm climate.

The Mount Mary Pinot Noirs do, however, resemble red burgundies more closely than do the majority of Australian Pinot Noirs, because they offer complex, secondary aromas rather than simply a mouthful of pretty fruit. Middleton deliberately keeps his wine in cask until the fruity and fermentation aromas have disappeared (which takes about two years). As a result, it needs to be kept for longer in bottle than most Australian Pinot Noirs – at least five or six years – before drinking.

PIPERS BROOK VINEYARD

Bridport Road, Pipers Brook, Tasmania 7254

Vineyard: 27 acres

Production: 30,000 bottles

Quality: 🍇🍇🍇   Price: ★★★★

Andrew Pirie chose the site of Pipers Brook in Tasmania in 1974 after carrying out a feasibility study to locate a region in Australia which could produce European-style wine. The study resulted in his receiving the first PhD in viticulture to be awarded by an Australian university.

The findings of his study led him to visit Tasmania, where he discovered Jean Miguet. Pirie remembers Miguet bringing up a jug of his Pinot Noir from his cellar. 'One sniff and I knew that Tasmania was the place.'

Pirie chose Tasmania rather than the mainland because there is much less evaporation during the growing season. He believes that the secret of making great wine lies in the vine's response to stress. Because Tasmania has a low evaporation rate he has been able to stress the vines by planting them close together – as is done generally in Burgundy, but very rarely in the New World. Close-planting is useless in high-evaporation climates because the vines simply dry up in summer. For his pains, Pirie has been accused of indulging in the wrong sort of viticulture, resulting in wines that taste minty and vegetal.

Pirie believes that the minty character is a feature of the best old Australian clone of Pinot Noir (MV6), and that mintiness turns into gameyness with age. It is not yet possible to determine the truth of this argument, because he did not produce a commercial size of crop until 1984, and did not produce a truly successful Pinot Noir until 1990. One of the reasons for his success in this vintage is that he made a selection of the best 15 per cent of his total crop. The wine has more depth and succulence than his previous efforts, whilst retaining its freshness and elegance. It smells and tastes very strongly of mint, camphor and eucalyptus, but then it is meant to.

TYRRELL' WINES

Broke Road, Pokolbin, New South Wales 2321

Quality: 🍇🍇🍇   Price: ★★★

The Tyrrells are descended from William Tyrrell, who emigrated from England to Australia in 1848 in order to become the Bishop of Newcastle. They were celebrated in the 1970s for their Vat 47 Chardonnay, the first varietal Chardonnay to have been made in Australia since the nineteenth century. In 1979 they became even better known for their Pinot Noir because the 1976 vintage was placed top of the Pinot Noir class in the Gault-Millau Wine Olympiad in Paris. Tyrrell

Pinot Noir was subsequently featured on the cover of *Time* magazine as one of the ten greatest wines in the world, alongside Chambertin and Romanée-Conti.

This was surprising, because Australian wine-show judges had rejected the 1976 vintage for 'not having any Pinot character' – and they had been right. Murray Tyrrell did not start producing top-class Pinot Noir until after his visit to Burgundy in 1977. He visited Gérard Duroché, a grower in Gevrey-Chambertin. During three weeks he went back six or seven times, because he liked the wines. Finally, Duroché started speaking to Tyrrell in English. He explained that he made the wine with uncrushed grapes. Since then Tyrrell, who made his 1976 Pinot Noir from crushed grapes, has used 50 per cent of uncrushed grapes. He says that it gives his wine softer fruit and softer tannin.

The Tyrrell Pinot Noirs are big, exuberant wines, with a lot of soft tannin and relatively little acidity. They are at their best quite young. Their character reflects the warm climate of the Hunter Valley, which most people would consider to be too hot for Pinot Noir. 'Oh no!' exclaims Bruce Tyrrell (Murray's son) when this idea is suggested. 'Pinot Noir needs some heat on it.' The Tyrrell Pinot Noirs may not taste much like burgundy but they do taste of Pinot Noir. This may have something to do with the soil. Murray Tyrrell says that they can produce great Pinot Noir seven years out of ten because the vines grow on limestone, as in Burgundy. Like Dick Graff of Chalone and Josh Jensen of Calera in California, the Tyrrells are *terroiristes* – among the few vine-growers in the New World to believe that soil is much more important than climate.

YARRA YERING VINEYARD

Briarty Road, Coldstream, Victoria 3770

Vineyard: 2 acres

Production: 3,500 bottles

Quality: 🍇🍇🍇🍇   Price: ★★★★★

The owner, Bailey Carrodus is a New Zealander who dresses and talks like an English gentleman. A plant physiologist, he conducted an extensive search across Australia before establishing his vineyard in the Yarra Valley in 1969. Until 1978 he was employed full-time by the government. He worked at the winery at weekends and picked the grapes during his annual holiday. He took his leave when the Shiraz and Cabernet Sauvignon vines ripened, by which time the Pinot Noir was two weeks over-ripe. He used to add it to his Shiraz-based Dry Red Wine No. 2. Pinot Noir, he says, goes well with Shiraz. (Merchants in Nuits-St-Georges have known this for years. That is why they add Rhône wines to their burgundies.)

Since 1978 Carrodus has made Pinot Noir on its own, but it took him until 1982 to find out the best way to do so. He vinifies it according to Burgundian principles, in open vats. 'I like the fruit to get warm – up to 34°C,' he says. 'I don't like squeaky-clean wines. I don't mind a bit of volatile acidity.' Volatile acidity is commonly regarded as a fault in Australian wine-making and Carrodus's wines have been accused of having too much. He points out that analysis shows their volatile acidity to be below perception level. He believes, however, that it is enough to bring out the wine's aroma, as it does in the case of red burgundies.

Like the best red burgundies, Yarra Yering Pinot Noir is an exciting wine, which sits on a knife-edge. It offers something which is lacking in most other Australian Pinot Noirs – finesse.

YERINGBERG

Maroondah Highway, Coldstream, Victoria 3770

Vineyard: 1 acre

Production: 1,000 bottles

Quality: 🍷🍷🍷–🍷🍷🍷🍷   Price: ★★★

Yeringberg was founded in 1862 by the de Pury family, emigrants from Neuchâtel in Switzerland. It has remained in the same hands ever since – the only nineteenth-century Yarra Valley vineyard still to do so. The collapse of the wine industry in the Yarra Valley caused Yeringberg to stop making wine after the 1921 vintage. It was revived at the end of the 1960s, when Guill de Pury replanted one-fifteenth of his grandfather's vineyard 'as a historical hobby'. He makes his money out of grazing cattle. 'We make wine as a means of self-expression,' de Pury says. 'We're trying to make the best wine regardless of price.'

The Yeringberg Pinot Noirs lack the up-front varietal character of most cool-climate Australian Pinot Noirs but they are serious, long, complex wines which need to be allowed to mature. 'Our best wines,' says de Pury, 'have been made from very ripe grapes. They are big, inelegant and difficult for the first five years. They taste bad in cask and bad when young. They do not win lots of prizes.'

CANADA

Canada has the potential to make fine Pinot Noir. Dick Ponzi, one of the founding fathers of Oregonian viticulture, looked in the Okanagan Valley in British Columbia before deciding to settle 300 miles to the south. He thought the climate was ideal, but the area was simply too remote. The south-western corner of British Columbia is the only vine-growing region in the New World which enjoys longer daylight hours in summer than Burgundy: the Okanagan Valley is situated at 50°N, even further north than Champagne. It is actually warmer than Champagne because heat is stored and reflected by the deep waters of Okanagan Lake, but most growers have planted German grape varieties or hybrids (crossings of European grape varieties with hardier American ones).

The main vine-growing region of Canada is the Niagara Peninsula between Lakes Erie and Ontario. At 43°N it is south of the Willamette Valley in Oregon, on a similar latitude to that of the area round Hobart in Tasmania and Canterbury in New Zealand in the Southern Hemisphere.

The Niagara Peninsula would be too cold for vine-growing in winter were it not for the Niagara Escarpment, which protects it from cold northerly winds, and it would be too hot in summer were it not for the cooling effect of the lakes. The region does not enjoy a good reputation because for many years the majority of the wines produced came from hybrids. A number of serious wineries were established in the 1970s and 1980s, however – in many cases under European influence. The best Pinot Noir is made at Inniskillin by an Austrian, Karl Kaiser. It is herbaceous, but has fruit. Château des Charmes ought to be good, given that the wine-maker, Paul Bosc, is a graduate of the University of Dijon in Burgundy, but he does not make the wine by Burgundian methods – it is fermented at a relatively low temperature in closed vats – and some vintages have been spoilt by bad oak casks. Promising Pinot Noirs have been made by some smaller estates, among them Cava Spring and Konzelmann, but as yet their vines are too young.

ENGLAND

Is England Too Cool to Grow Pinot Noir?

Bernard Theobald of Westbury Farm,* the one English vine-grower consistently to have produced a commercial Pinot Noir, believes fervently in the potential of English wine. 'Our fruit is the best in the world,' he explained in an interview with *Decanter* magazine. 'There is simply nothing to beat the best English apples, strawberries, cherries and plums. The grape is just another fruit, and we can produce some of the finest grapes in the world if we set about it properly.'

The problem is, England is not very warm. The average maximum temperature during the four months from June to September is only 24°C in southern England compared with 30°C in Rheims in Champagne and 31°C in Frankfurt in Germany. And neither Champagne nor Germany is renowned for making still red wines from Pinot Noir. Theobald believes, however, that the lack of warmth is compensated for by longer daylight hours. His vineyard is situated at 51.5°N compared with the German vine-growing area, which extends from 47.5°N to 51°N, and Champagne, which covers 48°N to 49.5°N. The Côte d'Or in Burgundy is at 47°N. The difference is hardly very significant. Moreover, it is not clear how much difference longer daylight hours make. Plants grow by absorbing carbon dioxide from the air which they photosynthesize. This can occur only in daylight hours but not necessarily in full sunlight. It is not known whether extra light compensates for less heat.

Does Pinot Noir ripen in England? Theobald insists that it does. He says that he picked his Pinot Noir grapes in 1989 at about 12.5 per cent potential alcohol – a level with which growers in Burgundy would have been happy – and other vintages at about 10 per cent – a level which is very common in Burgundy in poor years. Other growers report much lower sugar levels than this.

Theobald may pick grapes with decent sugar levels, but his wines have the distinct taste of having been made from under-ripe grapes. This does not, however, disprove his theory that good Pinot Noir can be made under English conditions, because he is growing the wrong clone on the wrong training system and vinifying it at too low a temperature. With his Geneva Double Curtain training system Theobald obtains crops of up to 85 hectolitres per hectare. If he halved his yield he might have a better chance of ripening his grapes. The one successful Pinot Noir so far produced in England was not made by Theobald but by a young Australian wine-maker, John Worontschak, at Thames Valley Vineyards in Berkshire, in 1989, his first vintage in the country. His earthy yet elegant 'Clocktower' bottling was made from a crop of 35 hectolitres per hectare, picked at 11.5 per cent potential alcohol, and vini-fied according to the latest Burgundian techniques – cold maceration before fermentation, warm fermentation, and minimal intervention before bottling.

The evidence of the abnormally hot 1989 vintage is not one from which it is possible to extrapolate, however. In most years Pinot Noir is fit only to be turned into sparkling wine – as Thames Valley Vineyards did with much of their 1990 and all of their 1991 harvest. Maybe the Pinot Noir-based sparkling wine which they are proposing to release as 'Leighton' in 1994 will silence those who argue that Pinot Noir grown under English conditions is the ideal grape variety for making spark-ling wine. Lamberhurst in Kent made sparkling wines based on Pinot Noir in 1984 and 1985, but the 1985 was not a success. They decided not to release it, and gave up on the experiment. They started again in 1988 and 1989, this time with more of the neutral-tasting hybrid grape variety Seyval Blanc and less of Pinot Noir. Stephen Skelton, the wine-maker, is not a fan of Pinot Noir. 'If you are growing grapes for sparkling wine,' he says, 'why grow a variety which has acid problems and which stinks like heaven in some years?'

There are two rays of hope for English Pinot Noir. One is the method of growing the grapes in plastic tunnels. Not only Pinot Noir but also Cabernet Sauvignon have been ripened successfully using this technique. Some people think this is cheating. Grapes grown in plastic tunnels are English grapes, grown in English soil but no longer in the English climate. Moreover, plastic tunnels are very expensive. A grower who can afford to grow Pinot Noir grapes in plastic tunnels can afford to try and ripen Pinot Noir outdoors by reducing the crop to 35, or even 20, hectolitres per hectare.

The other ray of hope is the greenhouse effect. This refers to the trapping of heat in the lower atmosphere by carbon dioxide and other industrially produced gases. Vine-growing (of white grapes) throve in England in the early Middle Ages, when the average annual temperature was 10 per cent warmer than its level in the nineteenth and early twentieth centuries. Thanks in part to the greenhouse effect the average annual temperature in both 1989 and 1990 was significantly higher than the level of the early Middle Ages.

In 1990 the Science Working Group of the United Nations Intergovernmental Panel on Climatic Change reported that if nothing is done to restrict the current emissions of industrial gases, the global mean temperature will rise by 7 per cent by 2025 and by 25 per cent by the end of the twenty-first century. Martin Parry, Professor of Environmental Management at Birmingham University, and one of the chairmen of the United Nations Science Working Group, believes that Britain will warm up more than the global average. He suggests that the climate of south-east England could come to resemble the present climate of south-west France – Bordeaux, in other words – with warmer, drier summers and warmer, wetter winters.

As Bernard Theobald told a reporter from the *Daily Telegraph*, 'When the greenhouse effect gets going, we shall be the only country in Europe able to produce fine wine because everywhere else will be so damned hot.'

*

WESTBURY FARM

Purley, Berkshire
Vineyard: 5 acres
Production: 10,000 bottles
Quality: 🍇–🍇🍇   Price: ★–★★★

Bernard Theobald, a naval officer turned farmer, planted a vineyard at Westbury in 1968 because, he says, 'I was fed up with milking cows. Wine seemed like a very good alternative.'

Wine is one thing, red wine made from Pinot Noir quite another. 'Other people said that you can't make red wine in England,' he explains. 'But they hadn't tried. They hadn't even thought about it. In almost every other vine-growing region white and black grapes are grown together. I could find no reason why England should be totally different from the rest of the world. Also I had in mind that I would need Pinot Noir if I was going at some point to make sparkling wine. I was hedging my bets.'

Each year from 1975 to 1989 Theobald turned his Pinot Noir into still red wine, using essentially Burgundian methods. The wines he made in his first fourteen vintages are green and mean. The 1989 vintage, however, is amazingly dark and extracted. I would not have identified it as Pinot Noir but it is undoubtedly an impressive achievement. Theobald has a clone from the South of France and 1989 was probably the first year it encountered the weather conditions for which it had been bred.

Having finally succeeded in making a decent still red wine, Theobald used all his 1990 crop of Pinot Noir to make a sparkling white one.

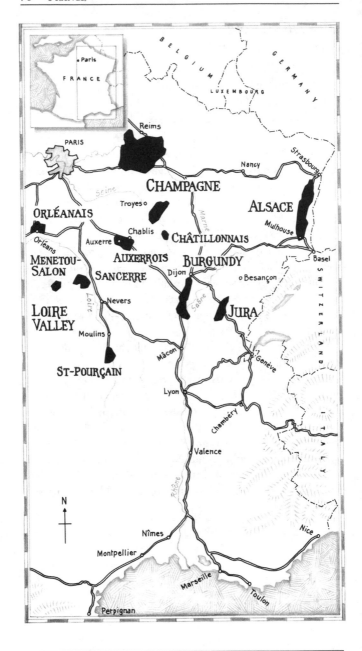

FRANCE

Alsace

At 48–9°N Alsace is as far north as parts of Champagne. It is famous for its white wines, made from Riesling, Gewürztraminer and Tokay-Pinot Gris. It would be reasonable to assume that it is not famous for its red ones because it is too cold. But this is not, in fact, the case. Alsace sits in a geological fault between the Vosges Mountains and the Black Mountains. The Vosges protect it from the prevailing westerly winds and therefore it enjoys a climate that is far drier and sunnier than other regions on the same latitude. In the summer and during September, which is the crucial month for ripening, it is both warmer and sunnier than Burgundy.

In theory it should be able to produce top-quality Pinot Noir. But it does not. Pinot Noir in Alsace suffers from the same problem as at Sancerre in the Loire Valley. It is not the most prestigious grape variety – Riesling is. This, and other white-wine varieties, are planted on the best-exposed, south-facing slopes. Pinot Noir is planted in the worst-exposed vineyards. As a result it generally produces a wine that is half-way between red and pink, without the flavour of either.

Some growers do make small quantities of serious Pinot Noir – but only in order to satisfy local demand for good red wine. Their wines are not generally seen abroad. Two proper Pinot Noirs which are exported are Réserve Personnelle from the merchants Hugel – an excellent wine with depth, made according to Burgundian principles – and Cuvée à l'Ancienne from the Turckheim Co-operative, which has been much touted by others, but by which I have not been impressed.

*

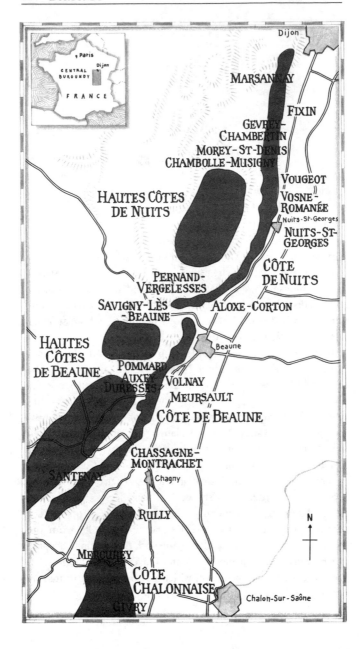

Burgundy

This book is principally concerned with the ways in which wine-makers handle Pinot Noir, rather than with the differences between villages and vineyards in Burgundy. The Burgundy entries have therefore been organized alphabetically by grower, rather than geographically by village. To do the latter would create insoluble problems, because many growers cultivate vineyards in more than one village, the result of the Burgundian practice of splitting each portion of one's property equally between all one's children, rather than giving each of them a different parcel of land. Moreover, the style of the grower generally dominates the characteristics of the village (see entries on Jean-Marc Bouley, Domaine Jean-Jacques Confuron, Maurice Écard, Robert Groffier, Domaine Jacqueson, Domaine Jayer-Gilles, Philippe Leclerc, Domaine Daniel Rion, and Christian Serafin, as well as the Accadian wines listed at the end of the section 'Colour – A Red Herring', on p. 22). The villages are listed towards the end of this introduction, with cross-references to all the growers in them who are given entries.

Growers and Merchants

The only producers who are not cross-indexed under the name of a village are the merchants, each of whom sells wine from many villages. Within each village, merchants buy wines from several growers, blend them together and bottle them under their own names.

Only ten merchants have been given entries in this book – Bouchard Père et Fils, Pierre Bourée, Doudet-Naudin, Drouhin, Louis Jadot, Jaffelin, Labouré-Roi, Louis Latour, Moillard, and Antonin Rodet – compared with 101 growers. Of these only two – Drouhin and Louis Jadot – produce wine that I would wholeheartedly recommend. The problem with merchants in Burgundy is that in general their wines are not very good. Indeed, many of those who are omitted from this book produce wines that it would be worth travelling a long distance in order to avoid.

The reason for this is partly a matter of history. Since their beginnings in the eighteenth century the principal rôle of merchants has been to adapt the wines made by growers in order to meet the taste of consumers. Often, this has meant making them fuller-bodied by blending them with wines produced in warmer climates. Growers who have criticized this adulteration have obviously been in difficulties when it has come to selling their own wines to merchants. This accounts for the origin of estate-bottling in the 1930s by growers such as Henri Gouges in Nuits-St-Georges and the Marquis d'Angerville in Volnay. From 1935 their wines were exported to the United States. However, this did not herald an explosion of estate-bottling. For the next two generations most burgundies were still bottled and distributed by merchants. Even in the early 1970s there were probably no more than fifty growers bottling their own wine.

The estate-bottling movement took off because of the economic crisis of 1973–4. Merchants stopped buying wines from growers, who therefore had no option but to start bottling and selling their wines themselves. They were assisted by the opening (in 1970) of the A6 motorway from Paris to Marseille via Beaune, which made it easy for Dutch and Belgian consumers to stop off to buy wines in Burgundy on their way to or back from a holiday in Italy or Spain.

The growers who started bottling their wines then are not yet as well known as the ones who have been bottling their wines since the 1930s, and certainly much less well known than merchants, who produce wines in a sufficiently large quantity to be able to market and advertise them internationally. The principal exception is Henri Jayer, who has served as a totem for all the small growers thinking of striking out on their own. He has proved that it is possible for a small grower to become an international superstar in the course of a few years. Jayer has also served as a symbol of the wide gulf in quality between growers' and merchants' wines. As more and more growers take to commercializing their own production, it is becoming increasingly difficult for merchants to find good wine. For example, when Frédéric and Michel Esmonin started bottling their own wines in 1985, merchants lost access to two of their best sources of Gevrey-Chambertin.

For the merchants the late twentieth century is a time of crisis. They are increasingly being restricted to buying either the less successful vats of good growers or wines made by growers who do not care enough about what they make to think of bottling it themselves. Some of them believe that the solution lies in buying grapes rather than wine, so that they can control the quality of the wine-making themselves. But this simply pushes the problem back another stage. The only way they can be sure of having good grapes is by buying the vineyards as well.

In 1985 Maison Louis Jadot, the most respected merchant firm in Burgundy, was sold by the Jadot family to its American importers Kobrand. The extra source of finance enabled Maison Louis Jadot to go and buy a third of the old Clair-Daü estate (42 acres of vineyards including the *grands crus* Le Musigny and Clos de Vougeot) and the merchant firm Maison Champy (15 acres, including another 6 acres of Clos de Vougeot). It is clear that Jadot was interested in Maison Champy – the oldest merchant company in Burgundy – only for its vineyards, because it immediately re-sold the company with its cellars but without its vineyards to the wine-broker Henri Meurgey.

It is possible for small merchants such as the new Champy, Pierre Bourée, Coron Père et Fils and Camille Giroud to produce good wines – because they can be selective in their purchases – but for larger merchants the future lies in giving up being merchants and becoming growers instead.

Classifications

The most famous region within Burgundy is the Côte d'Or, which means 'the hillside facing east'. Vines are planted on the eastern slopes of the Morvan plateau, where it runs down to the alluvial valley of the Sâone. The Côte d'Or extends for thirty-five miles, from south of Dijon to west of Chagny. On its periphery are the Côte Chalonnaise to the south, and the Hautes Côtes in the hills to the west. These are the regions that are generally thought of when one talks about red burgundy. There are, however, other, less important regions, such as the Auxerrois and the Châtillonnais. The characteristics of each region are described further below.

The wines produced in all these regions are divided by *appellation contrôlée* regulations – the laws covering the naming of wines – into several different classes. In ascending order, they are:

Bourgogne Grand Ordinaire. The lowest category. It can include some Pinot Noir but usually it is made from lesser grape varieties such as Gamay. It accounts for 2 per cent of the total crop of *appellation contrôlée* red and pink wines produced in the Côte d'Or, Hautes Côtes and Côte Chalonnaise.

Bourgogne Passe-Tout-Grains. A blend of Pinot Noir and Gamay. It must contain at least one-third of Pinot Noir but sometimes it has more. It is much more earthy and rustic than a wine made wholly from Pinot Noir, but can be very satisfying if drunk young. It accounts for 5–10 per cent of the total crop.

Bourgogne Rouge. Unless this comes from Beaujolais (in which case it has been made from Gamay), it is pure Pinot Noir. If it comes from a grower in the Côte d'Or, it will usually have been produced from vineyards on the plain, on the east side of the main road (N74) that runs from Dijon to Chagny via Beaune. It will usually offer a good introduction to the grower's style as well as excellent value for money. It accounts for 10–15 per cent of the total crop.

Regional *appellations*, covering several villages in a specific area of Burgundy. They are Bourgogne Côte Chalonnaise, Côte de Beaune-Villages, Côte de Nuits-Villages, Hautes Côtes de Beaune and Hautes Côtes de Nuits. They account for 20 per cent of the total crop.

Village *appellations*, such as Gevrey-Chambertin and Vosne-Romanée in the Côte d'Or, and Rully and Mercurey in the Côte Chalonnaise. In the Côte d'Or it is the worst-situated vineyards within each village which are entitled only to the simple village *appellation*: they lie either at the bottom of the slope (where the soil is too rich and there are problems with drainage in wet weather), or at the top of the slope (where the soil is too poor and the vines are too exposed to the elements). Village wines do not generally offer good value for money. This is particularly true in lesser vintages. In the last century many of the vineyards now entitled to a village *appellation* were planted with Gamay rather than Pinot Noir. Village *appellations* account for 25–30 per cent of the total crop.

Premiers crus. On the label they carry the name of the village followed by the name of the vineyard. They include the best-situated vineyards in the Côte Chalonnaise, and vineyards which are situated near the middle of the slope in the Côte d'Or. In general *premiers crus* are much higher in quality than simple village wines but not much higher in price. It is sensible to consider them as lesser – and much more affordable – versions of *grands crus* rather than as more elevated versions of village wines. One *premier cru*, Clos des Lambrays, was elevated to *grand cru* status in 1981, and official confirmation of La Grande Rue has been pending for some time now. Other top *premiers crus* as Gevrey-Chambertin Clos St-Jacques, Nuits-St-Georges Les St-Georges (which was provisionally classified as a *grand cru* in the nineteenth century) and Pommard Les Rugiens are equally worthy of the honour, but they are unlikely to receive it. *Premiers crus* account for 10–15 per cent of the total crop.

Grands crus. They account for 3 per cent of the total crop. They range from the very expensive to the ludicrously expensive. Are they the best?

The *grands crus* were established by the *appellation contrôlée* laws of 1935. These formalized the various attempts at classification which had been made in the previous eighty years and codified the viticultural developments of the previous two centuries. The vineyards which were given *grand cru* status were simply those which had been found to produce the best wine. In theory the *grands crus* are the vineyards which enjoy the best exposure. They are generally described as being situated in the belly-button (*le nombril*) of the hillside, at an altitude of about 850 feet above sea level. The middle of the Côte d'Or enjoys a slightly warmer climate than the lower and upper slopes, in part because of thermal inversion: the warm air that is created in the early morning settles in the middle of the slope.

In the case of the Clos de Vougeot, however, the award of *grand cru* status reflected historical reputation (as in the classification of Bordeaux) rather than the potential of the vineyard. The Clos de Vougeot runs from the middle right down to the bottom of the slope and therefore encompasses land of village, *premier cru* and *grand cru* quality. The reason why it was all classified as a *grand cru* was that in the nineteenth century Clos de Vougeot was sold as one single wine.

The Clos was split up at the end of the last century and is now divided between eighty different owners. In theory the best wine should come from growers with vines in the upper part of the Clos. But – to take one example – the wine made by Domaine Jean Grivot from old vines situated at the bottom of the Clos is more impressive than that made by Domaine Capitain-Gagnerot from relatively young vines in the upper part. Whether a bottle of wine deserves the name of the *grand cru* which it carries on the label or not depends principally on the age and quality of the vines and on the skill of the man who made the wine. Also, some *grands crus* are better than others. The greatest red burgundies are made by the best wine-makers from the oldest vines in one of eight super-*grands crus*. This is not an official title, but super-*grands crus* are easily distinguished from 'ordinary' *grands crus* by their much higher price. In the list of *grands crus* below, I have marked the super-*grands crus* with a dagger. *Grands crus* do not mention on their label the name of the village in which they are produced but are sold simply under their own name. Travelling from north to south (but alphabetically within each village), they are:

in Gevrey-Chambertin: Le Chambertin,† Chambertin-Clos de Bèze,† Chapelle-Chambertin, Charmes-Chambertin, Griotte-Chambertin, Latricières-Chambertin, Mazis-Chambertin, Mazoyères-Chambertin and Ruchottes-Chambertin

in Morey-St-Denis: Clos des Lambrays, Clos de la Roche, Clos St-Denis and Clos de Tart

in Chambolle-Musigny: Bonnes-Mares and Le Musigny†

in Vougeot: Clos de Vougeot

in Flagey-Échézeaux: Échézeaux and Grands Échézeaux

in Vosne-Romanée: Richebourg,† La Romanée,† La Romanée-Conti,† Romanée-St-Vivant† and La Tâche†

in Aloxe-Corton: Corton

The Regions of Burgundy

The Auxerrois

Light but well-structured red wines are produced in Irancy and Coulanges-la-Vineuse, two villages near Chablis, and in Épineuil, near Tonnerre. They produced a large quantity of red wine from Pinot Noir last century but after the vineyards were devastated by the phylloxera louse it was replaced by inferior grape varieties. Pinot Noir started to reappear in Irancy in the 1950s, in Coulanges-la-Vineuse in the 1970s, and in Épineuil in the 1980s.

Irancy produces the ripest and best wines of the three. The vineyards face south-west, and so receive more of the afternoon sun than the vineyards in Coulanges-la-Vineuse, which face south-east – with the exception of those of Serge Hugot, the best grower in the village. The wines of Irancy tend also to be more robust, because many of them contain between 5 and 10 per cent of the tannic César grape. An Irancy which includes César is capable of maturing in bottle for a decade.

The pre-eminence of Irancy was confirmed when it was awarded its own *appellation* in 1977. Coulanges-la-Vineuse and Épineuil are only entitled to the *appellation* Bourgogne Rouge. Although their names do appear on wine labels, their presence is tolerated only in practice and not in theory.

The best producers of Irancy include: Léon Bienvenu, Bernard Cantin, Gabriel Delalogue, Roger Delalogue and Jean Renaud.

The Châtillonnais

The Châtillonnais lies fifty miles north-west of the Côte d'Or, near the boundary between Burgundy and Champagne. As in the Auxerrois, a lot of Pinot Noir was grown here last century, but after phylloxera most vine-growers replaced it with Gamay. Today it is better-known for its oak (for making casks) than for its wine. In 1989 I visited Régine and Gilbert Brigand, the last remaining producers in the village of Massigny. They make a crisp, green, balanced wine, which is capable of lasting for many years.

The climate is different from that of the Côte d'Or. The winter is colder and vegetation is slower to start in the spring. The summer is slightly hotter and drier. There is no correspondence of vintages with the Côte d'Or. The 1988 vintage, for example, was only an average year. In some ways it is closer to that of Champagne. The Brigands are amused by the number of Champagne producers who try and buy grapes from them – for much less than they would pay on the other side of the border. They themselves make a sparkling wine from Pinot Noir, Pinot Blanc and Chardonnay which has a similar earthy character to Aube champagne.

The Côte Chalonnaise

The Côte Chalonnaise comprises three village *appellations* – Rully, Givry and Mercurey – and one generic *appellation*,

Bourgogne Côte Chalonnaise. It runs for thirty-five miles from the southern end of the Côte d'Or to the west of the town of Chalon-sur-Sâone. Whereas the Côte d'Or is made up of two east-facing hillsides, in the Côte Chalonnaise there are undulating hills and therefore a variety of microclimates. This explains why the new *appellation* Bourgogne Côte Chalonnaise was introduced in 1990: there are some very well-placed vineyards outside the three village *appellations* which deserve better than to be lost in the morass of the *appellation* Bourgogne Rouge.

In general the wines of the Côte Chalonnaise are lighter than those of the Côte d'Or. This is more a function of economics than of mesoclimate. The wines are lighter because they are sold less expensively and therefore the growers have to crop more heavily so the wines are lighter. Most Côte Chalonnaise wines are intended to be drunk young (although there are exceptions). One leading grower in Mercurey describes the region as 'the Beaujolais of the Côte d'Or'.

The best producers include:

in Givry: René Bourgeon,* Domaine Joblot, Domaine Ragot and Domaine Thénard

in Mercurey: Château de Chamirey,* Domaine de la Croix-Jacquelet, Domaine Jeannin-Naltet, Domaine Michel Juillot,* Domaine de Meix-Foulot and Domaine Suremain*

in Rully: Domaine Jacqueson*

(producers selling their wines as Bourgogne Côte Chalonnaise) in Bouzeron: Aubert de Villaine;* in Buxy: the Cave Coopérative de Buxy*

The Côte O'or

The principal wine-producing region of Burgundy, the Côte d'Or, is made up of two sequential hillsides, the Côte de Nuits (in the north) and the Côte de Beaune (in the south). Although the Côte de Beaune produces more red wine than the Côte de Nuits, it is better-known for its white wines – Meursault, Puligny-Montrachet, Le Montrachet, and so on. It is in the Côte de Nuits that most of the greatest red burgundies are produced. This is reflected in the fact that there are twice as many entries in this book for estates in the Côte de Nuits as for ones in the Côte de Beaune.

It is generally understood that the red wines of the Côte de Nuits are firmer and more tannic in their youth and richer and more intense in their maturity than those of the Côte de Beaune. This can partly be explained by differences of exposition and soil. In general the Côte de Nuits faces almost due east whereas the Côte de Beaune faces south or south-east. Contrary to popular belief, grapes on the east-facing slopes ripen sooner. The sun dries out the dew and the humidity of the soil from earlier in the day. Evening sun is less important. Despite its better exposition, grapes in the Côte de Nuits ripen up to a week later than those in the Côte de Beaune. This is because there is generally more clay in the soil. Clay soil is cooler: it retards ripening but produces fuller-bodied wines. In the Côte de Beaune there is more chalk. So it is generally more suited to the white grape, Chardonnay.

The Villages of the Côte O'or

Aloxe-Corton (Côte de Beaune). Best known for its white Corton-Charlemagne. The red wines (particularly from the *grand cru* Corton) can be surprisingly austere and tannic for the Côte de Beaune. The best producers include: Domaine Chapuis,* Michel Voarick, Domaine Daniel Senard.*

Auxey-Duresses (Côte de Beaune). Simple, pleasant red wines. The best producers include: Jean-Pierre Diconne.

Beaune (Côte de Beaune). More famous for its Hospices, its cobbled streets and its multitude of tourists than for its wines. They are neither as full-bodied as those of Pommard nor as elegant as those of Volnay. The best producers include: Domaine Besancenot-Mathouillet and Domaine Albert Morot.* There is also the Hospices de Beaune.*

Chambolle-Musigny (Côte de Nuits). Famous for producing the prettiest wines in the Côte de Nuits, scented with violets. The best producers include: Domaine Barthod-Noëllat,* Château de Chambolle-Musigny,* Domaine Daniel Moine-Hudelot, Domaine Georges Roumier,* Domaine Hervé Roumier,* Domaine Servelle-Tachot, Domaine Comte Georges de Vogüé* and Léni Volpato.

Chassagne-Montrachet (Côte de Beaune). Known only for its white wines, yet red wines account for approximately half the production. They are usually drunk young, yet they often have more stuffing than one might expect. The best producers include: Jean-Noël Gagnard, Château de la Maltroye, Jean-Marc Morey and Fernand Pillot.

Chorey-lès-Beaune (Côte de Beaune). Good, easy-drinking red wines. The best producers include: Château de Chorey-lès-Beaune, Domaine Maillard and Domaine Tollot-Beaut.

Côte de Beaune-Villages (Côte de Beaune). A catch-all *appellation* covering red wine from sixteen villages, of which twelve usually sell their wine under their own name.

Côte de Nuits-Villages (Côte de Nuits). This *appellation* covers the wines of Fixin and Brochon in the north of the Côte de Nuits and Prissey, Comblanchien and Corgoloin in the south. The best producers include: Domaine Chopin-Groffier* and Gérard Julien in Comblanchien.

Fixin (Côte de Nuits). Can also be sold as Côte de Nuits-Villages. The wines are similar to Gevrey-Chambertin, only even more rustic. The best producers include: Denis Berthaut and Domaine Pierre Gelin.

Gevrey-Chambertin (Côte de Nuits). The largest village in the Côte de Nuits, with nearly 1,500 acres under vines. It covers a multitude of different soils and therefore produces many different styles of wine. As a general rule, the wines are firm and tannic in their youth, and need time to mature. There are a number of famous, wealthy estates in the village, such as Domaine Camus, Domaine Damoy, Domaine Drouhin-Laroze,* Domaine Jean-Claude Fourrier,* Domaine Charles Rousseau* and Domaine Louis Trapet.* Of them only Rousseau produces top-class wines. There are a number of young growers who may not have holdings in the best *premier cru* and *grand cru* vineyards but whose wines often surpass those of the great estates, among them Denis Bachelet,* Domaine Lucien Boillot et Fils,* Alain Burguet,* Domaine Michel Esmonin,* Philippe Leclerc,* Domaine Charles Mortet,* Philippe Naddef,* Domaine Les Perrières,* Philippe Rossignol* and Christian Serafin.* Other good estates include Domaine Clos Noir,* Pierre Dugat, Frédéric Esmonin, Domaine Geantet-Pansiot, René Leclerc,* Bernard Maume,* Joseph Roty* and Domaine des Varoilles.*

Ladoix-Serrigny (Côte de Beaune). Decent, crisp wines. The best producers include: Edmond Cornu, Domaine Prince Florent de Mérode, Domaine André Nudant et Fils and Domaine Gaston et Pierre Ravaut.

Les Maranges (Côte de Beaune). An *appellation* created in 1989 to cover three obscure villages whose wine had in the past been sold as Côte de Beaune-Villages.

Marsannay (Côte de Nuits). It used to be famous for its pink wine, but this is now in decline. In 1987 it was given its own *appellation* for red wines. They are fruity and digestible. The best producers include: Domaine Philippe Charlopin, Bruno Clair,* Domaine Fournier, Domaine Lucien et Alain Guyard and Domaine Hugenot.

Meursault (Côte de Beaune). Very little red wine is produced. It is not as good as the white. The best producers include: Pierre Boillot, Domaine Coche-Dury* and Domaine Latour-Giraud.

Monthélie (Côte de Beaune). A lighter and less distinguished version of Volnay. The best producers include: Paul Garandet and Château de Monthélie Domaine Monthélie-Duhairet.

Morey-St-Denis (Côte de Nuits). Lying between Gevrey-Chambertin and Chambolle-Musigny, it is less well known than either, partly because it is a small village, and partly because it has no single style of its own: some of the wines taste more like Gevrey-Chambertin, others more like Chambolle-

Musigny. The best producers include: Pierre Amiot,* Clos de Tart,* Domaine Dujac,* Robert Groffier,* Georges Lignier,* Hubert Lignier,* Domaine Ponsot,* Domaine Bernard Serveau* and Domaine Vadey-Castagnier.

Nuits-St-Georges (Côte de Nuits). Firm, tannic wines. In theory (but not always in practice) it is possible to draw a distinction between the rounder, if still tannic, wines produced to the north of the town, towards Vosne-Romanée, and the more austere wines produced south of the town, some of them in the village of Premeaux, which sells its wines as Nuits-St-Georges. The best producers include: Bertrand Ambroise,* Domaine de l'Arlot,* Jean Chauvenet,* Domaine Georges et Michel Chevillon,* Robert Chevillon,* Georges Chicotot,* Domaine Chopin-Groffier,* Domaine Jean-Jacques _ Confuron,* Domaine Robert Dubois,* Domaine Henri Gouges,* the Hospices de Nuits, Domaine Machard de Gramont,* Alain Michelot,* Gilles et Henri Remoriquet* and Domaine Daniel Rion.*

Pernand-Vergelesses (Côte de Beaune). The red wines enjoy a good reputation, but I have generally found them to lack stuffing. The best producers include: Domaine Marius Delarche, Domaine Dubreuil-Fontaine, Domaine Laleure-Piot, Roland Rapet and Domaine Rollin.

Pommard (Côte de Beaune). Soft, rich, full-bodied wines. The best producers include: Domaine Billard-Gonnet, Jean-Marc Boillot, Domaine du Clos des Épenots,* Domaine Coste-Caumartin; Domaine de Courcel,* Jean Garaudet,* Michel Gaunoux, Domaine Armand Girardin,* Domaine Lejeune,* André Mussy,* Domaine Parent, Domaine Pothier-Rieusset.*

St-Aubin (Côte de Beaune). Next door to Chassagne-Montrachet. Similar, if slightly lighter, wines. They offer good value for money. The best producers include: Jean-Claude Bachelet, Hubert Lamy, Domaine Henri Prudhon.

St-Romain (Côte de Beaune). Better-known for its white than for its red wines, which can offer good value but are sometimes too austere. The best growers include: Bernard Fèvre and Alain Gras.

Santenay (Côte de Beaune). Generally too rustic for its own good. The best growers include: Adrien Belland, Vincent Girardin, Domaine Lequin-Roussot and Domaine Prieur-Brunet.

Savigny-lès-Beaune (Côte de Beaune). Well-structured, light but quite earthy wines, which develop in the medium term. The best producers include: Domaine Simon Bize,* Domaine Capron-Manieux, Domaine Chandon de Briailles,* Maurice Écard* and Jean-Marc Pavelot.*

Volnay (Côte de Beaune). Fine, elegant, long-lasting wines. The best producers include: Domaine Marquis d'Angerville,* Domaine Bitouzet-Prieur, Jean-Marc Bouley,* Yvon Clerget, Domaine Lafarge,* Hubert de Montille, Domaine de la Pousse d'Or* and Joseph Voillot.*

Vosne-Romanée (Côte de Nuits). This village produces the finest, most sumptuous wines in the whole of Burgundy (and therefore in the world). The best producers include: Robert Arnoux,* Domaine Cacheux-Blée,* Sylvain Cathiard, Domaine du Clos Frantin,* Domaine Confuron-Cotetidot,* Domaine René Engel, Jean Faurois, Domaine Grivot,* Domaine Anne et François Gros, Domaine Jean Gros,* Domaine Gros Frère et Soeur,* Domaine Haegelen-Jayer,* Henri Jayer,* Domaine Lamarche,* Domaine Leroy,* Domaine Méo-Camuzet,* Domaine Mongeard-Mugneret,* Domaine Mugneret-Gibourg,* Domaine Pernin-Rossin,* Bernard Rion, Domaine de la Romanée-Conti,* Emmanuel Rouget and Jean Tardy.

Vougeot (Côte de Nuits). Famous for the *grand cru* Clos de Vougeot, which is divided among eighty different growers. The only estate actually situated in the Clos itself is Château de la Tour.* In the village Domaine Bertagna,* Georges Clerget and Alain Hudelot-Noëllat produce good wines.

*

The Hautes Côtes

The Hautes Côtes are a secondary wave of hills running parallel to and to the west of the Côte d'Or. In general the Hautes Côtes de Beaune have remained in cultivation for centuries but the vineyards in the Hautes Côtes de Nuits were devastated by the phylloxera louse at the end of the nineteenth century and were not replanted until the 1960s. A new type of cultivation was introduced. Instead of small, low bushes close together, the vines were planted high and wide, and far apart. This system made cultivation cheaper – because a machine could plant, work and (in many cases) harvest the vines.

The problem with high-trained vines, it is said (particularly by growers in the Hautes Côtes de Beaune who have low-trained vines), is that they ripen grapes later than low-trained ones. It is pointed out that because the grape is further from the ground, the sap has further to run. The argument is not proven, however. One might equally well say that high-trained vines ripen the grapes faster because they have a greater reserve of energy. Vines in the Hautes Côtes ripen later than those in the Côte d'Or regardless of whether they are high-trained or not. This is because they are grown at a higher altitude – generally at between 1,000 and 1,300 feet, compared with between 700 and 1,000 feet in the Côte d'Or. The higher the vineyard, the more difficulty the grower has in ripening the grapes in cool years. In warm vintages, nobody has any problems.

The best producers include:

(in the Hautes Côtes de Beaune) in Nantoux: Jean Joliot et Fils;* in Meloisey: Domaine Mazilly;* in Échevronne: Domaine Lucien Jacob*

(in the Hautes Côtes de Nuits) in Messanges: Thierry Vigot; in Marey-lès-Fussey: Domaine Thévenot le Brun; in Magny-lès-Villers: Domaine Jayer-Gilles*

(growers in the Hautes Côtes with cellars in the Côte d'Or) in Beaune: the Cave co-opérative des Hautes Côtes;* in Vosne-Romanée: Domaine Michel Gros*

Vintage Guide

As I have stated earlier, vintage guides are misleading. For those people who wish to be misled:

1980	4–8/10	Initially condemned. In fact, some excellent wines were made, principally in the Côte de Nuits. Most of them need drinking up.
1981	2–4/10	Initially condemned, and with reason.
1982	4–8/10	Initially condemned for producing a huge crop of pale, watery wines. Many of them have mysteriously taken on colour and body in bottle and are quite delicious now. But do not hang on to them.
1983	2–9/10	Initially lauded as the vintage of the century. It then transpired that some wines had been spoilt by hail (avoid Chambolle-Musigny and Vosne-Romanée) and others had been ruined by rot. There are successful wines, but they are still very tannic and few of them will be ready to drink before the end of the century.
1984	3–5/10	Initially condemned because of the wines' high levels of acidity. It is true that the grapes did not ripen fully. But many of the wines have turned out to be pleasant, if rather light.
1985	8–9/10	Initially lauded as the vintage of the century. Now written off for

producing wines that were delicious when young but have been going downhill since 1988. It is true that they have low levels of acidity (which in theory should reduce their life-span) but it is well worth hanging on in there.

1986   4–7/10   Variable. Some of the wines from the Côte de Nuits are good but lean and tannic; others are just lean. Many of the wines from the Côte de Beaune are best forgotten. This was the vintage that made the 1982s look good.

1987   6–8/10   Obviously destined to be a forgotten vintage. It can be compared to 1979, which also produced very nice, balanced, ripe wines that drank well young but continued to drink well for many years. Unfortunately, overshadowed by the following vintage.

1988   9–10/10   Initially praised, but regarded as a bit too aggressive. Now acknowledged as possibly the vintage of the century. Similar to the 1978s – long, balanced, built to age – but perhaps even more concentrated.

1989   6–9/10   Initially lauded as the vintage of the century until people realized that they were confusing Burgundy with Bordeaux. It was very hot at harvest, and many of the wines fermented too fast. They are very pretty, but can lack substance.

| 1990 | 8–9/10 | By this time no one could be bothered to talk about vintages of the century. The wines are quite delicious. They combine the backbone of the 1988s with the ripeness of the 1985s. |

BERTRAND AMBROISE

Premeaux, 21700 Nuits-St-Georges

Vineyard: 37 acres

Production: 50,000 bottles

Quality: 🍇🍇🍇–🍇🍇🍇🍇   Price: ★★★–★★★★

Bertrand Ambroise is a friendly young man who makes approachable but extracted wines by macerating the grape skins in the wine for as long as possible – two and a half weeks on average. His wines have lots of ripe, slightly pruney fruit and no lack of tannin. They lack the elegance of the wines made by his brother Alain Ambroise, the manager of Domaine du Clos Frantin, however. This reflects the difference between Nuits-St-Georges, where Ambroise has most of his vines, and Vosne-Romanée, where the Domaine du Clos Frantin is situated.

PIERRE AMIOT

21740 Morey-St-Denis

Vineyard: 25 acres

Production: 50,000 bottles

Quality: 🍇🍇🍇   Price: ★★★–★★★★

Pierre Amiot is a plump and engaging man. When I told him how difficult it was to fix appointments to see the better growers in Burgundy, he said, 'I'm ready to receive anyone.'

His wines are plump and engaging, too. For my taste, they are too glycerous, too inelegant and I looked in vain for a core of pure Pinot Noir fruit but they are undoubtedly the sort of burgundies that a lot of people like. Although he has most of his vines in Morey-St-Denis, his best wine is probably the Gevrey-Chambertin *premier cru* Les Combottes.

Pierre Amiot should not be confused with Bernard Amiot, an unrelated grower in the next-door village of Chambolle-Musigny.

DOMAINE MARQUIS D'ANGERVILLE

Volnay, 21190 Meursault

Vineyard: 32 acres

Production: 50,000 bottles

Quality: 🍇🍇🍇🍇   Price: ★★★★

This is one of the great estates of Burgundy. The Marquis d'Angerville became famous in the 1930s because he fought against the dishonest practices of merchants, who therefore stopped buying his wine, forcing him to bottle and to sell direct. The present Marquis (Jacques) d'Angerville took over the estate on his father's death in 1952. He says that he makes wine by the same methods, except that he bottles it after one and a half rather than two and a half years in cask. He enjoys a reputation for making light, delicate wines – but I have found them to be serious, concentrated wines which need keeping. He makes his best wine from the Volnay *premier cru* Clos des Ducs, a vineyard of which he enjoys monopoly ownership.

DOMAINE DE L'ARLOT

Premeaux, 21700 Nuits-St-Georges

Vineyard: 30 acres

Production: 35,000 bottles

Quality: 🍇🍇🍇🍇   Price: ★★★★

This estate was bought from Maison Jules Belin in 1987 by the insurance company AXA. It comprised the whole of two *premier cru* vineyards in Nuits-St-Georges: Clos de l'Arlot and Clos des Forêts St-Georges. Half an acre of the *grand cru* Romanée-St-Vivant has since been added – at the cost of a further nine million francs. AXA also owns Châteaux Pichon-Baron, Cantenac-Brown and Petit-Village in Bordeaux. It has invested in vineyards partly for financial reasons and partly as a public relations exercise.

The estate is run on AXA's behalf by Jean-Pierre de Smet (who, despite his Dutch surname, comes from Nice). He is a disciple of Jacques Seysses, the owner of Domaine Dujac in Morey-St-Denis, whom he met when they both took part in a skiing competition. He worked at Domaine Dujac for several harvests. 'Jacques Seysses is my model,' he says. 'I like his way of working: his openness of mind and his willingness to enter into discussion with other growers.'

De Smet has adoped Seysses's method of vinification. He puts whole bunches in the vat and crushes them by foot. The purpose is not to prolong the fermentation but for some of the grapes to ferment whilst they are still unbroken, which brings complexity to the wine. The wines resemble those of Domaine Dujac – they are long and balanced, with dry tannins – but they are not yet quite in the same class.

ROBERT ARNOUX

21670 Vosne-Romanée

Vineyard: 27 acres

Production: 50–60,000 bottles

Quality: 🍇🍇–🍇🍇🍇🍇   Price: ★★★–★★★★

Robert Arnoux is unusual among vine-growers in Vosne-Romanée in that he actually exhibits an interest in selling his wines. He displays a direct sales sign beside the main road outside his cellars, and is always happy to reel off his opinions to visitors at high speed in a thick accent apparently of his own invention – in a passable imitation of a second-hand car salesman.

Surprisingly, his wines are quite good, although they suffer from overcropping in years of naturally high yields such as 1989. His *premiers crus* from Vosne-Romanée are generally long, fruity wines and his Romanée St-Vivant can be quite wonderful.

DENIS BACHELET

54 route de Beaune, 21220 Gevrey-Chambertin

Vineyard: 6 acres

Production: 10–15,000 bottles

Quality: 🍇🍇🍇🍇   Price: ★★★–★★★★

An enthusiastic young wine-maker, who took over from his father (now living in Belgium) in 1983, Denis Bachelet is nevertheless suspicious of journalists. He was unwilling to tell me how he makes his wine, on the grounds that he has secrets that he does not want his neighbours to know. All he would say was, 'There are twelve hours when you must be present at the fermentation. These are the key to making good wine. They are as likely to start at 3 a.m. as at midday.'

However he does it, Bachelet makes really clean, pure, fruity wines from vines in the village of Gevrey-Chambertin which were planted in the 1930s and from vines in the *grand cru* Charmes-Chambertin which were planted last century.

DOMAINE BARTHOD-NOËLLAT

21770 Chambolle-Musigny

Vineyard: 12 acres

Production: 25,000 bottles

Quality: 🍇🍇🍇🍇🍇   Price: ★★★—★★★★

Gaston Barthod is naturally reticent but becomes more forth-coming if one shows enthusiasm over his wines. He says that he was taught a great deal by his father-in-law in the 1930s – such as the importance of sorting out rotten grapes in the vineyard yourself rather than leaving it to the harvesters.

Officially he handed over the running of the estate to his daughter Ghislaine in 1986 but he continues to impart his mark on the wine. In their tidy cellars they make a beautiful Chambolle-Musigny which has elegance as well as depth.

DOMAINE BERTAGNA

21640 Vougeot

Vineyard: 70 acres

Production: 100,000 bottles

Quality: 🍇🍇🍇—🍇🍇🍇🍇   Price: ★★★—★★★★

The reputation of this estate – which owns vineyards throughout the Côte de Nuits – was established in the 1960s and 1970s by the Bertagna family, immigrants from the Côte de Bone in Algeria. In 1982 it was bought by Eva Reh, whose sister Annegret runs the Reichsgraf von Kesselstatt estate based in Trier in the Mosel Valley.

Eva Reh has remodelled the estate and spent a lot of money on stainless-steel fermentation vats and new oak casks for maturation. But the style of wine has not changed. Roland Massé, the cellar-master, says that he tries to make elegant wines. They may not reach the highest class – not even when made from old vines in the *grands crus* vineyards Clos St-Denis, Clos de Vougeot and Le Chambertin – but they are clean, quite lean and very accessible. They are the best sort of 'commercial' red burgundy.

In 1988 the Reh family bought the merchant house of Geisweiler but this is run separately (by Eva Reh's husband Mark Siddle).

DOMAINE SIMON BIZE

> rue Chanoine Donion, 21420 Savigny-lès-Beaune
>
> Vineyard: 40 acres
>
> Production: 80,000 bottles
>
> Quality: 🍇🍇🍇   Price: ★★★

Simon Bize has been bottling wine from his vineyards in Savigny-lès-Beaune – rather than selling it in bulk to merchants – since before the Second World War. The wine is now made by his son Patrick but still in a traditional style: firm in its youth but round and quite rustic, becoming gamey with age.

DOMAINE LUCIEN BOILLOT ET FILS

> rue de l'Église, 21220 Gevrey-Chambertin
>
> Vineyard: 45 acres
>
> Production: 60,000 bottles
>
> Quality: 🍇🍇🍇–🍇🍇🍇🍇   Price: ★★★–★★★★

'Why is Henri Jayer so famous?' I was asked by Louis and Pierre Boillot, the two young brothers who run this estate, when I visited them in 1989. 'We want to be like him.' They have already gone a long way in a short time. Their father emigrated to Gevrey-Chambertin from Volnay many years ago – the reason being that he did not get on with his father, the wine-maker Henri Boillot – but he did not buy any vines until 1978. Louis and Pierre have made the wines since they returned from the army in the early 1980s.

Their first efforts were not wonderful but since the 1987

vintage they have produced intense, dark wines – particularly from their holding in Nuits-St-Georges, which they say includes some ungrafted vines planted last century. Robert Parker links the improvement with their abandonment of filtration. I tasted both filtered and unfiltered versions of their 1987 Gevrey-Chambertin and the latter was infinitely more profound.

MAISON BOUCHARD PÈRE ET FILS

rue du Château, 21200 Beaune

Vineyard: 150 acres

Production: 300,000 bottles

Quality: 🍇–🍇🍇🍇   Price: ★★★–★★★★

Of the two merchant houses in Burgundy which bear the name Bouchard, this is the original one. In 1750 the oldest son of the family (Bouchard Aîné) left his father's business (Bouchard Père) and set up on his own. It is also the more prestigious. Indeed, it has been suggested that it was because of their prominence that in 1989 Claude Bouchard and his son Jean-François were prosecuted for adding an excessive amount of sugar in the 1987 vintage and for illegally adding acid. (See 'Harvesting Pinot Noir', on pp. 17–20.) Ironically this prosecution results from the Bouchards' attempts to improve their wine. Since the 1982 harvest, in which they saw good grapes being badly handled, they have converted from buying in wine to buying in grapes and making the wine themselves. If they had still been buying in wine rather than grapes, then there would have been no reason to prosecute them.

In 1984 the Bouchards constructed a new winery with automatic closed fermentation tanks. According to Jean-François Bouchard, the wines made in these tanks 'have more fruit in their youth but also have a better balance for ageing. They are particularly good in lesser years like 1984.' The wines the Bouchards have made in their new tanks have received positive reviews from many journalists, whom they receive in the most hospitable manner. The wines they make from their holdings in the Beaune *premier cru* Les Grèves and the *grand cru* Le Corton have been singled out for special praise. I disagree. There is nothing actually wrong with the wines, but I find them both over-extracted and excessively simple. The Vosne-Romanée *premier cru* Les Reignots and the *grand cru* La Romanée, which are made in traditional open vats under their supervision at the Château de Vosne-Romanée, are much more exciting, exotic, mushroomy wines.

JEAN-MARC BOULEY

Volnay, 21190 Meursault
Vineyard: 32 acres
Production: 50,000 bottles
Quality: 🍇🍇🍇🍇   Price: ★★★★

'In each village there are three or four names that everyone in the world knows and who sell their wine more expensively and more easily,' says Jean-Marc Bouley, who owns vines in both Volnay and Pommard. 'I want to be one of them.' An ambitious young man, Bouley did not start selling the majority of his production in bottle until the 1985 vintage. He was provided with the finance to set up on his own by the wine-broker Alain Corcia, whose company is called Prestige des Vins de France.

Bouley has sought to establish his reputation by making *vins de garde*. They are long, elegant and well-structured. 'People who think that Volnay is delicate are amazed that my wines are so powerful,' he says. 'This is a problem commercially – except for selling to the United States, where Robert Parker likes this style. I am better known abroad than in France.'

MAISON PIERRE BOURÉE

21220 Gevrey-Chambertin
Production: 100–200,000 bottles
Quality: 🍇🍇🍇   Price: ★★★★
Other label: Vallet Frères

Pierre Bourée is a small, old-fashioned merchant house owned by the Vallet family. They buy in only a small amount of wine, preferring to make most of the wine they sell themselves. They ferment whole bunches of grapes, complete with stalks, at a high temperature for three weeks. The resulting wines are undoubtedly serious and complex – particularly from Gevrey-Chambertin 'Clos de la Justice', a vineyard which they own, and from the *grand cru* Charmes-Chambertin. Some of their other wines taste awkward or just plain dull. Serena Sutcliffe thinks that they are 'too alcoholic and top-heavy'.

RENÉ BOURGEON

Jambles, 71640 Givry
Vineyard: 17 acres
Production: 35,000 bottles
Quality: 🍇🍇–🍇🍇🍇   Price: ★★

'I want to make *vins de garde* like Côte de Nuits,' declares René Bourgeon, who makes wines in the Côte Chalonnaise under the Bourgogne Côte Chalonnaise and Givry *appellations*.

In order to fulfil his ambition, in the early 1980s Bourgeon took up with the controversial oenologist Guy Accad. By 1990 he was cold-macerating the grapes for twelve days before fermentation – cooling them to 2°C and then gradually letting them warm up – and fermenting them for a further twelve days at a maximum temperature of 28°C. The resulting wines are clearly well-made but they do not have the structure of burgundies: they are too aggressive; they lack finesse. Moreover, they do not taste obviously of Pinot Noir.

ALAIN BURGUET

18 rue de l'Église, 21220 Gevrey-Chambertin
Vineyard: 14 acres
Production: 20,000 bottles
Quality: 🍇🍇🍇🍇   Price: ★★★

Every time Alan Burguet is written about it is pointed out that it is a great pity that he does not have any *premier cru* vineyards on which to exercise his skills. These are undoubted. A small, aggressive-looking man, he produces tough, complex wines from ordinary village vineyards in Gevrey-Chambertin. He makes wines in a reduced style – that is to say, they retain their fermentation gases for a long time in cask and mature very slowly. His *vieilles vignes cuvée* from 1978, the vintage which created his reputation, is still not fully developed.

CAVE COOPÉRATIVE DE BUXY

71390 Buxy
Vineyard: 582 acres
Production: 1,100,000 bottles
Quality: 🍇🍇–🍇🍇🍇   Price: ★★

The Buxy co-operative in the south of the Côte Chalonnaise enjoys a pre-eminent status among French co-operative wineries, whose products usually range from the dire to the disappointing. Although the wines it produces are entitled to nothing grander than the Bourgogne and Bourgogne Côte Chalonnaise *appellations*, it does make a special bottling of wine made from grapes from older, lower-yielding vines. This is matured in oak casks, of which one-fifth are new, and is sold under the label 'Fûts de Chêne'. It is more complex than the co-operative's other wines and offers excellent value for money.

The director of the co-operative, Roger Rageot, has invested a great deal of money and energy in improving the wines, including the invention of special fermentation tanks in which robots replicate the treading that was traditionally done by foot. In this light of his efforts, the wines – although they are all nice, light and crisp – ought to be even better than they are.

Rageot admits that the wines suffer from being filtered three times before bottling. In order to avoid having to do this, he wants to introduce another stage – a cellar for refining the wines – between the maturation in bulk and the bottling. He has been carrying out secret tests on such a cellar for the last three years. 'It will be something unique in Burgundy. By the end of the century we will be able to launch wines on the market that are ready to drink and are more elegant than the ones we make today.'

DOMAINE CACHEUX-BLÉE

21670 Vosne-Romanée

Vineyard: 14 acres

Production: 10,000 bottles

Quality: 🍇🍇🍇🍇   Price: ★★★–★★★★

Jacques and Patrice Cacheux do not bow to fashion. Although they have some new oak casks, they only buy them because they have to replace old ones. Patrice says that the taste of new oak is very flattering, but it does not bring quality to a wine. They make quite tough wines from vineyards in Nuits-St-Georges and Vosne-Romanée. This was particularly true in 1986 when the fermentation stopped for a week. For this reason Patrice is not keen to sell to the United States, where he believes people like wines which are more immediately appealing.

Surprisingly, their supplest wine comes from the *grand cru*

Les Échézeaux, where their vines are fifty years old. A 1982 Échézeaux tasted in 1989 had a remarkably deep colour for such a diluted vintage; it was soft, rich, complex and still quite tannic. It had not been aged in new oak at all.

CHÂTEAU DE CHAMBOLLE-MUSIGNY

21770 Chambolle-Musigny

Vineyard: 10 acres

Production: 10,000 bottles

Quality: 🍇🍇🍇–🍇🍇🍇🍇   Price: ★★★★–★★★★★

This domaine in Chambolle-Musigny was created by Frédéric Mugnier's great-great-grandfather, a manufacturer of black-currant liqueur in Dijon, in about 1910. Until 1978 the vines were rented out to the merchant company Faiveley. Frédéric took over in 1985, but he is still finding his way. 'I vinify experimentally,' he says. 'I try out new things each year. I vinify different parcels by different methods. In general I have been vatting for longer and longer each year. The purpose is to extract more.'

Mugnier makes toasty, glycerous wines which should appeal not only to people who like 'old-fashioned' burgundy but also to those who think that these 'old-fashioned' wines are heavy and inelegant. His *grand cru* Le Musigny is fabulous.

CHÂTEAU DE CHAMIREY

Chamirey, 71640 Mercurey

Vineyard: 55 acres

Production: 100,000 bottles

Quality: 🍇🍇🍇   Price: ★★★

This estate, in Mercurey in the Côte Chalonnaise, is owned by Bertrand Devillard, the managing director of the merchant house Antonin Rodet. The wine is distributed exclusively by Rodet, but it is made separately from Rodet's wines and is far superior to them. It has beautiful, crisp fruit, and can be drunk very young.

DOMAINE CHANDON DE BRIAILLES

rue Soeur Goby, 21420 Savigny-lès-Beaune

Vineyard: 27 acres

Production: 50,000 bottles

Quality: 🍇🍇🍇   Price: ★★★

This is an aristocratic estate, whose owners are related to the Chandons of Moët et Chandon. It includes vineyards in the *grand cru* Le Corton as well as in the village of Savigny-lès-Beaune. The wine is made by Comtesse Nadine de Nicolay, with the help of the broker Henri Meurgey, in an aristocratic style.

Meurgey rescued the Comtesse de Nicolay in the late 1980s, when she had all but fallen into the hands of the oenologist Guy Accad. 'Guy Accad offered to make wines for me that exploded in the mouth,' said the Comtesse. 'I didn't want that. I like severe wines. I don't like to chaptalize. My 1988s only have 10–11 per cent alcohol. I try and compensate for the lack of alcohol by having concentration.'

The wines are long, lean and classically structured. They are capable of ageing for a very long time in bottle but do not always succeed in shaking off the sulphurous smells which sometimes spoil them.

DOMAINE CHAPUIS

21920 Aloxe-Corton

Vineyard: 22 acres

Production: 40,000 bottles

Quality: 🍇🍇🍇   Price: ★★★★

This estate has been producing wine (although not under the Chapuis name) for eight centuries. Its reputation is based principally on its white Corton-Charlemagne. The red wines (with the exception of the excellent Corton-Perrières, from a *grand cru* vineyard) are a little too lean and light, and they certainly cannot be accused of being flattering in their youth.

'It is our role,' says Maurice Chapuis, 'to make wine which is difficult to judge at the start. I try to make wine which is closed at first and which does not explode in the mouth during the first few years. That is not how Pinot Noir tastes.'

JEAN CHAUVENET

rue de Gilly, 21700 Nuits-St-Georges

Vineyard: 16 acres

Production: 25–30,000 bottles

Quality: 🍇🍇🍇   Price: ★★★★

Jean Chauvenet, the president of the Nuits-St-Georges vine-growers union, works with the oenologist Guy Accad (see 'Colour – A Red Herring', on pp. 20–22) but only takes part of his advice. Since 1982 he has, on Accad's instructions, cold-macerated his grapes before fermentation for four or five days – but he follows this with a traditional fermentation at a warm temperature which lasts for ten days more. The end result is a Nuits-St-Georges which is attractive in its youth but still tastes as people would expect red burgundy to do.

DOMAINE GEORGES ET MICHEL CHEVILLON

24 and 41 rue Henri de Bahèzre, 21700 Nuits-St-Georges

Vineyard: 20 acres

Production: 25,000 bottles

Quality: 🍇🍇🍇   Price: ★★★—★★★★

This is the less prestigious of the two Chevillon estates in Nuits-St-Georges. The jovial, rotund Michel Chevillon makes elegant, accessible wines without much staying power which resemble those of the Gouges estate more closely than the wines made by his more famous cousin Robert. His best wine comes from the most famous vineyard in Nuits-St-Georges, the *premier cru* Les St-Georges.

ROBERT CHEVILLON

68 rue Félix Tisserand, 21700 Nuits-St-Georges

Vineyard: 32 acres

Production: 30,000 bottles

Quality: 🍇🍇🍇🍇🍇   Price: ★★★★

Generally regarded as the most prestigious wine-producer in Nuits-St-Georges, Robert Chevillon is a simple man who is horrified by the idea of stardom. He stresses the importance of little details, such as doing his own bottling (rather than employing a mobile bottling line) so that he can choose the best day. He is not forthcoming about the details of his fermentation techniques but it is clear that he macerates the grape skins in the wine for a very long period. His wines are tough in their youth but they are long and extremely elegant compared with the general run of Nuits-St-Georges.

Chevillon makes wonderfully concentrated wines from vines in the *premiers crus* Les Cailles and Les Vaucrains, which were planted just after the end of the First World War, but his best wine is a supremely complex yet restrained *premier cru* Les St-Georges, from the most famous vineyard in Nuits-St-Georges.

GEORGES CHICOTOT

12 rue Paul Cabet, 21700 Nuits-St-Georges

Vineyard: 15 acres

Production: 30,000 bottles

Quality: 🍇🍇🍇   Price: ★★★★

'I am a peasant,' says Georges Chicotot, who makes wines from a range of vineyards in Nuits-St-Georges. 'I believe in doing things simply.' Similar opinions have been expressed by many of Burgundy's greatest wine-makers, but Chicotot is not one of them. He is a cocky Jack-the-Lad, whose wines taste like they have been made for him by an oenologist. As indeed they have – or rather they have been made in concert with the oenologist Guy Accad. Chicotot described to me in detail his bizarre fermentation method but threatened physical damage if I was to repeat it. (For details about the methods used by all the wine-makers advised by Accad, see 'Colour – A Red Herring', on pp. 20–22.)

Chicotot's wines are remarkably deep-coloured and at first they impress you with their depth of fruit and tannin, but then you realize that they have no middle to them. There is no evidence that they become more interesting with time. At six years of age a Nuits-St-Georges Les Pruliers 1984 was still young and green, well-made but charmless.

DOMAINE CHOPIN-GROFFIER

21830 Comblanchien

Vineyard: 25 acres

Production: 35,000 bottles

Quality: 🍇🍇🍇🍇   Price: ★★★–★★★★

Daniel Chopin's estate is spread all over the Côte de Nuits – the result of combining his family's vineyards with those of his wife, who is the cousin of Robert Groffier, a wine-maker in Morey-St-Denis.

Chopin, who has been making wine since 1959, follows traditional methods. He always includes some stalks in the vat and ferments the wine for an average of two weeks. But his wines are not hard in their youth. They are round and glycerous, with Pinot Noir fruit in their core. This is no less true of his Clos de Vougeot – which is outstanding – than it is of his good-value Côte de Nuits-Villages, made from vines in Comblanchien, where he lives. 'The important thing,' he says, 'is to have an agreeable sensation when drinking the wine – whether young or old.'

BRUNO CLAIR

5 rue du Vieux Collège, 21160 Marsannay-la-Côte

Vineyard: 37 acres

Production: 85,000 bottles

Quality: 🍇🍇🍇🍇   Price: ★★★–★★★★

Bruno Clair's grandfather Joseph came to Marsannay from Santenay at the southern end of the Côte d'Or immediately after the end of the First World War. Hitherto the vineyard of Marsannay had been planted in Gamay and produced table-wine for consumption in Dijon. It was Clair who planted Pinot Noir and made it into a pink wine which he called Bourgogne Rosé de Marsannay. This was later given its own *appellation*.

Joseph Clair built up an extensive domaine (Domaine Clair-Daü), with holdings throughout the Côte de Nuits. This was split up in 1985, as the result of a family dispute. One-third of the vineyards (including the *grands crus* Clos de Vougeot and Le

Musigny) were sold to Maison Louis Jadot. Bruno Clair has retained mostly village and *premiers crus* vineyards in Marsannay and Gevrey-Chambertin, together with the *grand cru* Chambertin-Clos de Bèze.

Whereas the old Clair-Daü estate enjoyed a reputation for making long-lasting, tannic wines, the young Bruno Clair makes wines in a much more modern style. They are balanced, elegant and quite fruity, and are capable of being drunk either young or old. The principal exception to this rule comes from the one vineyard Clair owns in the Côte de Beaune: he makes a surprisingly concentrated wine from vines in the Savigny-lès-Beaune *premier cru* La Dominode, which were originally planted in 1902.

DOMAINE DU CLOS DES ÉPENOTS

21630 Pommard

Vineyard: 12 acres

Production: 15,000 bottles

Quality: 🍇🍇🍇   Price: ★★★★

This estate is unusual in Burgundy in having a large parcel of vines in a single block (within the *premier cru* Pommard Les Épenots). The vineyard has not been divided up because it has been owned since the beginning of the century by the Comtes Armand. They have always been absentee landlords who have employed a manager to run the estate for them. From 1950 until 1984 the manager was Philibert Rossignol, a native of Volnay. In her book *Great Vineyards and Wine-makers* Serena Sutcliffe described his wine as 'complete' and 'multi-dimensional' but I have never been impressed by what I have tasted from this period.

In 1985 the wine-making was taken over by Pascal Marchand, a young French-Canadian. He has reduced the yields in the vineyard, purchased equipment for controlling the temperature of fermentation and extended the fermentation period. He has transformed the wine. Marchand says that he looks for concentration and depth of fruit, and he certainly achieves his aim. His wine can be accused of lacking finesse, but it is quite delicious.

DOMAINE DU CLOS FRANTIN

21670 Vosne-Romanée

Vineyard: 37 acres

Production: 50,000 bottles

Quality: 🍇🍇🍇–🍇🍇🍇🍇   Price: ★★★★

Like the Clos de Tart in Morey-St-Denis, the Domaine du Clos Frantin is owned by a firm of merchants, Bichot, which (fortunately) does not seek to influence the wine-making. The manager, Alain Ambroise, is full of ideas. He macerates the grape skins in the wine for a total of three weeks, having developed the theory that if you have a little sugar left after the end of fermentation and continue to macerate, the sugar turns to glycerol.

Whatever the explanation, the wines he makes are plump and attractive. They cover twelve *appellations* throughout the Côte de Nuits, but they are best from Vosne-Romanée, particularly the *premier cru* Les Malconsorts.

DOMAINE CLOS NOIR

11 rue du Gaizot, 21220 Gevrey-Chambertin

Vineyard: 15 acres

Production: 15–30,000 bottles

Quality: 🍇🍇🍇   Price: ★★★★

Second label: Domaine Philippe Batacchi

'I am crazy about trying out different methods of vinification,' says Philippe Batacchi. 'Between 1972, when I started, and 1985 I carried out experiments on whole vintages. None of these years taste the same.' In 1983 he tried hot maceration of the grapes before fermentation, heating them to 45–50°C. This extracted colour but he found that it did not last. In 1985 he tried cold maceration of the grapes before fermentation. Then he fermented at a high temperature, up to 34°C – in order to extract fat. In 1990 he started working with the oenologist Guy Accad, who extended his period of cold maceration from four to fifteen days and afterwards fermented the wine at a low temperature, never exceeding 28°C.

Batacchi's wines have good fruit but they lack depth and complexity. This is no less true of the *grand cru* Clos de la Roche than of his village Gevrey-Chambertin. They give the impression of being made by someone who likes playing around with different methods of wine-making rather than putting his heart into his wines.

CLOS DE TART

21740 Morey-St-Denis

Vineyard: 19 acres

Production: 25,000 bottles

Quality: 🍇🍇🍇🍇   Price: ★★★★

The Clos de Tart, a *grand cru* in the village of Morey-St-Denis, has since 1932 been wholly owned by the merchants Mommessin – but the manager Henri Perraut says that he continues to follow the wine-making methods which were practised at the Clos before Mommessin bought it. He ferments whole bunches of grapes complete with the stalks. He says that this produces harder wines which need to be kept at least seven or eight years before drinking. However, he rounds them out by maturing them entirely in new oak – another practice which he says is traditional at the Clos.

Because they are made from old, low-yielding vines, the wines stand up well to the new oak. They turn out rich, glycerous and complex, with dry tannin from the stalks and some vanilla from the oak. They may not be the most elegant wines made in Burgundy, but they are among the most reliable. In 1990 I tasted the wine Perraut had made in the much-reviled 1975 vintage. It was remarkably good.

DOMAINE COCHE-DURY

9 rue Charles Giraud, 21190 Meursault

Vineyard: 6 acres

Production: 15,000 bottles

Quality: 🍇🍇🍇–🍇🍇🍇🍇   Price: ★★★–★★★★

Jean-François Coche enjoys a reputation as one of the very best producers of white burgundy. On the whole, successful producers of white burgundy make disappointing red wines.

'You generally have to vinify the two at the same time,' Coche explains. 'People tend to forget about the red wines. But, in fact, there is no problem with white wines once they are fermenting in cask. Red wines have to be surveyed and worked every day. With white wines it is enough to be very methodical. With red wines you always have to ask questions. You have to change your method every year. The most difficult thing is to produce red wines which both have finesse and are long in the mouth. The longer a wine is, the more alcoholic and concentrated it is: it lacks finesse.'

Coche makes elegant, understated, serious red wines from vineyards in the villages of Auxey-Duresses, Meursault, Monthélie and Volnay. They may not be easy to drink in their youth but they both have finesse and are long in the mouth.

DOMAINE JEAN-JACQUES CONFURON

Premeaux, 21700 Nuits-St-Georges
Vineyard: 17 acres
Production: 35,000 bottles
Quality: 🍇🍇🍇🍇   Price: ★★★★

Since Jean-Jacques Confuron's death in 1983 the wine has been made by his young, friendly daughter Sophie Meunier. She makes elegant, pretty wines which are hardly typical of Nuits-St-Georges. Robert Parker says that they are spoilt by a vegetal taste but I found them rather classy.

DOMAINE CONFURON-COTETIDOT

21670 Vosne-Romanée
Vineyard: 20 acres
Production: 30,000 bottles
Quality: 🍇🍇🍇🍇   Price: ★★★★

A small, funny man of indeterminate age, Jacky Confuron was the first client in Burgundy of the oenologist Guy Accad. It was by working with Confuron that Accad developed his now famous wine-making method. This involves cold maceration of the grapes for one week, followed by fermentation of uncrushed grapes for a further two weeks or so. (See 'Colour – A Red Herring', on pp. 20–22.)

Oddly enough, Confuron condemns 'modern methods' and says that he makes 'powerful wines' by 'the old method'. 'I make wines which are hard at first, not wines which are supple and good to drink young,' he explains. 'Because of the way in which I make my wines, I do not need to age them in new oak. They would be undrinkable for thirty years if I put them in new oak. The 1983s need thirty to forty years anyway.'

These comments are not borne out by a tasting of his wines,

made from vineyards scattered throughout the Côte de Nuits. They are soft and sweet, with ripe fruit, although they certainly have plenty of tannins underneath. They are among the best of the wines made by the Accadian method. The Vosne-Romanée *premier cru* Les Suchots is particularly impressive – yet this is the wine of which the 1987 vintage was famously rejected by the official tasting board for having a taste of 'bitter cocoa'. The only possible explanation for its rejection is that someone wanted to get, through Confuron, at Guy Accad.

DOMAINE DE COURCEL

21630 Pommard

Vineyard: 15 acres

Production: 25–30,000 bottles

Quality: 🍇🍇🍇🍇🍇   Price: ★★★★

This estate is owned by Gilles de Courcel, who works for the wine-merchants Calvet in Bordeaux, and managed on his behalf by Yves Tavant, the third generation of his family to perform this rôle.

The self-effacing Tavant makes probably the most profound wines in Pommard – wonderfully ripe, balanced and concentrated. It is a mystery how he manages this, as he ferments the grapes for only ten days and at a relatively low temperature. Much of the quality must be attributed to the age of the vines, which in their 12-acre holding in the *premier cru* Les Épenots – the source of their best wine – are between thirty and sixty-five years old.

MAISON DOUDET-NAUDIN

rue Henri Cyrot, 21420 Savigny-lès-Beaune

Vineyard: 15 acres

Production: 5–10,000 bottles

Quality: 🍇   Price: ★★★

Doudet-Naudin is a small merchant firm which is famous for practising what it describes as the 'ancient method' (*méthode ancienne*) of vinification. This involves little destalking and maceration periods of between two and three weeks.

Yves Doudet's father started in 1955 by selling the wines from a cellar he had walled up in 1943 to conceal it from the Germans. 'We have always made wines to drink old,' Doudet explains. 'We make wines as they were made before the War. My father liked old things. He did not have a telephone, and we did not buy our first tractor until 1983. My father learnt wine-making from his father in the late 1920s. If the wines from that period are still good now, it is because they were very hard in their youth.'

If the only problem with these wines were hardness in their youth, then there would be little reason to criticize them. I am frankly astonished that Robert Parker can have described Doudet-Naudin's wines as 'concentrated, full and rich'. In my experience these wines – whether from the humble village of Pernand-Vergelesses or the *grand cru* Le Corton – are earthy, dirty and common. I can only agree with Anthony Hanson when he wrote, 'If this is how the ancients did it, I am all for progress.'

MAISON JOSEPH DROUHIN

7 rue d'Enfer, 21200 Beaune

Quality: 🍇🍇🍇🍇   Price: ★★★–★★★★★

Robert Drouhin is the highest-profile merchant in Burgundy. A marketing genius, he understands why consumers pay inflated prices for burgundies. 'We're not selling wine,' he explains. 'We're selling luxury. We're selling the image of the cobbled streets of Beaune.'

Robert Drouhin took over the direction of the company founded by his great-uncle in 1957 at the age of twenty-three. The wines he made in the 1960s were uninspiring. It was the destruction of his bottling plant and much of his stock of wine by fire in 1973 that led him to rethink his approach to wine-making. He commissioned a market-research analysis which showed that consumers were generally disappointed by red burgundies, which they considered to lack colour, flavour and longevity. Beginning with the 1976 vintage he extended the fermentation period to two weeks, and the wines improved dramatically.

Today, Drouhin enjoys a better reputation than any merchant other than Louis Jadot. It is significant that Robert Drouhin names Jadot as the only other merchant for whom he has any respect. The wines are not quite as good as those of Jadot, but then they are made in a very different style. Whereas Jadot's are difficult to taste in their youth, those of Drouhin are very accessible, with lots of fruit but sometimes lacking a little in depth and complexity. Drouhin's flagship vineyard is the Beaune *premier cru* Clos des Mouches but there is a remarkable consistency throughout a very large range of wines.

DOMAINE DROUHIN-LAROZE

20 rue Gaizot, 21220 Gevrey-Chambertin

Vineyard: 31 acres

Production: 50,000 bottles

This estate, which is based in Gevrey-Chambertin, includes vineyard holdings in some of the most famous *grands crus* in Burgundy, among them Bonnes-Mares, Clos de Vougeot and Chambertin-Clos de Bèze. It is beautifully maintained, and it is well worth trying to get to see the cellars, which have been built without walls at the end, so that visitors can see how the subsoil differs over a few yards. Managing to reach the cellars may pose something of a problem, however. In order to have an introduction, I had my visit arranged by a broker whom Bernard Drouhin dealt with and knew well. When I arrived for my appointment, Drouhin asked me where the broker was. I said that I had no idea. He said that, in that case, he could not receive me. He showed me round the cellars and gave me a glass of Bonnes-Mares 1987 (good but hardly profound) 'out of friendship' but said that he could not give me a tasting unless the broker was there. I have often found growers in Burgundy to be suspicious of journalists, but never to this extent.

DOMAINE ROBERT DUBOIS

Premeaux, 21700 Nuits-St-Georges

Vineyard: 45 acres

Production: 120,000 bottles

Quality: 🍇🍇🍇   Price: ★★★

Régis Dubois, Robert's son, regards himself as 'a pioneer'. He sells two or three times as much wine in bottle as most other vine-growers in Burgundy. He owns vineyards in the Côte de Beaune as well as in various parts of the Côte de Nuits: that way, he says, he can offer a range of different wines without having to turn himself from a grower into a merchant. 'I have a totally different sense of commercialization from other growers,' he adds. 'I have very modern installations.' He has some automatic roto-tanks which ferment a wine in one week rather than two, without any physical labour. He admits, however, that wine made in these tanks is more tannic and has less finesse than wine made more slowly in open vats.

The quality of Dubois's wines suffers a little from his devotion to efficiency. In their youth they have an odd fruit character which does not bring to mind Pinot Noir. Dubois worries that they lack primary aromas, which he says present fashion demands. This is hardly surprising, given that most of them come from Nuits-St-Georges, which does not enjoy a reputation for producing pretty wines. They do become more elegant with age, but they lack concentration.

DOMAINE DUJAC

21740 Morey-St-Denis

Vineyard: 30 acres

Production: 50–60,000 bottles

Quality: 🍇🍇🍇🍇   Price: ★★★★–★★★★★

In a former life Jacques Seysses was the director of Nabisco, France, and a great wine-lover. Then he decided to indulge his hobby, choosing Burgundy because it was easier to build up an estate there than in Bordeaux. He settled in Morey-St-Denis simply because that was where an estate became available: he bought it in 1968 from a man who had no sons and whose wife wanted to go back to live in Nice.

As an outsider – with an American wife – Seysses has served as first port of call for many New World producers wanting to learn how Pinot Noir is made in Burgundy. His wine-making method has been adopted by Joseph Swan and Josh Jensen at Calera in California and by James Halliday at Coldstream Hills and Gary Farr at Bannockburn in Australia. This method is very simple. Seysses puts whole grapes, with their stalks, into the vat and allows them to ferment. He explains that this produces a slower fermentation and more complex wines. Some of the grapes ferment whilst still unbroken, which is bad for the colour but brings complexity.

Seysses's wines are undoubtedly excellent but the rave reviews he has received should probably be attributed to his personality (and to the fact that he speaks English). Robert Parker says that they are ripe wines which drink well young. Actually, they are long, lean, dry and austere wines which need time to mature. This is particularly true of his top wines, from the *grands crus* Bonnes-Mares and Clos de la Roche, which can remain undrinkable for a decade.

MAURICE ÉCARD

rue Chanson Maldant, 21420 Savigny-lès-Beaune

Vineyard: 30 acres

Production: 50,000 bottles

Quality: 🍇🍇🍇–🍇🍇🍇🍇   Price: ★★★

Maurice Écard has been making wines in Savigny-lès-Beaune since 1948. Compared with the general style of the village, his wines have more depth and ripeness. He explains that he likes a challenge: 'If I were a grower in Pommard, I'd try to make light wines; as I am here, I try to make round ones.'

DOMAINE MICHEL ESMONIN

1 rue Neuve, 21220 Gevrey-Chambertin

Vineyard: 15 acres

Production: 8,500 bottles

Quality: 🍇🍇🍇🍇   Price: ★★★★

Michel Esmonin only started to bottle his own wines in 1987 when his daughter Sylvie graduated from university. They still sell the majority of their production to merchants, but what they bottle under their own label is the cream of their crop. Their village Gevrey-Chambertin is made from grapes on the hillside; what they sell to merchants is made from grapes grown on the plain. Their best wine is the Gevrey-Chambertin *premier cru* Clos St-Jacques.

Their wines are balanced and elegant, with a salty, smoky-bacon character. Sylvie Esmonin says that they use Châtillon-nais oak casks made by Flaive in Dijon because they are 'very discreet' and 'harmonize well with the wine'. In fact, it is these same casks which give the Richebourg from Domaine Jean Gros its extraordinary smell of toast.

*

MAISON FAIVELEY

> 8 rue Tribourg, 21700 Nuits-St-Georges
>
> Vineyard: 250 acres
>
> Production: 625,000 bottles
>
> Quality: 🍇🍇🍇   Price: ★★★–★★★★★

I am prepared to be proved wrong about these wines. Faiveley is a merchant company, but its vineyard holdings are so large that it is able to make most of its wine from grapes it has grown itself. These holdings are dominated, in terms of quantity, by the Domaine de la Croix Jacquelet in Mercurey in the Côte Chalonnaise, and in terms of quality by several *grands crus*, of which the most concentrated is a portion of Le Corton which was officially classified in the 1930s as Clos des Cortons Faiveley. There is no reason why Faiveley's wines should suffer from the defects of other merchants' burgundies. Certainly, they are complex and have a core of real Pinot Noir fruit. Moreover, both Robert Parker and Clive Coates are great fans. But I find them too earthy and too coarse.

DOMAINE JEAN-CLAUDE FOURRIER

> 7 route de Dijon, 21220 Gevrey-Chambertin
>
> Vineyard: 20 acres
>
> Production: 35,000 bottles
>
> Quality: 🍇🍇🍇   Price: ★★★★–★★★★★

'I try to make elegant, fruity wines,' says Jean-Claude Fourrier, who has inherited the estate of his great-uncle Fernand Pernot, who acquired a great reputation for the wines he made during the 1960s from his vineyards in Gevrey-Chambertin.

The wines are much lighter than they used to be. Robert Parker says that they suffer from excess production and carelessness in the cellar. They are not quite as bad as Parker suggests, however. Fourrier explains that he works with a lot of restaurateurs, who do not want the wine to dominate the food. When I told him (in 1989) how much I liked his straight 1987 Gevrey-Chambertin, which had more stuffing than most, he replied that restaurateurs had found it too aggressive for their cooking.

JEAN GARAUDET

21630 Pommard
Vineyard: 14 acres
Production: 20,000 bottles
Quality: 🍇🍇🍇🍇   Price: ★★★★

Jean Garaudet says that he tries to make wines that are not excessively tannic because he sells mostly to restaurants. It is true that his wines have light and pretty fruit but – with the exception of his Monthélie – they are backed up by acidity and tannin and need to be kept. They are undoubtedly long and elegant, but in some cases I wonder if there is enough fruit and flavour behind all that structure. Garaudet's best wine, Pommard *premier cru* Les Charmots, made from vines planted at the beginning of the century, is certainly not suitable for drinking young in restaurants.

DOMAINE ARMAND GIRARDIN

21630 Pommard
Vineyard: 11 acres
Production: 12,000 bottles
Quality: 🍇🍇🍇🍇   Price: ★★★★

Henri Girardin took over the running of the family estate after his father and brother died in the Second World War. At heart, he is a traditionalist. 'I make wines that are tough in their youth,' he says. 'In general the style of Pommard is more robust than that of Volnay.' Girardin is not immutable, however. In 1985 he was persuaded by his American importer, Robert Kacher, to mature the portion of his wine that he exports to the United States in a mixture of new and one-year-old oak casks. He continues to mature the rest of his production in old casks, as before.

The wine that is aged in new oak is exuberant and tremendously appealing in its youth, but this does not mean that it has a better potential for ageing than the wine matured in old casks. The concentration of Girardin's wines does not come from being aged in new oak but from being made from old vines. His best wines, the Pommard *premiers crus* Les Épenots and Les Rugiens, are made partly from vines planted in 1900.

DOMAINE HENRI GOUGES

7 rue du Moulin, 21700 Nuits-St-Georges

Vineyard: 22 acres

Production: 40–50,000 bottles

Quality: 🍷🍷🍷🍷　　Price: ★★★★

'The wines of Domaine Henri Gouges,' writes Matt Kramer, 'are second-rate and have been for years. No estate has coasted longer on a once-lustrous reputation than this one. The wines are so thin that in some vintages they border on the anorexic.'

Domaine Henri Gouges is arguably the most prestigious small estate in Burgundy. It was Henri Gouges who led the battle against mercantile fraud and the movement towards estate-bottling in Burgundy in the 1920s. He died in 1967 and it is said that the wines have not been the same since.

Given that all the vineyards owned by the Gouges estate are Nuits-St-Georges *premiers crus* and that three-quarters of the vines are forty years or older, one might expect the wines to be intense and concentrated. Instead, they are well-balanced and mid-weight. 'Our reputation,' says Henri's grandson Pierre, 'is to make wines which are delicate rather than tannic.' Their house-style is a product of unusual (for Burgundy) wine-making methods. The grapes are fermented in closed tanks at a relatively low temperature (28°C); some of them are unbroken and ferment intercellularly, as in the Beaujolais. Pierre says that this method produces wines with more fruit and perfume.

There is nothing new about it, however. It was introduced by Henri Gouges himself. The wines at this estate have always been relatively restrained. In 1988 I tasted a Nuits-St-Georges Les Pruliers 1964 which had become meaty with age but was still crisp and even.

DOMAINE GRIVOT

21670 Vosne-Romanée

Vineyard: 37 acres

Production: 50,000 bottles

Quality: 🍇–🍇🍇🍇   Price: ★★★★–★★★★★

Nowadays Domaine Grivot is talked about as much as any other estate in Burgundy because it is the most prestigious domaine to have taken on Guy Accad as its consultant oenologist.

The beautiful, charming young Étienne Grivot, who received a number of proposals of marriage by post from America after his face appeared on the cover of the *Wine Spectator*, started taking Accad's advice on soil treatments as soon as he arrived in the Domaine in 1982. Accad, he explains, was 'the first person I met who spoke coherently about the problems of Burgundy'. It took five years for the soil to be sufficiently well-adjusted for Accad to start advising Grivot on his vinification. This appears to have caused a rift between Étienne and his father Jean, supposedly his partner in running the domaine. 'Burgundy is a conservative region,' Jean Grivot told Harry Eyres in *Wine Dynasties of Europe*. 'We are not here to overturn tradition. I am not in favour of revolutions.'

At first Accad's advice changed Grivot's wines for the better. The 1986s had been hard and thin. The 1987s were ripe and approachable. 'For the first time,' declared Étienne Grivot, 'I have managed to produce a *vin de garde* which can also be drunk young.' The 1988s appear to be excellent, although it is only possible to speculate as to their ultimate quality. In 1990 Étienne Grivot described them as 'monolithic' and 'Cartesian'. The 1989s, in contrast, were 'spontaneous' and 'spiritual'. I can see what he meant. They were over in an instant and, when you thought about it, there was nothing to them at all.

ROBERT GROFFIER

21740 Morey-St-Denis

Vineyard: 20 acres

Production: 20,000 bottles

Quality: 🍇🍇🍇   Price: ★★★★

Robert Groffier has his fans. 'One of my favourite growers in Burgundy,' writes Clive Coates. 'His wines are always classically elegant.' I beg to disagree. Groffier, who ferments with a lot of stalks and matures his *premiers crus* in at least 50 per cent new oak, produces a rich, glycerous, 'old-fashioned' burgundy, which is enjoyable to drink but heavy-handed. He would do better if he had his vineyards in Morey-St-Denis, where he lives. In fact, they are in Chambolle-Musigny. He fails to express the elegance of Chambolle, whereas his methods would counterbalance the austerity of Morey. He is more successful in tough years such as 1986 than in flattering ones such as 1987.

DOMAINE GROS FRÈRE ET SOEUR

21670 Vosne-Romanée

Vineyard: 32 acres

Production: 40,000 bottles

Quality: 🍇🍇–🍇🍇🍇🍇   Price: ★★★★

Bernard Gros, who makes the wine at this estate (owned by his aunt Colette), is the opinionated brother of Michel Gros, wine-maker for the Domaine Jean Gros. Some of the wines come from the same *appellations*, in the village of Vosne-Romanée. But they could not be more different. 'I try to make wines as supple and round as possible,' Gros explains. '*Vins de garde* don't interest me. Wine has been democratized. People without cellars have the right to drink fine wine. A great wine is a contradiction. It is both strong and soft. Only *grands crus* arrive at a perfect contrast.'

It is true that the higher you ascend in the scale of Gros's wines, the more they are strong and soft at the same time. The strongest and softest (and by far the best) is the *grand cru* Richebourg. All of Gros's wines taste of fruit. But none of them taste as though they were made of Pinot Noir.

DOMAINE JEAN GROS

21670 Vosne-Romanée

Vineyard: 25 acres

Production: 30,000 bottles

Quality: 🍇🍇🍇🍇🍇   Price: ★★★★–★★★★★

This is one of the great names of Burgundy. It once was even greater. With substantial holdings in the *grands crus* of Richebourg, Clos de Vougeot, Grands Échézeaux and Échézeaux, Domaine Gros-Renaudot, as it was then known, was in the status of its vineyards second only to the Domaine de la Romanée-Conti.

In 1963 the estate was split into four parts, one of them being Domaine Jean Gros, run since his death by his son Michel, and two of them being combined into Domaine Gros Frère et Soeur, run by Michel's brother Bernard. A portion of the

Domaine Jean Gros was given to Michel's and Bernard's sister Anne-Françoise in 1988. Her estate, Domaine Anne-Françoise Gros, should not, of course, be confused with Domaine Anne et François Gros, which is the fourth part of the old Gros-Renaudot estate.

The best of the wines produced by Domaine Jean Gros come from the Vosne-Romanée *premier cru* Clos des Réas (which it owns exclusively) and from the super-*grand cru* Richebourg. They are distinguished from the wines made by the other Gros estates by the fact that they are matured entirely in new oak. The Richebourg smells more of toast – of grilled oak – than any other red burgundy I have tasted. Michel Gros buys some of his casks from Flaive in Dijon, who toast their casks very heavily. He has tried to persuade the other two coopers from whom he buys casks to toast them more heavily but (he says) they are too set in their ways. He believes that a heavily toasted cask marries better with the wine.

Like the wines of Henri Jayer in the same village, which are matured entirely in new oak, the wines of Domaine Jean Gros combine the richness appreciated by lovers of 'old-fashioned' burgundy with the pure Pinot Noir fruit sought by modernists. They are of the highest class.

DOMAINE MICHEL GROS

Chevrey, 21700 Nuits-St-Georges

Vineyard: 12 acres

Production: 20,000 bottles

Quality: 🍇🍇🍇   Price: ★★★

Michel Gros runs Domaine Jean Gros in Vosne-Romanée on behalf of his mother, brother and sister. He owns this estate in the Hautes Côtes de Nuits himself. The Gros family came to Vosne-Romanée from the Hautes Côtes 150 years ago. When Michel's late father Jean bought land in the Hautes Côtes in 1967 it was (says his widow) because he felt nostalgic for the wide open spaces.

Because the climate is cooler than in the Côte d'Or, Michel goes to elaborate lengths in order to ensure that the grapes ripen. He prunes the vines much more severely than he does in the Côte d'Or and therefore achieves a smaller crop, only 30 hectolitres per hectare. He also harvests the grapes a week later than at Vosne-Romanée. As a result, the wines, although light, do not lack ripeness or concentration. They offer excellent value for money.

DOMAINE HAEGELEN-JAYER

21670 Vosne-Romanée

Vineyard: 12 acres

Production: 25–30,000 bottles

Quality: 🍇🍇🍇–🍇🍇🍇🍇   Price: ★★★★–★★★★★

For people who insist on having the name Jayer on a bottle of burgundy, here is another one – because Alfred Haegelen married a cousin of the great Henri Jayer.

Haegelen has his cellars in Vosne-Romanée, like Henri Jayer, and has holdings in some of the same *appellations*, but the wines do not taste at all similar. Haegelen says that he makes 'perfumed, spicy wines' by including the stalks in the fermentation vat and ageing all his wines in at least 50 per cent new oak. They certainly have plenty of flavour but they lack finesse. They are toasty, tannic, gamey wines of a style which doubtless appeals to lovers of 'old-fashioned' burgundy. By far the best of them is the *grand cru* Clos de Vougeot.

CAVE COOPÉRATIVE DES HAUTES CÔTES

route de Pommard, 21200 Beaune

Vineyard: 750 acres

Production: 1.5 million bottles

Quality: 🍇🍇–🍇🍇🍇   Price: ★★

This co-operative, which was formed in 1968, has played a major part in the revival of the Hautes Côtes, since it has enabled growers to obtain a fair price for their grapes without having to invest individually in buildings and materials. It has also performed a propaganda function thanks to its ostentatious situation on the main road out of Beaune towards Cluny.

Although it has 220 members, with vineyards in a number of villages throughout the Côte d'Or, 80 per cent of its production comes from the Hautes Côtes de Nuits and Hautes Côtes de Beaune, and it is on these wines that its reputation is based. Vinification in automatic tanks produces crisp, lean, quite stylish wines that offer excellent value for money.

HOSPICES DE BEAUNE

21200 Beaune

Vineyard: 143 acres

Production: 200,000 bottles

Quality: 🍇🍇–🍇🍇🍇🍇   Price: ★★★★★

The buildings of the Hospices de Beaune, which were established in the fifteenth century as a charitable institution for the sick and the poor, are the greatest tourist attraction in Burgundy. Over the years a great many vineyards have been donated to the Hospices, the vast majority of them in the Côte de Beaune. Most are *premiers crus*, but the name of the vineyard does not appear on the label. The produce of different vineyards is blended together and labelled with the name of the benefactor. The Cuvée Rousseau-Deslandes, for example, is a blend of four *premier cru* vineyards in Beaune.

The intention behind the donations was that the wine should be auctioned and the proceeds used to fund the Hospices' good works – and the auctions are still held, on the third Sunday of November each year. The prices the wines fetch have by custom been allowed to set the general level of prices for the burgundies of that year. This is absurd, as buyers at the auction always pay too much. The wines have rarely been worth ordinary prices, let alone high ones. They reached their nadir in 1976, when many of them were ruined by being put in defective barrels. The next year, the Hospices hired a new wine-maker, André Porcheret, who by producing concentrated wines from only the older vines made it possible for them to be matured entirely in new oak barrels. From 1977 to 1987 the Hospices enjoyed a brief period of glory. In 1988 Porcheret left to make the wine at the new Domaine Leroy. His successor has managed, in the naturally concentrated vintages of 1988, 1989 and 1990, to produce wines that are far too light to support the new oak in which they continue to be matured.

In the March following the vintage the wines are moved in cask from the cellars of the Hospices to those of each of the merchants who has bought wine or who has been nominated by a purchaser to mature and bottle his wine for him. The eventual quality of the wine in question therefore depends on the quality of the merchant. The largest purchaser of Hospices wines is usually André Boisseaux, the owner of Patriarche, which is not the best merchant firm in Burgundy.

DOMAINE JACQUESON

Rully, 71150 Chagny
Vineyard: 10 acres
Production: 20,000 bottles
Quality: 🍇🍇🍇–🍇🍇🍇🍇   Price: ★★★

Henri Jacqueson produces the best red wines in the Côte Chalonnaise. They disprove the theory that red wines from Rully are lighter than those from Mercurey. His Rullys are deep in colour, with plenty of extract and a core of Pinot Noir fruit. When I told him that, had I tasted them blind, I would not have taken them for coming from the Côte Chalonnaise at all, he replied, 'That's what all the buyers say.'

The colour is produced by heating a portion of the must to

80°C before fermentation. This method was fashionable in Burgundy in the 1970s but nowadays growers who want to extract colour prefer to adopt the technique of cold maceration that is preached by the oenologist Guy Accad, and Jacqueson has been left on his own. The extract is obtained by fermenting the wine at 30°C for two to three weeks. The glycerol that this method produces, says Jacqueson, is 'the beauty of wine. That is what the Côte Chalonnaise is about – the beauty of wine. You don't have to keep it for ten years. You can drink it young.'

MAISON LOUIS JADOT

5 rue Samuel Legay, 21200 Beaune

Production: 2,000,000 bottles

Quality: 🍇🍇🍇🍇–🍇🍇🍇🍇🍇   Price: ★★★–★★★★★

Jadot are the most reputable, the most honourable and the best wine merchants in Burgundy. Much of the credit for this state of affairs should be given to André Gagey, who has run the company since the death of Louis Jadot III in 1962, first on behalf of the Jadot family and now on behalf of Kobrand, its American agents, to whom the Jadot family sold the firm in 1985.

Gagey's approach is demonstrated by the manner in which he buys from growers. Merchants prefer to buy grapes so that they can control the vinification; growers prefer to sell them wine because they are paid more for it. Merchants usually end up having to buy wine. Gagey buys grapes but pays the growers as though they had sold him wine. So both sides are happy. His hyperactive wine-maker Jacques Lardière makes the wine in a mixture of traditional open vats and automatically rotating tanks. He does not make the same mistake as many people who try to use roto-tanks to abbreviate the fermentation. 'Our aim,' he says, 'is always to macerate for as long as possible. Roto-tanks are better for this.'

Jadot make outstanding wines from a vast range of vineyards

throughout the Côte d'Or. It would be invidious to single out any of them for special praise. They are all true to the character of their *appellations*. Nevertheless, I have often heard Jadot's wines criticized at trade tastings – the reason being that they are difficult to drink in their youth. As Gagey points out, 'Wines which taste very nice in cask are not wines that one can keep for many years.'

MAISON JAFFELIN

2 rue du Paradis, 21200 Beaune
Production: 280,000 bottles
Quality: 🍇🍇🍇–🍇🍇🍇🍇   Price: ★★★–★★★★★

It is sometimes suggested that Jaffelin is simply a second label for the Drouhin wines. It is certainly owned by Drouhin but it is run quite separately by the outgoing young Bernard Repolt.

Jaffelin's wines do not come too far behind those of Drouhin in terms of quality but the style is different. Jaffelin own no vineyards and buy proportionately more ready-made wine than Drouhin do, but Repolt believes that it is easier to create a house-style from wines you have bought in than from wines you have made yourself. He maintains quality by declassifying wines if they are not up to scratch. His most impressive wines – relatively speaking – often come from lesser villages such as Monthélie, Santenay and Pernand-Vergelesses.

Repolt says that Drouhin likes more 'feminine' wines than he does. He says his wines take longer to evolve – in part because of his preference for new oak. 'I like new oak a lot. I do not say that I am right.' One should not, however, exaggerate the differences between Drouhin and Jaffelin: Repolt himself is not an oenologist, so he employs Drouhin's oenologists to make his wine.

HENRI JAYER

21670 Vosne-Romanée

Quality: 🍇🍇🍇🍇🍇   Price: ★★★★–★★★★★

The appearance of Henri Jayer can be compared with that of a comet or of a shooting star. For a brief moment he illuminated all of Burgundy, then he disappeared.

Jayer was born in 1922 and started making wine in 1945. Despite cultivating vines in some of the finest vineyards in Vosne-Romanée – including the *premiers crus* Clos Parantoux and Les Brûlées and the *grands crus* Échézeaux and Richebourg – he did not start bottling his own wine until the recession of 1973–4. It was not until the 1978 vintage that his reputation was established, both in France and on the West Coast of the United States. His wines were not imported into Britain until 1982. Six years later, when he had just started to become a household name, he retired.

For ten brief years Jayer exerted greater influence than any other grower on the wine-makers of Burgundy and the wine-drinkers of the world. He served as the symbol of the whole generation of vine-growers who started bottling their own wine during the recession of the 1970s and brought together the old generation of wine-drinkers who thought red burgundies were full-bodied wines and the new generation who thought that they ought to taste of Pinot Noir. By the time he retired, Jayer had attained such an iconic status that his various relatives – among them Alfred Haegelen, who married Henri's cousin and created Domaine Haegelen-Jayer, and Robert Jayer in the Hautes Côtes de Nuits – benefited from having the Jayer name on their label. (They are all descended from four Jayer brothers who came to Burgundy at the start of the century.)

When I visited Jayer just before his retirement, I asked him if he had a secret. 'If there is a secret, it is simplicity: to intervene as little as possible; to let nature do its own work. Oenologists say that you should get the fermentation started as quickly as possible, that you should put the wine through its malolactic fermentation as early as you can, and that you should rack the wine off its lees immediately afterwards. I do the opposite.'

Among the methods which he developed in opposition to the oenological teachings of his time were a cold maceration of the juice before fermentation – he had been doing this for years before the proselytizing oenologist Guy Accad appeared on the scene – followed by a long fermentation, more maceration afterwards, and the maturation of all his wines – except his Bourgogne Rouge – for about eighteen months in 100 per cent new oak. These methods produced gorgeous, intensely fruity wines, which he intended to be enjoyed relatively young. 'I make wines which taste of fruit,' he explained.

Because of the quality of his wines, and his willingness to help the younger generation, Jayer's once-revolutionary methods are widely practised today. In particular, they are practised at Domaine Méo-Camuzet, whose vineyards he used to work under a sharecropping arrangement and whom he now advises on both vine-growing and wine-making techniques. They are also practised by his nephew Emmanuel Rouget, to whom he has leased his own vineyards. Jayer has not really disappeared; his wines live on through the inspiration he gives to others.

DOMAINE JAYER-GILLES

Magny-les-Villers, 21700 Nuits-St-Georges

Vineyard: 22 acres

Production: 50,000 bottles

Quality: 🍇🍇🍇🍇   Price: ★★★★

The vineyards owned by Robert Jayer span the great (the *grand cru* Les Échézeaux) and the humble (most of his vines are in the Hautes Côtes de Beaune and Hautes Côtes de Nuits). He makes all his wines in the same way, using techniques which closely mirror those of his more celebrated cousin Henri. He denies that they have developed these methods together, but clearly they have discussed them.

In the mid-1980s Robert Jayer adopted two of his cousin's more celebrated methods: cold maceration of the grapes for four days before fermentation, in order to extract colour; and the maturation of all his red wines – even from the Hautes Côtes – in new oak. This may well be connected with the fact that he exports a quarter of all his production to the United States via Robert Kacher, a great fan of new oak.

For their *appellation*, his Hautes Côtes wines are quite staggering. They have an amazing depth of colour and long, intense, clean, black-cherry fruit. They do not taste excessively oaky. All they lack is a bit of charm: they are a bit too aggressive, a bit too oenological. Moreover, for Hautes Côtes wines they are very expensive. 'I sell wine according to its quality not its *appellation*,' Jayer explains.

DOMAINE JEAN JOLIOT ET FILS

Nantoux, 21190 Meursault

Vineyard: 21 acres

Production: 40,000 bottles

Quality: ♟♟♟♟   Price: ★★–★★★

Jean-Baptiste Joliot produces the classiest wines in the Hautes Côtes de Beaune. Many growers in the Hautes Côtes have difficulty ripening grapes in normal years, let alone cold vintages such as 1984, but Joliot's Hautes Côtes de Beaune 1984 is a delicious, elegant wine. 'With reasonable yields,' he explains, 'you can get ripe grapes even in years like 1984. There is no secret. Quality is linked to the yield.'

Wines from the Hautes Côtes are generally regarded as being lighter than ones from the Côte d'Or, but Joliot says that his wines are not so much light as hard (because of their higher level of acidity). 'If other Hautes Côtes wines tend to be light,' he says, 'it is because of a high crop.'

Joliot also makes a Pommard, which is rounder, softer and more concentrated than his Hautes Côtes de Beaune. He admits that he ferments his Pommard for longer, in order to extract more tannin. 'Perhaps I don't extract all that I ought to from my Hautes Côtes wines because I want to differentiate them from my wines from the Côte d'Or,' he explains.

DOMAINE MICHEL JUILLOT

Mercurey, 71640 Givry

Vineyard: 62 acres

Production: 100,000 bottles

Quality: 🍇🍇🍇–🍇🍇🍇🍇   Price: ★★★

Michel Juillot has sold wine under his own name in bottle since the late 1950s and is generally regarded as the leading producer in Mercurey in the Côte Chalonnaise. I visited the estate in 1989, and was shown round by Laurent, Michel's son. The previous year, at the age of twenty-one, he had worked harvests in six different regions, including California, Australia and New Zealand. This experience had left him full of new ideas. 'We do lots of experiments here,' he said.

I tasted the results of various experiments, including a 1987 Mercurey which had been heated to 40°C and then sealed in its fermentation vat for two months. It smelt of geraniums but was long, rich and complex on the palate. I also tasted a 1988 Mercurey from three different types of cask, two of them made from French oak and one from Polish. They were so different that I told Laurent that I would not have said that the three were the same wine. He replied that lots of people had told him this.

Altogether, there were so many experiments that it was difficult to come to a conclusion about the overall quality of the wines that were actually on sale. As far as I could tell, the estate deserved its reputation, and produced serious, mid-weight wines which needed a little while in bottle to show of their best.

MAISON LABOURÉ-ROI

B.P. 14, 21700 Nuits-St-Georges

Production: 1,500,000 bottles

Quality: 🍇🍇🍇   Price: ★★★—★★★★

This merchant company was bought by the Cottin family in 1973. It is run by two brothers, Louis and Armand; another brother, Philippe, is a director of Château Mouton-Rothschild in Bordeaux.

The company vinifies and distributes the wines of Domaine Chantal Lescure, which is based in Nuits-St-Georges but has most of its vineyard holdings in Pommard. Otherwise it has virtually no vineyards of its own from which to make wine. Nevertheless, all the wines sold under the Labouré-Roi label conform to a distinctive house-style.

Louis Cottin has strong views on wine-making. 'I cannot abide tannin,' he says. 'We try to make wines that are as fruity and as low in tannin as possible.' They do so by fermenting the grapes at a low temperature – about 27°C, the temperature at which Beaujolais is normally fermented. It is hardly surprising that the wines taste more like Beaujolais than any other red burgundies I have encountered. They are pleasant, pretty wines but they are hardly serious.

DOMAINE LAFARGE

Volnay, 21190 Meursault

Vineyard: 25 acres

Production: 50,000 bottles

Quality: 🍇🍇🍇🍇🍇   Price: ★★★★—★★★★★

The Lafarge wines have been enjoying an international reputation since they have been sold in bottle – rather than in bulk to merchants – since 1935. The reputation is fully justified. Michel Lafarge's Volnay *premiers crus* Clos des Chênes and Clos du Château des Ducs are wonderful wines – long, elegant, perfectly balanced and built to last.

DOMAINE DES COMTES LAFON

rue Pierre Goignet, 21190 Meursault

Vineyard: 10 acres

Production: 15,000 bottles

Quality: 🍇🍇🍇🍇   Price: ★★★★

The Domaine des Comtes Lafon is famous for making rich, intense, dramatic white wines. Its reputation was created by René Lafon in the 1960s and 1970s. He rather ignored the red wines. René has now handed over the wine-making to his self-assured son Dominique. 'For the red wines,' says Dominique, 'I have taken some ideas from the whites. I want a long fermentation which starts slowly. My father fermented for a week or so. I ferment for two.'

Dominique Lafon makes his red wines mostly from *premier cru* vineyards in Volnay. They are long, elegant and classical, and well worth buying on their own account.

DOMAINE LAMARCHE

21670 Vosne-Romanée

Vineyard: 21 acres

Production: 30–50,000 bottles

Quality: 🍇🍇🍇–🍇🍇🍇🍇   Price: ★★★★–★★★★★

Like Trapet in Gevrey-Chambertin and Gouges in Nuits-St-Georges, the Lamarche estate in Vosne-Romanée is generally reckoned to be living on past glories. The last vintages produced by Henri Lamarche (who died in 1985) were disappointing, and – although he is hardly a young man – it has taken his son François a little while to find his feet. But since 1988 – perhaps encouraged by the imminent elevation of his monopoly vineyard La Grande Rue to *grand cru* status – he has started to make lovely, ripe, velvety wines, which should be ready for drinking at six to eight years of age. Lamarche's best wine is not, in fact, La Grande Rue but the already extant *grand cru*, Grands Échézeaux. His Vosne-Romanée *premier cru* Les Malconsorts is also delicious.

MAISON LOUIS LATOUR

18 rue des Tonneliers, 21200 Beaune

Vineyard: 40 hectares

Production: 500,000 bottles

Quality: 🍷🍷–🍷🍷🍷   Price: ★★★–★★★★★

Ten years ago the merchant company Louis Latour was the focus of a major controversy which has since been largely forgotten. The fact that it pasteurized its wines was considered to be the most shocking of several revelations made by Anthony Hanson in his book on Burgundy, which appeared in 1982.

The precise effect of pasteurization is not known, but there can be little doubt that the wine is altered by the thermic shock of being heated to 70°C. Louis Latour has sought to justify pasteurization – also practised by one other major merchant company, Moillard – by saying that it is a less brutal process than sterile filtration – the treatment preferred by the majority of the many mediocre merchant companies in Burgundy. This may be so, but Louis Latour does not pasteurize as an alternative to filtration. It filters, then pasteurizes, then filters again – if necessary – before bottling. It is so cautious that it removes sediment from old vintages with a siphon before shipment.

The significance of pasteurization is that it places the Maison Louis Latour in the context of the technology of a hundred years ago. The company adopted the practice because the present Louis Latour's grandfather, also called Louis Latour, took a scientific degree at the end of the nineteenth century, when Pasteur's discoveries were all the rage. It is a moot point whether the Maison Louis Latour has progressed since. The present Louis Latour says that it has always made its wines in the same way. It gets fermentation under way at once by heating part of the must in large double-skinned copper bowls, and then ferments the wine for only five or six days.

Surprisingly for wines fermented for so short a period, they are big, brutish and old-fashioned; they lack that prerequisite of red burgundy, delicacy. This is particularly true of Latour's most famous red wine, Château Corton-Grancey, a blend of grapes from several vineyards in the *grand cru* Le Corton. The problem may not lie so much in the pasteurization or the vinification method as in the fact that Latour appears to give priority to its white wines. Most of the white wines are bought as grapes whereas most of the reds are bought as wine. The company justifies this distinction by saying that red-wine vintages are less reliable and that it is sometimes necessary to reject some of them completely. Among the years it has rejected are 1980 and 1987 – two perfectly good vintages.

PHILIPPE LECLERC

13 rue des Halles, 21220 Gevrey-Chambertin

Vineyard: 17 acres

Production: 40,000 bottles

Quality: 🍇🍇🍇🍇🍇   Price: ★★★–★★★★

Philippe Leclerc, one of the stars of Gevrey-Chambertin, has been described by Robert Parker as someone who walks to the

beat of a different drummer and who could double as a member
of a Hell's Angels motorcycle gang. 'I make wines for myself,'
he says. 'I make wines which are very hard at the start, very
powerful, and good to drink when between ten and twenty
years old. I want to recreate the full-bodied wines of the past.'
He points out that the crop was much smaller then and that he
has therefore had to adopt different methods.

Leclerc crushes but does not destalk the grapes, macerates
them for one week, ferments them for two weeks, then macerates them for a further week. Then he matures his *premiers crus*
entirely in new oak. 'Ten years ago,' he remembers, 'people
said that what I did was crazy. Now they are all copying me. But
it is very dangerous to follow the general principles if you do
not know all the little details. It is like a chef giving you a list of
ingredients without saying when he uses them.'

No one makes wines quite like Philippe Leclerc. They are
rich and toasty, long and strong, very complex and not at all
heavy-handed. The best for value is the Bourgogne Rouge, the
best for quality the Gevrey-Chambertin *premier cru* La Combe
au Moine, from vines which were planted before the First
World War. They can be purchased, at reasonable prices, from
an 'Olde Worlde' shop which Leclerc owns in the centre of the
village.

RENÉ LECLERC

28 route de Dijon, 21220 Gevrey-Chambertin

Vineyard: 25 acres

Production: 20–30,000 bottles

Quality: 🍷🍷🍷–🍷🍷🍷🍷   Price: ★★★★

There are two well-known Leclercs in Gevrey-Chambertin,
René and his younger brother Philippe. They worked together
until 1980, when René left, saying that he found his brother
impossible to work with. Their wine-making methods are quite
similar, however – with the exception that René does not

mature his wines in new oak. He says that he tried 20 per cent new oak in 1986 – under the influence of Robert Parker – but has since given up. 'New oak,' he says, 'only brings the taste of oak. You can put any old rubbish in new oak and people will like it. It hides bad tastes.'

Because he does not use new oak, René's wines are much more difficult to taste in their youth than those of his brother. They are big, rich and awkward, and can develop well. But I cannot help feeling that new oak suits this style of wine-making. Like his brother, René makes his best wine from the Gevrey-Chambertin *premier cru* La Combe au Moine.

DOMAINE LEJEUNE

21630 Pommard

Vineyard: 15 acres

Production: 25,000 bottles

Quality: 🍇🍇🍇–🍇🍇🍇🍇   Price: ★★★★

François Jullien de Pommerol, who used to work as an agronomist in Africa, spent from 1977 until 1989 teaching oenology at the Lycée Viticole in Beaune, whilst making the wine at his family estate part-time. He has developed a unique vinification method, which combines a week of *macération carbonique* with two weeks of traditional Burgundy fermentation, punching down the grapes three times a day. He says that this method enables him to have a long fermentation at a high temperature – normally you have to choose between one and the other.

Jullien's wines do not exhibit any of the aromas of *macération carbonique* but are round and glycerous with sweet fruit. It has been suggested that they will not age, but I cannot agree. There is plenty of tannin hidden under all that fruit. One might more fairly criticize them for being rather old-fashioned and lacking in elegance. They are best from the two Pommard *premiers crus* vineyards, Les Argillières and the famous Les Rugiens.

DOMAINE LEROY

21670 Vosne-Romanée

Vineyard: 73 acres

Production: 100,000 bottles

Quality: 🍇🍇🍇🍇🍇   Price: ★★★★★

In 1988 it was reported in the press that the Japanese were trying to buy the Domaine de la Romanée-Conti. In fact, the Japanese company Takashimaya had offered to buy one-third of Maison Leroy, of which it was the Japanese agent. The connection with the Domaine de la Romanée-Conti was that Maison Leroy was owned by Lalou Bize-Leroy, the co-proprietor of the Domaine, and that Maison Leroy distributed the wines of the Domaine all over the world (except in the United States and Great Britain). This was sufficient to persuade the Minister of Agriculture, Henri Nallet, to swear that he would block the sale. 'Romanée-Conti is like a cathedral,' he declared. In the end Takashimaya bought just under 20 per cent of Maison Leroy as at that level it did not need government approval.

With Takashimaya's money Lalou Bize-Leroy went and bought the old Noëllat estate in Vosne-Romanée. Maison Leroy was principally a merchant company, for which she had bought the best possible wines – paying very high prices if need be – but she had not made the wines herself. The purchase of Domaine Noëllat gave her the opportunity to make wine from many of the most celebrated vineyards of the Côte d'Or, including Clos de Vougeot, Richebourg, Romanée-St-Vivant and Le Musigny. She is now running down Maison Leroy – she will continue to buy wine only at the level of generic Bourgogne Rouge – in order to concentrate on Domaine Noëllat, which she has renamed Domaine Leroy.

Bize-Leroy says that she bought Noëllat because the vineyards were planted with 'an extraordinary type' of Pinot Noir, with very small grapes. The vines are very old, between forty-five and fifty years on average. She has converted the vineyards to bio-dynamic methods – an even more rigorous version of organic cultivation, which involves organizing vineyard work according to the phases of the moon.

According to her, the wines Noëllat made from their wonderful vineyards were 'terrible'. To make her wines, Bize-Leroy seduced André Porcheret from the Hospices de Beaune, whose wines he had turned round in the early 1980s.

The wines Porcheret is now making for Leroy are quite fabulous. In some respects they resemble the wines of the Domaine de la Romanée-Conti – the grapes are not destalked, so the wines are hard in their youth – but they are not the same. Porcheret makes more effort to keep the wine away from air than does Bernard Noblet at the Domaine de la Romanée-Conti. 'I want my wines more severe than those of the Domaine,' Bize-Leroy told a journalist from the American magazine the *Wine Spectator*. 'I want them very clean. I want to emphasize the fruit.' She denies that she is setting herself up in competition with the Domaine de la Romanée-Conti, but nobody believes her – not least because she offered the 1988s at prices just as high as those of the Domaine. No wine merchant in Britain bought any of them.

GEORGES LIGNIER

21740 Morey-St-Denis

Vineyard: 32 acres

Production: 50,000 bottles

Quality: 🍷🍷–🍷🍷🍷🍷   Price: ★★★–★★★★

According to the American wine-writer Matt Kramer, Lignier's wines taste too much of Pinot Noir and not enough of their *appellations* (Kramer, it should be pointed out, is a *terroiriste*). His theory is not borne out by a tasting of the wines, however. It is true that Lignier's village wine from Morey-St-Denis lacks stuffing. This may have something to do with the fact that he prefers the Bordeaux fermentation method of pumping the juice back over the cap of skins to the Burgundy one of punching the cap down. On the other hand, the wines he makes from three *grands crus* vineyards in Morey-St-Denis – Clos St-Denis, Clos de la Roche and Bonnes-Mares – are long, clean and intense, and certainly taste of their *appellations*. Nowhere else in Burgundy have I encountered such a great discrepancy between a grower's lesser and greater wines.

HUBERT LIGNIER

21740 Morey-St-Denis

Vineyard: 17 acres

Production: 15–20,000 bottles

Quality: 🍇🍇🍇🍇   Price: ★★★★

Robert Parker regards Hubert Lignier as one of the greatest wine-makers in Burgundy. This is rather a strange opinion to hold. Hubert Lignier makes good, mid-weight wines from vineyards in Chambolle-Musigny, Morey-St-Denis and Gevrey-Chambertin. They are more consistent than those of his cousin Georges, but they are hardly stunning. The most impressive is a separate bottling of wine from 55-year-old vines (*vieilles vignes*) in the Morey-St-Denis *premier cru* Les Chaffots. The name of this vineyard does not appear on the label, because it is pronounced the same way as *l'échafaud*, meaning 'scaffold'.

DOMAINE MACHARD DE GRAMONT

Prissey, 21700 Nuits-St-Georges

Vineyard: 40 acres

Production: 60,000 bottles

Quality: 🍇🍇🍇–🍇🍇🍇🍇   Price: ★★★–★★★★

Arnaud de Gramont is given to diatribes about the state of Burgundy today. He agrees that the wines were generally too light between 1965 and 1975 but says that people are now returning to traditional long vinifications. 'The wines are less commercial. I am accused of making wines that need to mature for too long before drinking.'

De Gramont makes good, firm, balanced wines from vineyards scattered throughout the Côte d'Or. His most impressive wines do not come from Nuits-St-Georges, where the estate is based, but from the *premiers crus* Les Guettes in Savigny-lès-Beaune and Clos Blanc in Pommard. The most interesting Nuits-St-Georges is a village wine from the Hauts Poirets vineyard, which is given spice and softness by the presence of 5 per cent Pinot Gris. These wines do not take quite as long to mature as de Gramont suggests.

Domaine Machard de Gramont should not be confused with Domaine Bertrand de Gramont, which was set up by Arnaud's older brother a few years ago.

BERNARD MAUME

56 route de Beaune, 21220 Gevrey-Chambertin

Vineyard: 10 acres

Production: 15,000 bottles

Quality: 🍇🍇🍇🍇   Price: ★★★★

Bernard Maume lives in Gevrey-Chambertin but commutes daily to Dijon, where he teaches biochemistry at the university. As befits a deliberate-talking academic, he makes long, firm, austere wines which take time to develop. His *grand cru* Mazis-Chambertin is outstanding.

DOMAINE MAZILLY

21950 Meloisey

Vineyard: 27 acres

Production: 45,000 bottles

Quality: 🍇🍇🍇   Price: ★★–★★★

The Mazilly estate in the Hautes Côtes de Beaune dates back to the sixteenth century. It includes vines in Pommard as well as in the Hautes Côtes, but its most remarkable products are two single-vineyard wines from the Hautes Côtes, Le Clou and Clos du Bois Prévot. The latter is situated 200 yards as the crow flies from the edge of the Pommard *appellation*. These wines do not taste like Pommard, as they taste of cherries rather than raspberries or strawberries and have a structure more reminiscent of Bordeaux than burgundy. At half the price of Pommard, they offer outstanding value for money. 'Everyone says this,' agrees Frédéric Mazilly. 'But it is like the difference between champagne and other sparkling wines. When you are celebrating, you open a bottle of champagne – whether it offers good value for money or not.'

DOMAINE MÉO-CAMUZET

21670 Vosne-Romanée

Vineyard: 27 acres

Production: 30–40,000 bottles

Quality: 🍇🍇🍇🍇–🍇🍇🍇🍇🍇   Price: ★★★★–★★★★★

This estate in Vosne-Romanée has come into the limelight because of its connection with the legendary Henri Jayer, who rented some of its vines until 1988 and has since then worked as its consultant. It combines the Méo family vineyards with those of Étienne Camuzet (the member of parliament for the Côte d'Or and one of the key figures in drawing up the *appellation contrôlée* legislation in 1935) which were inherited by Jean Méo in 1959. He was busy with his work as a director of the government-owned Elf petrol company and as a technical adviser to Général de Gaulle, so before the 1983 vintage he sold hardly any of the wine in bottle.

Until 1988 the vines were worked by four local growers, Jean and Jacques Faurois, Jean Tardy and Henri Jayer, under a sharecropping arrangement: they made the wine and gave Jean Méo half their production as rent (which Méo promptly sold in bulk to local merchants). The position today is very different. Jayer's vines have reverted to Domaine Méo-Camuzet, and the wines are made by Jean Méo's son Jean-Nicolas. The latter has modelled his methods on those of Jayer – the grapes are destalked, macerated cold before fermentation to extract colour, and matured entirely in new oak – and the wines resemble those of Jayer, too. People who are wistful for the wines Jayer used to produce are recommended to purchase the Vosne-Romanée *premiers crus* Les Brûlées and Clos Parantoux of Domaine Méo-Camuzet, which has finally become one of the great estates of Burgundy.

ALAIN MICHELOT

8 rue Camille Rodier, 21700 Nuits-St-Georges

Vineyard: 18 acres

Production: 30–35,000 bottles

Quality: 🍇🍇🍇🍇   Price: ★★★★

A large man with a red beard, Alain Michelot makes expansive wines, supported by firm tannins, from his vineyards in Nuits-St-Georges. They are velvety – but in the rustic style of Nuits-St-Georges rather than in the elegant manner of Vosne-Romanée.

MAISON MOILLARD

2 rue François Mignotte, 21700 Nuits-St-Georges

Vineyard: 54 acres

Production: 4,000,000 bottles

Quality: 🍇–🍇🍇🍇   Price: ★★–★★★★

Founded by Symphorien Moillard in 1850, this company has for many years enjoyed a reputation as the banker of the burgundy trade, holding stocks of wines from vineyards throughout Burgundy for others to draw on. It has not been reputed for its quality.

Beginning with the 1983 vintage Moillard has taken to fermenting its Pinot Noir grapes in automatic roto-tanks which, says Henri-Noël Thomas (a descendant of Symphorien Moillard), extract colour and glycerine better than traditional open vats. The wines have improved enormously. At a tasting in 1989 wines from 1983 and subsequent vintages were ripe and clean, with plenty of Pinot Noir fruit. A 1985 Clos de Vougeot was outstanding. Two earlier wines (a 1980 Fixin and a 1982 Nuits-St-Georges) were quite simply worn out. Thomas described them as 'useless'.

One should not exaggerate the improvement, however. The main reason for using roto-tanks is commercial: the wines finish fermenting sooner, within six days, so the tanks can all be used at least twice during the harvest. The drawback of such a rapid fermentation is that the tannins are not fixed properly and the wines do not last very long. Moillard would argue that they are not intended to. Its wines are sold mostly in French supermarkets, and are drunk very young. Thomas criticizes years like 1983 and 1988 as being bad vintages for consumers (although they are good for connoisseurs). There is also another problem. Although Moillard's wines have acquired two eminent supporters in Clive Coates and Robert Parker, I find them too extracted to be really enjoyable. The Beaune *premier cru* Les Grèves, which was appreciated more than any of its other wines by most of the people attending one

London tasting, tastes more like Châteauneuf-du-Pape than burgundy.

DOMAINE MONGEARD-MUGNERET

21670 Vosne-Romanée

Vineyard: 50 acres

Production: 70,000 bottles

Quality: 🍇🍇🍇🍇   Price: ★★★★–★★★★★

Jean Mongeard's father died during the Second World War and he made his first vintage at his family estate in Vosne-Romanée in 1945 at the age of fifteen. He was introduced by Henri Gouges to the American wine-merchant Frank Schoonmaker, to whom he sold his entire crop in bottle.

Today Mongeard, who is president of the Vosne-Romanée vine-growers' union, cultivates an estate four times as large as his father's. He says that his wine-making methods are the same. 'There are not thirty-six ways to make wine,' he explains. 'But it would not be true to say that the wines I make are like the wines of fifty years ago. The average quality is much better now. I don't know what my parents would have done with a 1984. My Grands Échézeaux 1984 is magnificent.' Mongeard had run out of this wine by the time of my visit, but I did try his 1984 Échézeaux. It was slightly green but undoubtedly con-centrated, and quite exceptional for such a poor year. He also makes an impressive Clos de Vougeot, from forty-year-old vines.

Since Mongeard's wines are generally rich and tannic, it is unwise to follow his advice to drink them at between five and ten years of age. In 1989 the 1978 Grands Échézeaux was still quite harsh.

DOMAINE ALBERT MOROT

avenue Charles Jaffelin, 21200 Beaune

Vineyard: 17 acres

Production: 15–35,000 bottles

Quality: 🍇🍇🍇🍇   Price: ★★★–★★★★

Albert Morot was a merchant who gradually sold off his merchant business to concentrate on his estate. This is run today by his grand-daughter, Mademoiselle Françoise Choppin, a lady of indeterminate age. She makes quite beautiful wines – intense, ripe and balanced – from a range of *premier cru* vineyards overlooking the town of Beaune. She does not offer them for sale until, in her view, they are ready to drink: when I visited in 1991 she was selling the 1984s.

DOMAINE CHARLES MORTET

22 rue de l'Église, 21220 Gevrey-Chambertin

Vineyard: 22 acres

Production: 40,000 bottles

Quality: 🍇🍇🍇🍇   Price: ★★★★

This estate in Gevrey-Chambertin is quite a new one by Burgundian standards, having been built up by Charles Mortet in the 1950s. It came to prominence in the late 1980s because of the wine-making skills of his boyish-looking son Denis, who is in his thirties.

Although he is wary of giving away too many details of his wine-making methods, Denis Mortet can be (by Burgundian standards) remarkably candid. When I visited him in 1989 he told me that the reason why other growers were all saying that their 1988s were better than their 1985s was that they had sold their 1985s. He also admitted that the ten casks of Gevrey-Chambertin he sold each year to the merchant firm Rodet came from the younger vines whose produce he did not consider good enough to sell under the Mortet label. 'I can't cheat myself,' he said. 'I keep the best to myself.'

The wines he keeps are very good indeed. By the standards of Gevrey-Chambertin they are elegant, very long on the palate and can be drunk quite young. The Gevrey-Chambertin *premier cru* Les Champeaux is particularly impressive.

DOMAINE MUGNERET-GIBOURG

21670 Vosne-Romanée

Vineyard: 12 acres

Production: 27,000 bottles

Quality: 🍇🍇🍇🍇   Price: ★★★★–★★★★★

Other label: Domaine Georges Mugneret

This estate, which is based in Vosne-Romanée but includes vineyards throughout the Côte de Nuits, was built up by Georges Mugneret, a consultant ophthalmologist, who died in 1988. He was famous for making good wines in bad vintages. His widow explains that 'as a doctor he was used to curing the sick'.

The wines are now made by his daughter Marie-Christine, a pharmacist. She says that she goes for fruit, but her wines are not ripe and velvety like those of other estates in Vosne-Romanée; they are serious, tight, green, austere wines, built for long-term ageing. Her best wines, from the *grands crus* Ruchottes-Chambertin and Clos de Vougeot, need twenty years to mature.

ANDRÉ MUSSY

21630 Pommard

Vineyard: 15 acres

Production: 25,000 bottles

Quality: 🍇🍇🍇–🍇🍇🍇🍇   Price: ★★★★

André is the twelfth generation of the Mussy family to make wine in Pommard. He was born in 1914, and his first vintage was 1928. 'At the beginning,' he remembers, 'we didn't have a plough. We did all our work by hand. We bought our first mule in 1931. Tractors did not arrive until the 1950s.'

It was not until the crisis of the mid-1970s that Mussy started to commercialize his wine in bottle rather than sell it all in bulk to merchants. Today he is well-known in both Britain and the United States. Mussy believes that what has made his reputation abroad is the difference between his bottlings of different vineyards, including two *premiers crus* in Beaune and two in Pommard.

It is difficult to judge this theory as Mussy insists that visitors taste his wines with a flat metal tastevin. 'The tastevin,' he explains, 'is made to criticize wine; a glass improves it.' As far as I could tell, the wines are ripe, rich and long, although a little more finesse would be preferable. 'I like making "masculine", powerful wines,' Mussy declares. The most powerful – and the best – comes from the famous Les Épenots vineyard in Pommard, where the vines were planted when Mussy was ten years old.

PHILIPPE NADDEF

30 rue Jean-Jaurès, Couchey, 21160 Marsannay-la-Côte

Vineyard: 12 acres

Production: 20–25,000 bottles

Quality: 🍇🍇🍇🍇   Price: ★★★★

Philippe Naddef is a young man who has built up a new estate, mostly in Gevrey-Chambertin, since 1983. He created his reputation with his first vintage – which is hardly surprising, since by macerating the grape skins in the wine for three weeks

or more and maturing the result entirely in new oak he produces firm, long, clean (but not oaky) wines with a penetrating
taste of red fruit. He makes two Gevrey-Chambertin *premiers
crus*: Les Champeaux, which is delicious in its youth, and Les
Cazetiers, which is classy and concentrated; and one *grand cru*,
Mazis-Chambertin, which is simply stunning.

JEAN-MARC PAVELOT

1 passage Guettote, 21420 Savigny-lès-Beaune

Vineyard: 26 acres

Production: 25–50,000 bottles

Quality: 🍇🍇🍇–🍇🍇🍇🍇   Price: ★★★

Jean-Marc Pavelot is a conscientious wine-maker whose wines
are the quintessence of Savigny-lès-Beaune: firm, digestible, a
little earthy, well worth ageing for five or ten years. The exception is his best wine, the *premier cru* La Dominode. He points
out that this is much more concentrated than people expect
Savigny-lès-Beaune to be – with the result that they often
identify it as coming from Volnay.

DOMAINE PERNIN-ROSSIN

21670 Vosne-Romanée

Vineyard: 20 acres

Production: 25–30,000 bottles

Quality: 🍇🍇🍇–🍇🍇🍇🍇   Price: ★★★★–★★★★★

André Pernin, a small grower in Vosne-Romanée, is usually
spoken of as a disciple of the oenologist Guy Accad (see 'Colour
– A Red Herring', on pp. 20–22). When I visited him in the
summer of 1990, I asked him if this was true. 'I am not a disciple
of Accad,' he replied. 'We employ him as our oenologist.'

Pernin has worked with Accad since 1980, longer than anyone except Jacky Confuron in Vosne-Romanée. It was reported at the end of 1990 that he had given Accad the sack, on the grounds that he no longer seemed to have enough time to spare.

It is a pity for Accad that he has lost Pernin, as he was the exponent of Accad's methods who most successfully combined the fruity, bubblegum tastes of cold maceration and cool fermentation with tannin, extract and vineyard character. His Morey-St-Denis is minty and rather bizarre but his Vosne-Romanées are ripe and well-balanced and his Nuits-St-Georges *premier cru* La Richemone, made from a parcel of old vines which he rents from the actor and wine-fanatic Gérard Depardieu, is deep, concentrated and outstanding.

DOMAINE LES PERRIÈRES

rue Planteligone, 21220 Gevrey-Chambertin

Vineyard: 30 acres

Production: 30,000 bottles

Quality: 🍷🍷🍷–🍷🍷🍷🍷   Price: ★★★★

This is a combination of two estates, Domaine Les Perrières at Gevrey-Chambertin, an old family estate, and Domaine La Tassée in Chambolle-Musigny, which François Perrot has built up since 1978. Perrot is a serious young man who makes wines that are austere and tannic in their youth but have good length and structure, and develop well. His style of wine-making suits the muscular nature of Gevrey-Chambertin much better than it does the generally more delicate style of Chambolle-Musigny.

CHÂTEAU DE POMMARD

21630 Pommard

Vineyard: 50 acres

Production: 80,000 bottles

Quality: 🍷🍷🍷–🍷🍷🍷🍷   Price: ★★★★

Château de Pommard is the only estate in the Côte d'Or that is organized for the reception of tourists. The owner, Jean-Louis Laplanche, a psychology professor at the Sorbonne in Paris, sells the majority of his crop to visitors who have been shown round by one of his three guides. Visitors do not need to book but can just turn up between 8.30 a.m. and 6.30 p.m. on any day between Easter and mid-November. They are shown the vineyards, the winery and the cellars – all of which are impressive – and given a tasting of a recent vintage. This costs 20 francs. It used to be free, but apparently people used to abuse the service by turning up twice a day to take an aperitif.

The wine – only one is made – is presented in a tacky pseudo-eighteenth-century bottle. It is not cheap, nor is it elegant, but it is full and rich and precisely conforms to the popular idea of how red burgundy should taste.

DOMAINE PONSOT

21740 Morey-St-Denis

Vineyard: 22 acres

Production: 35,000 bottles

Quality: 🍷🍷🍷🍷–🍷🍷🍷🍷🍷   Price: ★★★★–★★★★★

Other label: Domaine de Chézeaux

Hippolyte Ponsot in Morey-St-Denis was one of the frst growers to start bottling his own wine, rather than selling it in bulk to merchants, in the 1930s. His son Jean-Marie started working at the estate when he came back from the army in 1948. 'At the end of the war our generation modernized everything,' he says. 'People thought that everything new was good. But I was never one for modernization. We have not changed our methods since my father's time.' He warns, however, that 'if people talk about traditional methods, it is a marketing argument. It gives the consumer security.'

Whatever the reason, Ponsot is a traditionalist. He ferments the grapes with a certain portion of the stalks, producing quite austere but very long and elegant wines. They are reputed to be wonderful in vintages with good natural concentration such as 1985 and 1988 and insipid in years of high yields such as 1986 and 1989, but I have not found the difference to be quite as marked as that. His most famous, and best, wine is a separate bottling of the produce of forty-year-old vines (*vieilles vignes*) in the *grand cru* vineyard Clos de la Roche.

DOMAINE POTHIER-RIEUSSET

21630 Pommard

Vineyard: 20 acres

Production: 30,000 bottles

Quality: 🍇🍇🍇🍇   Price: ★★★★

Virgile Pothier is short, fat, talkative and philosophical. Robert Parker rightly describes him as epitomizing the popular perception of a French wine-maker. He is famous for the quality of wine he makes in off-vintages from his holdings in *premiers crus* vineyards in Pommard. In 1989 I tasted a delicious Pommard Les Charmots 1977 which was at its peak. I asked him how he had made the wine. He said, 'I can't remember exactly. It was a succession of small things. In the morning before I made the wine I did not know what I was going to do.' The wine had only 11.5–12 per cent alcohol. 'I never chaptalize a lot,' he explained. 'It's not worth it. It puts the wine out of balance. The other day I showed a client a 1942 made during the war when there was no possibility of chaptalization. It had 10.5–11 per cent alcohol. It was still good, if light.'

Because they can be low in alcohol, Pothier's wines are not always flattering in their youth, but they are perfectly balanced and mature for years. In this respect they resemble the wines made by Hubert de Montille nearby in Volnay. 'People always drink wine too soon,' says Pothier. 'My 1977s were not good at the start.'

DOMAINE DE LA POUSSE D'OR

Volnay, 21190 Meursault

Vineyard: 30 acres

Production: 50–60,000 bottles

Quality: 🍷🍷🍷🍷🍷   Price: ★★★★

Before the French Revolution this estate was part of the Domaine de la Romanée-Conti. It is usually thought that it is owned today by Gérard Potel. In fact, he manages it on behalf of a consortium of French and Australian owners. This and other misconceptions arise from his talking so fast and being so full of ideas that it is difficult actually to have a conversation with him.

'Making wine,' he says, 'is like acting in the theatre. What you do does not often work – and when it does you keep banging on trying to repeat it.' He macerates the wine in contact with the grape skins for two weeks or more. 'Pinot Noir,' he explains, 'does not have any taste. It is not like Cabernet Sauvignon. A simple varietal wine is not possible. You need a long vatting time to extract the character of the soil.'

Potel makes long, clean, persistent wines. They can be aggressive in their youth, and need to be allowed to mature to show of their best. His Volnay *premiers crus* Les Caillerets 'Clos des Soixante Ouvrées' and Clos de la Bousse d'Or can be quite wonderful, but only after ten or even twenty years in bottle. (The estate used to be named Domaine de la Pousse d'Or, after the vineyard, but this was changed in 1967 after a decree was passed forbidding an estate from calling itself after one vineyard if it also included other vineyards. The exception to this rule is the Domaine de la Romanée-Conti.)

DOMAINE JACQUES PRIEUR

68 rue des Santenots, 21190 Meursault

Vineyard: 22 acres

Production: 30–40,000 bottles

Quality: 👑–👑👑👑   Price: ★★★★–★★★★★

For some years this estate has been making tragically insipid wines from vineyard holdings in some of the greatest sites in the Côte d'Or, among them Musigny, Chambertin and Chambertin-Clos de Bèze. In 1988 50 per cent of the estate was sold to the merchant firm of Antonin Rodet. Jean Prieur used the proceeds to finance a year-long sailing trip round the world and the wine-making (beginning with the 1990 vintage) was taken over by his son Martin.

Martin makes much more serious wines than his father. He draws off juice before fermentation where necessary; he has increased the number of times the cap of skins is punched down into the juice from one a day to three; he has extended the period of maceration to two weeks. His 1990s are a bit too flattering for their own good, but they are undoubtedly a quantum leap above his father's intensely disappointing 1988s. I have every confidence that the wines made at this estate will continue to improve.

DOMAINE HENRI ET GILLES REMORIQUET

25 rue Charmois, 21700 Nuits-St-Georges

Vineyard: 18 acres

Production: 35,000 bottles

Quality: 👑👑👑👑   Price: ★★★★

Henri Remoriquet, an old grower in Nuits-St-Georges, is a mine of information about Burgundy. When it is suggested to him that growers crop too heavily nowadays – in 1982 the Remoriquets produced over 60 hectolitres per hectare – he points out that this is no larger than the yield in 1944, which was achieved without the benefit of fertilizer. He also says that their methods of vinification remain the same as they were fifty years ago and the wines taste similar. These are now made by his son Gilles and are ripe, slightly rustic, and can be enjoyed relatively young.

DOMAINE DANIEL RION

Premeaux, 21700 Nuits-St-Georges

Vineyard: 35 acres

Production: 80,000 bottles

Quality: 🍇🍇🍇🍇   Price: ★★★★

In 1989 the American wine magazine the *Wine Spectator* published an extraordinary article suggesting that the 32-year-old Patrice Rion might become the next Henri Jayer. In fact, Patrice, who took over from his father in 1980, makes a very oenological, even Californian, style of wine. Whereas most Burgundians allow their wines to be fermented by natural vineyard and cellar yeasts, Rion follows the New World practice of adding a yeast strain that has been selected in a laboratory. He adds a champagne yeast because, he says, it produces a pure wine, with very little volatile acidity.

Rion says that he makes a modern style of burgundy and that his wines are fresh, quite low in alcohol, and often high in acidity. After I tasted a range of his wines, he inquired whether I had found them too aggressive. In general, I found that they were. Rion's technology-driven approach suits the more direct and fruity style of Nuits-St-Georges better than the more delicate and perfumed character of Vosne-Romanée. His best wine is his Nuits-St-Georges *premier cru* Les Hauts Pruliers, which is complex and not too aggressive. Rion makes more impressive wines in lesser vintages than in greater ones, because they present him with more of a challenge. He made disappointing wines in 1985 but supremely elegant ones in the more difficult vintage of 1986.

*

MAISON ANTONIN RODET

71640 Mercurey

Vineyard: 225 acres

Production: 2,500,000 bottles

Quality: 🍇   Price: ★★–★★★★

This large merchant house is situated, unusually, in Mercurey in the Côte Chalonnaise rather than in Beaune or Nuits-St-Georges, but it buys wine from producers throughout Burgundy. Its wines have received a fair amount of favourable publicity in recent years.

They have certainly improved – but only to the extent that they now all taste very similar. Rodet say that they are looking for wines which are good to drink young but have a potential for ageing, but this is not evident from a tasting of them. They are not bad, but they are not good. They taste rather sweet and confected. They appear to have been sacrificed on the altar of accessibility.

In 1991 a majority shareholding in Antonin Rodet was purchased by the champagne house Laurent-Perrier.

DOMAINE DE LA ROMANÉE-CONTI

21670 Vosne-Romanée

Vineyard: 62 acres

Production: 100,000 bottles

Quality: 🍇🍇🍇🍇🍇   Price: ★★★★★

I must begin with an apology. In 1988 I published a book called *Wine Snobbery* in which I referred to the practice of late picking at the Domaine de la Romanée-Conti. I said that I had never tasted its wines and therefore cited the opinions of three expert writers on Burgundy: Serena Sutcliffe, who said that the grapes were picked too late, Clive Coates, who said that the wine spent too long in contact with the grape skins in the fermentation vat, and Anthony Hanson, who said that the wines were 'made with a heavy hand'. The Domaine de la Romanée-Conti is the most famous estate in Burgundy. More nonsense has been written about it than about any other.

I have now tasted the range of the wines produced by the Domaine on five occasions. They comprise the produce of the two best vineyards in Burgundy, Romanée-Conti and La Tâche, both of them in the village of Vosne-Romanée and both owned exclusively by the Domaine; two other super-*grands crus*, Richebourg and Romanée-St-Vivant; and two ordinary *grands crus* (if such a thing is possible), Grands Échézeaux and Échézeaux. With the possible exception of the Richebourg, it would be ridiculous to accuse them of being made with a heavy hand. They are the quintessence of burgundies: they express themselves not by their size but by their finesse and by their length on the palate. This is particularly true of the best vineyard, Romanée-Conti itself.

It may be that the wines have changed since Sutcliffe, Coates and Hanson made their observations. I have tasted a full range of the wines only since the 1985 vintage, which was when the manager of the Domaine, André Noblet, died and was succeeded by his son Bernard. According to local gossip, Bernard has abandoned his father's practice of late picking and now gathers the grapes at the same time as everyone else. Those who spread such gossip misunderstand the way the Domaine works, however. It is owned by a dozen shareholders from two families, Leroy and de Villaine, and managed jointly by two of Burgundy's most prominent figures, Lalou Bize-Leroy and Aubert de Villaine. Bernard Noblet is their employee.

Noblet does not speak (at least not to journalists), but according to Bize-Leroy he 'follows very meticulously the methods of his father. We have not changed our policy. We harvest the grapes when they are ripe. In the 1970s there were a lot of wet summers so we often picked late. In the last few years there has been no need to pick late. If other people in Vosne-Romanée imagine that we harvest earlier than we used to, that is because they are harvesting later than they used to.'

The wine-making methods remain essentially unchanged. They consist of minimum intervention. Whole bunches are put, uncrushed, in a vat; fermentation starts slowly and lasts for about three weeks. The wines are then matured entirely in new oak, spending as long in contact with their fermentation lees as possible. One change that has been introduced since Bernard Noblet took over from his father is that the wines are no longer bottled directly from cask but the casks are blended beforehand. There is therefore no longer as great a variation between bottles as there used to be.

The only respect in which it is now reasonable to criticize the Domaine's wines is their price. It should be pointed out that it is not merely the Domaine which permits itself generous profit margins but also its agents and wine merchants. At the beginning of 1991 the going price for Romanée-Conti 1988 was £400 (approximately $650) a bottle.

PHILIPPE ROSSIGNOL

61 avenue de la Gare, 21220 Gevrey-Chambertin

Vineyard: 8 acres

Production: 15,000 bottles

Quality: ♥♥♥♥   Price: ★★–★★★★

Since he left school in 1974 Philippe Rossignol, the son of a local farmer, has gradually been building up his vineyard holdings. As yet he does not make anything grander than a straight Gevrey-Chambertin, however. His most remarkable wine is his humble Bourgogne Rouge, from vineyards in Couchey and Marsannay. It is matured, like all his other wines, in between one-third and one-quarter new oak casks. It is similar in style to his Gevrey-Chambertin – rich and tannic, turning gamey with age – and offers outstanding value for money.

JOSEPH ROTY

24 rue du Maréchal de Lattre, 21220 Gevrey-Chambertin

Quality: 🍇🍇🍇   Price: ★★–★★★★

Joseph Roty is not like other vine-growers in the Côte d'Or. He is friendly – too friendly. During my visit to his estate in Gevrey-Chambertin, he talked incessantly whilst I was attempting to concentrate on his wines, plying me with a blend of medieval history and bad jokes. He drank cider and smoked non-stop. Clearly, he is no fan of critics, since he began by reminding me that the restaurateur Paul Bocuse had compared critics to eunuchs who know how to talk about love but do not know how to make it.

Roty does not make wines like those of other vine-growers in the Côte d'Or, either. Since a direct question is more likely to elicit another anecdote than a direct answer, it is impossible to say precisely what methods he uses. However, he has been playing with cold maceration of the grapes before fermentation since long before the oenologist Guy Accad came upon the scene. He says that this helps you to have the maximum of aromas in the wine. For the same reason, he ferments at a low temperature, between 20 and 25°C, and as a result the wines taste of fruit juice. They are not bad, for all that, but they lack elegance. Roty's most famous wine, the *grand cru* Charmes-Chambertin, is also, in my view, his least elegant.

Roty also makes a kosher Bourgogne Rouge, to which he adds no chemical product, not even sulphur dioxide at bottling to preserve it. He describes this as 'the ancient method', pointing out that the first book of oenology was the Bible.

DOMAINE GEORGES ROUMIER

21770 Chambolle-Musigny

Vineyard: 35 acres

Production: 50,000 bottles

Quality: 🍇🍇🍇🍇🍇   Price: ★★★★–★★★★★

Domaine Georges Roumier has now taken over from the Domaine Comte Georges de Vogüé as the most prestigious estate in Chambolle-Musigny. Ironically, it was under the management of Georges Roumier's son Alain that Domaine Comte Georges de Vogüé reached its apogee. The style of wine-making at the two estates is very different, however. Georges Roumier, a lawyer and wine-merchant, established a reputation before the Second World War for making rich, powerful wines. His son Jean-Marie preferred a lighter, suppler style – as was the trend in the 1960s and 1970s, and is still practised at Domaine Comte Georges de Vogüé.

Christophe, son of Jean-Marie, has made the wine since 1982. He believes that burgundy was too light for a period. He tries to make wines with more structure than his father did. 'People tell me that I make wines like my grandfather.' He has resurrected his grandfather's technique of taking the wine off its skins before the end of fermentation and finishing the fermentation in barrel. This enables him to ferment the wine for longer, which he says 'produces glycerol and makes the wine rich in the mouth'.

Christophe is not a fan of new oak – which means that his wines are less flattering in their youth than those of some other producers. They are round and tannic, but they do not lack elegance. The Musigny is staggering.

DOMAINE HERVÉ ROUMIER

21770 Chambolle-Musigny

Vineyard: 22 acres

Production: 20,000 bottles

Quality: 🍇🍇🍇🍇   Price: ★★★★

This estate in Chambolle-Musigny is a new one, but it already has a complicated history. Hervé is the son of Alain Roumier, the former manager of the Domaine Comte Georges de Vogüé, and the cousin of Christophe, who now runs Domaine Georges Roumier. Hervé used to work with his father at the Domaine Comte Georges de Vogüé and use its equipment to make his own wine at weekends. In 1986 Comte Georges de Vogüé died and his daughter told Hervé that he could no longer use the equipment. Hervé and Alain left Domaine Comte Georges de Vogüé and set up in business together.

The wines I have tasted have been lean and elegant, with lovely Pinot Noir fruit. The village Chambolle-Musigny is delightful, the *grand cru* Bonnes-Mares quite wonderful – and more stylish than the heavyweight version produced by Christophe Roumier down the road. Other visitors have been less complimentary, precisely because the wines are lighter than those of Domaine Georges Roumier, and more comparable to those of Domaine Comte Georges de Vogüé.

DOMAINE ARMAND ROUSSEAU

place de la Cure, 21220 Gevrey-Chambertin

Vineyard: 32 acres

Production: 50,000 bottles

Quality: 🍇🍇🍇🍇🍇   Price: ★★★★–★★★★★

Armand Rousseau in Gevrey-Chambertin was one of the first growers in Burgundy to start bottling his wines, rather than selling them in bulk to merchants, in the 1930s. His son Charles, who took over the estate in 1959 after his father was killed in a car accident, says that he still practises essentially the same methods as his father did fifty years ago.

Short, bull-headed and fast-talking, Charles Rousseau is surprisingly modest given the reputation his wines enjoy. He admits that they went through a bad patch in the late 1970s because of a fungal infection in the cellar. Today they are long, pure, clean, concentrated and very classy. His most famous and most intense wine is the *grand cru* Le Chambertin but it would really be invidious to single out any of his wonderful array of *grands crus* – Charmes-Chambertin, Mazis-Chambertin, Ruchottes-Chambertin, Chambertin-Clos de Bèze and Clos de la Roche – either from each other or, indeed, from his amazing Gevrey-Chambertin *premier cru* Clos St-Jacques.

DOMAINE DANIEL SENARD

21920 Aloxe-Corton

Vineyard: 20 acres

Production: 30,000 bottles

Quality: 🍇🍇🍇–🍇🍇🍇🍇   Price: ★★★★

I met Philippe Senard early in 1989, just after he had taken up with the oenologist Guy Accad. He had gone over to the Accadian camp after tasting the 1987s made by Étienne Grivot in Vosne-Romanée, which he described as 'fantastic'. I compared his pre-Accadian 1987s with his Accad-inspired 1988s. The former showed much more finesse but much less consistency; the latter were simpler and more direct. This would seem to support the proposition that the Accad method standardizes different wines – but it is still not hard to distinguish his Corton *grands crus*, and especially the wonderful Clos du Roi, from his simple Aloxe-Corton.

CHRISTIAN SERAFIN

7 place du Château, 21220 Gevrey-Chambertin

Vineyard: 11 acres

Production: 25,000 bottles

Quality: 🍇🍇🍇   Price: ★★★★

Christian Serafin, a vine-grower in Gevrey-Chambertin, only started bottling the majority of his crop in 1985, when he was discovered by the American importer Robert Kacher. It was at Kacher's behest that he started to mature virtually all his wines for up to two years in new oak.

Through Kacher Serafin got known by the American writer Robert Parker, another fan of new oak. 'Since the 1985 vintage my experience has been one of unequivocal joy and conviction that Mr Serafin does indeed know how to make great wine,' Parker wrote in his newsletter, the *Wine Advocate*, in October 1989. I beg to disagree. Serafin's wines have plenty of sweet, round Pinot Noir fruit but they lack elegance and complexity, and are excessively dominated by the taste of new oak. The most impressive is not a *premier* or *grand cru* but a separate bottling of wine made from old vines (*vieilles vignes*) entitled only to the simple village *appellation* Gevrey-Chambertin.

DOMAINE BERNARD SERVEAU

21740 Morey St-Denis

Vineyard: 17 acres

Production: 22,000 bottles

Quality: 🍇🍇   Price: ★★★★

In his book on Burgundy, Matt Kramer describes Serveau as 'the supreme producer in Morey-St-Denis'. In other words, Kramer considers the wines to be superior to those of Dujac and Ponsot.

It is true that Jean-Louis Serveau (Bernard's son) makes decent, complex, quite full-bodied wines that age well. The best of them is the Morey-St-Denis *premier cru* Les Sorbets, but even this never develops the length or finesse of great burgundy. This is not surprising, given that the grapes have been fermented for only a week.

DOMAINE DE SUREMAIN

Mercurey, 71640 Givry

Vineyard: 45 acres

Production: 135,000 bottles

Quality: 🍇🍇🍇   Price: ★★★

Remarkably, this shambolic estate in Mercurey in the Côte Chalonnaise was in the forefront of progress at the beginning of the last century. It can hardly have advanced since. 'My great-grandfather was very modern,' says Yves de Suremain; 'we are very traditional.'

I tasted the wines in the depths of mid-winter, in a cellar that was colder than the snow-filled air outside. As far as it was possible to judge, the wines are lean and austere in their youth. They develop very slowly by the standards of the Côte Chalonnaise, but are well worth keeping for a few years – provided that you are not bothered by a gamey, bacterial bouquet.

CHÂTEAU DE LA TOUR DE VOUGEOT

21640 Vougeot

Quality: 🍇🍇🍇🍇   Price: ★★★★

Château de la Tour, a mock fortress built in 1890, should not be confused with the Château du Clos de Vougeot, the site of the old Cistercian monastery, where the Confrérie des Chevaliers de Tastevin now holds its meetings.

Château de la Tour owns the largest portion of the Clos de Vougeot, 13.5 out of 124 acres. It used to belong to the merchant Jean Morin but on his death passed to his two daughters. The wine is made for them by François Labet (memorably described by Robert Parker in his book on Burgundy as 'the young, attractive Françoise Labet') under the supervision of the oenologist Guy Accad.

Labet first heard of Guy Accad through reading an article in the *Revue du Vin de France* about Jacky Confuron. He went and tasted Confuron's 1986s, then started working with Accad, beginning with the 1987 vintage. He now makes really good, dark, concentrated wines which stand alongside those made by Jacky Confuron and André Pernin as the best of those made by the Accad method. (See 'Colour – A Red Herring', on pp. 20–22.)

DOMAINE LOUIS TRAPET

53 route de Beaune, 21220 Gevrey-Chambertin

Vineyard: 30 acres

Production: 50,000 bottles

Quality: 🍇🍇🍇–🍇🍇🍇🍇   Price: ★★★★–★★★★★

This Gevrey-Chambertin estate is generally acknowledged to be riding on the reputation it established in the 1950s and 1960s. The wines are very good – very long on the palate – but they lack concentration. From vines planted in Chambertin in 1919 – sold as a separate *vieilles vignes* bottling in top vintages – one is entitled to expect something more than what Trapet has recently produced. Some, but not all, of the blame should be laid on the mobile bottling firm which has filtered and sulphured the wines to excess.

It may be that one will see an improvement in the half of the estate which the affable, rambling Jean Trapet handed over in 1990 to his nephew Nicolas Rossignol. This wine will be sold under the label Rossignol-Trapet.

DOMAINE DES VAROILLES

rue de la Croix des Champs, 21220 Gevrey-Chambertin

Vineyard: 31 acres

Production: 30,000 bottles

Quality: 🍇🍇🍇🍇–🍇🍇🍇🍇🍇   Price: ★★★★–★★★★★

For such a cautious man, Jean-Pierre Naigeon, the owner both of Domaine des Varoilles in Gevrey-Chambertin and of the merchant business Naigeon-Chauveau, is disarmingly honest. When I visited him in 1989, the vintages he had for sale were 1986 and 1987. He told me that neither was much cop.

He cultivates six acres of the *grand cru* Clos de Vougeot. Some of his vines are at the bottom of the Clos, which is supposed to produce poor wine. He says that when he told the wine-writer Hugh Johnson where his vines were situated Johnson replied that he was the first grower not to have told him that his vines were in the upper part of the Clos.

Naigeon can afford to be honest because he makes wonderful wines, largely from old, low-yielding vines. They are hard and sometimes awkward in their youth, but they develop great complexity with age. The most impressive of them are probably the Gevrey-Chambertin *premier cru* Clos des Varoilles, which is entirely owned by the estate (hence its name), and the *grand cru* Charmes-Chambertin.

AUBERT DE VILLAINE

Bouzeron, 71150 Chagny

Vineyard: 10 acres

Production: 30,000 bottles

Quality: 🍇🍇🍇   Price: ★★–★★★

Aubert de Villaine, the co-owner of the Domaine de la Romanée-Conti, lives at Bouzeron in the Côte Chalonnaise, where he owns a small estate. He says that he vinifies his Pinot Noir grapes essentially in the same way as at the Domaine – except that he destalks three-quarters of the grapes before fermentation. The wines, however, do not in any way resemble those of the Domaine but have simple, ripe fruit and are delicious if drunk very young. 'Wines from the Côte Chalonnaise are at their best when they are young,' says de Villaine. 'They can age but they become much less interesting.' His American wife Pamela disagrees. She points out that wine-makers spend so much of their time tasting young wines that they end up preferring them.

DOMAINE COMTE GEORGES DE VOGÜÉ

21770 Chambolle-Musigny

Vineyard: 30 acres

Production: 20,000 bottles

Quality: 🍇🍇🍇🍇–🍇🍇🍇🍇🍇   Price: ★★★★★

Situated in the tiny village of Chambolle-Musigny, this is one of the great estates of Burgundy. It has been selling wine direct to consumers since the fifteenth century. It is generally considered to have reached its apogee during the first half of Alain Roumier's tenure as wine-maker, from 1955 until 1972. After that, the quality of the wines declined markedly.

In 1986 the Comte Georges de Vogüé died. The estate was taken over by his son-in-law, Gérard de Causans, but he died a year later of cancer. Alain Roumier retired, saying that he did not get on with the people who were now in charge, and was replaced by a young oenologist, François Millet, who looks like a civil servant and treats journalists with the contempt of one. When I asked him why he macerated the grape skins in the wine for two weeks after the end of the alcoholic fermentation, he replied, 'You know the answer perfectly well.'

Millet makes excellent, elegant wines, if not quite up to the level achieved by Alain Roumier in the 1960s. For an estate which owns three-quarters of the *grand cru* Le Musigny the wines lack the expected spark of excitement. They are precisely what one might expect of an oenologist who neither owns nor lives on the estate. When I visited it seemed that the only creature to live there was a savage-looking Alsatian which had belonged to Gérard de Causans and appeared to obey no other master.

JOSEPH VOILLOT

Volnay, 21190 Meursault

Vineyard: 30 acres

Production: 20–25,000 bottles

Quality: 🍇🍇🍇🍇🍇   Price: ★★★★

Joseph Voillot is a thoughtful, self-effacing man who shows no interest in the commercial aspects of a wine-maker's job. He still sells off half his crop in bulk to merchants because, he says, he is a vine-grower and not a salesman. He points out that in the past the job of a vine-grower was to cultivate his vineyard but today increasingly people ignore vineyard work in order to concentrate on vinifying and selling wine. This gives him great concern for the future.

His approach to wine-making means that Voillot has not received the fame he has deserved. I am utterly astonished at the faint praise that has been doled out by other writers on Burgundy. Robert Parker goes so far as to suggest that he would do well to seek advice from an oenologist. Nothing would be more disastrous. Voillot's wines may not be flattering in their youth but they are perfectly balanced and fantastically long in the mouth. His Volnay *premiers crus* Les Caillerets and Les Champans are among the best wines made in the village; his Pommard *premier cru* Les Rugiens is nothing less than the Romanée-Conti of the Côte de Beaune – not the biggest but the best.

Champagne

Sparkling Wines and Climate

Much of the best sparkling wine has been made by people who plant Pinot Noir in order to produce red wine but find that their climate is too cool. This is what happened in Champagne. At some point during the Middle Ages the Pinot Noir grape was introduced there from Burgundy and growers tried to make wine from it that was similar to red burgundy – the most famous wine in France. They failed. Pinot Noir in Champagne produced a red wine with less alcohol and less colour than burgundy. However, Nicolas Brûlart, the Chancellor of France, and a major vineyard-owner in Champagne, managed to persuade the Court that a pale-coloured wine (which just happened to be the only type he could produce) was better than a red wine.

In the seventeenth and eighteenth centuries Champagne produced a still pink wine (*vin gris*). The paler it was, the more it was appreciated. So that the colour should be as pale as possible the juice was fermented in contact with the grape skins for a very short time. It did not extract the tannins from the grape skins which would be able to protect it from oxidation. As a result, champagne was even more fragile than red burgundy. Most wine was sold in cask, but champagne was put in bottle in order to preserve it. Often, it had not completely finished fermenting by the winter, when it was bottled. This would not have mattered had it been kept in cask – it would have started fermenting again in the spring but the gases would have escaped – but in bottle the gases were trapped. Lo! a sparkling wine.

The same phenomenon – of a sparkling wine rising from the ashes of a still one – has been repeated in the New World. In 1970 Barry and Audrey Sterling planted Chardonnay and Pinot Noir at Iron Horse Vineyards at the western edge of the Russian River valley in Sonoma County in California, among apple orchards. They intended to make the grapes into still wine but discovered that the site was cooler than they had originally thought: there was a cool breeze and this air sat in a hollow in the middle of their vines. After the Pinot Noir crop failed in 1980 they decide to convert to sparkling-wine production. Since 1985 they have made the best sparkling wine in California.

It is not as cool at Iron Horse as in Champagne, however. Barry and Audrey Sterling's daughter Joy points out that in Champagne they pick the grapes (depending on the year) at between 9 and 10 per cent potential alcohol, whereas Iron Horse picks at 10.5 per cent. Because the grapes are riper, less sugar needs to be added at the end of manufacture to conceal the harsh acidity of unripe fruit. She says that before 1985 their sparkling wines were too austere because they were harvested too early. She believes that sparkling-wine producers in California should turn their warmer climate into an advantage.

The problem with Joy Sterling's attitude is that it encourages producers to make sparkling wines in regions that really are warm enough to make still Pinot Noir. The experience of the Anderson Valley in Mendocino County in California should serve as a salutary lesson. It is a relatively young viticultural region: the first vineyards were planted only twenty years ago. It suddenly attracted the spotlight in 1985 when the champagne company Louis Roederer decided, after looking all over the United States, to site its American sparkling-wine facility there. Roederer was encouraged to make its decision by the large diurnal (day-to-night) temperature fluctuation, which ensures good acidity levels in the grapes.

Hans Kobler, who arrived in the Anderson Valley in 1973, believes that it will be taken over for sparkling-wine production. He doubts the wisdom of this, however. He believes that the Anderson Valley is really too warm for sparkling wine, for which people start picking the grapes at the end of July. 'If an area is right for still wine, it is too warm for sparkling. I'm sorry that the champagne people have come because we really could have made a name for Pinot Noir here.'

The best climate for sparkling wines is not just cool by viticultural standards but positively cold. To make a balanced sparkling wine you need a base wine which is too low in alcohol and too high in acid to be drunk on its own. The addition of sugar before the second fermentation in bottle produces a one-tenth increase in the alcohol content, and during this fermentation the acid levels drop by about 30 per cent.

It is hard to find a climate as perfect as that of Champagne. Champagne is hardly a warm region, but because it is so far north (49°) it has longer hours of sunlight in summer than other vine-growing regions. Also, the vineyards are luminous – the light is unexpectedly bright, probably because of the chalk soil. The grapes ripen very slowly, and to just the right extent. 'Champagne is unique because of its luminosity,' says Yves Bénard, chairman of Moët et Chandon. 'You can't go far enough north in America or south in Australia.' But you can find the same chalk soil, and even longer daylight hours, in England.

In the early eighteenth century the gentleman-farmer Charles Hamilton planted two vine varieties, both of them probably clones or mutations of Pinot Noir, at his vineyard in Cobham in Surrey. The first wine he made was red, but he was not pleased with it. 'The wine was so harsh and austere that I despaired of ever making red wine fit to drink; but through the harshness I perceived a flavour something like that of small French white wines, which made me hope I should succeed with white wine. That experiment succeeded far beyond my most sanguine expectations; for the first year I made white wine, it nearly resembled the flavour of champagne; and in two or three years more, as the vines grew stronger, to my great amazement, my wine had a finer flavour than the best champagne I ever tasted; the first running was as clear as spirits, the second running was *oeil de perdrix* [the pink of a partridge's eye], and both of them sparkled and creamed in the glass like champagne.'

'It would be endless to mention how many good judges of wine were deceived by my wine,' he added, 'and thought it superior to any champagne they ever drank; even the Duc de Mirepoix preferred it to any other wine. But such is the prejudice of most people against anything of English growth, I generally found it most prudent not to declare where it grew, till after they had passed their verdict upon it.'

Is the Best Sparkling Wine Made from Pinot Noir?

One of the reasons why English sparkling wine does not fulfil the promise shown by Charles Hamilton's experience more than two centuries ago is that it is not made from Pinot Noir. Instead, it is made from Germanic grape varieties such as Reichensteiner, which has the advantage of tasting ripe at a low sugar level, but this ripeness comes in the form of a strange grapey taste which appeals more to consumers of German wine than to those of champagne. English wine-makers argue that they use Reichensteiner because they are not 'befuddled by tradition' – they are not obliged to copy champagne but can use the grape varieties that are best suited to their climate. They criticize producers of sparkling wine in America and Australasia for trying to copy champagne rather than making their own indigenous style of sparkling wine.

It is true that wine-makers in the New World make their sparkling wines from Pinot Noir and Chardonnay because that is what is done in Champagne – but they do this not because they are incapable of thinking for themselves but because they have learnt from history. Champagne became famous for its sparkling wines partly because it had an ideal climate but also because it made its sparkling wine predominantly from Pinot Noir – a grape variety whose taste perfectly combines with the yeasty character produced by a long, slow fermentation in bottle.

In the eighteenth century Chardonnay was added not for its taste but because Pinot Noir on its own did not produce enough fizz: because it has a high protein content, Chardonnay produces a wine with more carbon dioxide – more bubbles – than does Pinot Noir. Then champagne was made by a dif-

ferent method from the one used today: it was only fermented
once, and it sparkled because it was bottled before the first
fermentation had finished.

Since the introduction last century of the 'champagne
method', in which sugar and yeast are added to the finished still
wine to make it ferment a second time, champagne producers
have been able to control the amount of fizz themselves. They
no longer need to add Chardonnay to Pinot Noir. So why do
they do so? For commercial reasons. The reputation of
champagne as the *sine qua non* of celebration has been created
by the big champagne companies, which sell their products
worldwide. In order to have a sufficient quantity to commercialize, they have to blend together wines from all over the
Champagne region. These are made not only from Pinot Noir
and Chardonnay but from a third grape, Pinot Meunier, which
is a less distinguished mutation of Pinot Noir. It is also essential
for the big houses to be able to blend wines from different
origins together in order to neutralize their taste. Their job is
to create, retain and promote a particular house-style, a particular taste – they do not want the taste of individual grapes in
individual villages to get in the way.

Since it is the big houses who have created the international
reputation of champagne it is their wines which producers in
other regions have tasted and copied. So they blend Pinot Noir
with Chardonnay. For the moment, they are right to do so:
unless Pinot Noir comes to be planted in appropriately cold
climates in the New World, it is unlikely that it will be able to
produce top-class sparkling wine on its own. Some of the finest
champagnes, however, are produced entirely from Pinot Noir –
in particular from the four villages in the Montagne de Reims
which were traditionally the *grands crus* for black grapes:
Ambonnay, Aÿ, Bouzy and Verzenay. (They have since been
joined by seven other *grands crus* nearby.) These champagnes
have a very particular taste, which can come as quite a shock to
someone brought up on the blended champagnes of the big
companies. They are much richer, much more like *wine*. The
best producers include: in Ambonnay, André Beaufort
(organic), Henri Billiot and Pierre Fauvet; in Aÿ, Maison

Collery; in Bouzy, Maison Barancourt and Georges Vesselle; in Verzenay, Michel Arnould.

Red Wine from Champagne

In the beginning champagne was a still red wine. Sparkling champagne was invented in the late seventeenth century (not, it should be pointed out, by Dom Perignon). For the next 150 years the two types of champagne fought for supremacy. Sparkling champagne was condemned by connoisseurs. The wine-merchant Bertin de Rocheret described it as an 'abominable drink', pointing out that bubbles destroyed the flavour of the individual vineyards and that 'effervescence . . . is a merit in an inferior wine and the property of beer, chocolate and whipped cream'.

Sparkling champagne only took over conclusively with the introduction of the 'champagne method' in the middle of the nineteenth century. Within a generation the English wine-merchant Thomas George Shaw was able to describe still red wine from Champagne as something that was practically unknown. Yet, in his opinion, it was finer than the red wine made in Burgundy. Are red wines of this quality to be found in Champagne today?

The growing conditions were different in the past and favoured the production of still red wines more than they do today. Towards the end of the last century the vines were devastated by the phylloxera louse and had to be pulled out and replanted with vines grafted on to American vine rootstock, which was resistant to phylloxera.

It is generally felt that ungrafted vines ripen sooner, and better, than grafted ones. Certainly this is the experience of Christian Bizot, the managing director of Bollinger, who has preserved a small parcel of ungrafted Pinot Noir vines in his vineyards at Bouzy and Aÿ. The sparkling wine which he makes from these vines – Vieilles Vignes Françaises – has been memorably described by Jancis Robinson as having 'the unctuous power of a very fine cough syrup'.

Another reason why more red wine was made in the past is that the yields were much smaller. The average yield in Champagne has increased from 25 to 30 hectolitres per hectare fifty years ago to 80 or 90 today. Yield is the major factor which differentiates still red wines from Champagne – officially called Coteaux Champenois – from red burgundy. Georges Vesselle, a vine-grower in Bouzy, says that he has planted Burgundy clones of Pinot Noir in Champagne and they make very good red wines. They are not very different from Champagne clones except that they have a lower yield.

Growers who wish to make still red wine from Pinot Noir grapes in Champagne are faced with a major problem. The plants have been selected for high yields and low colours – exactly the opposite of what they need. Moreover, because the vines are forced to crop heavily they tire early and have to be replaced very young. The majority of wine in Champagne is made from what in Burgundy would be considered excessively young vines.

Vesselle says that you have to select the oldest and lowest-producing vines to make red wine. In 1990 his average crop was 80 hectolitres per hectare but some vines produced the equivalent of only 35 and it was from these that he made red wine. His Bouzy Rouge is a light wine, with a pretty taste of strawberries. It does not taste like burgundy, and certainly lacks its length on the palate. I would not have thought it capable of long-term ageing but Vesselle told me that Bouzy should only be drunk after twenty years in bottle, by which time it has developed the characteristics of a top red burgundy.

During 1991 I tasted both a Bouzy and a Verzenay from the 1976 vintage. They were interesting, complex wines – but they did not prove the theory that a fundamentally light wine is capable of developing, as a result of bottle ageing, the con-centration of red burgundy. The best producers of Coteaux Champenois include: in Aÿ, Bollinger; in Bouzy, Maison Barancourt and Georges Vesselle. However, these wines *never* offer good value for money: they are produced from grapes that would otherwise be turned into *grand cru* champagne and therefore have to be sold for an equivalent price.

Rosé de Riceys

According to legend it was with Rosé de Riceys that the masons building the royal château at Versailles refreshed themselves. One day King Louis XIV, watching them at work, tasted the wine and approved of it. Nicholas Faith, author of *The Story of Champagne*, believes that today's Rosé de Riceys is an 'ancient relic' which 'bears a marked resemblance to the wine which Louis XIV drank'.

Faith may well be right. Rosé de Riceys is a still pink wine made from Pinot Noir grapes grown in the vineyards around the village of Les Riceys in the Aube department in southern Champagne. Fewer than half the Pinot Noir vineyards in the village – the ones facing south – are allowed to produce grapes for Rosé de Riceys. If a grower intends to make a Rosé de Riceys, the I.N.A.O. (Institut National des Appellations d'Origine des Vins: the government body in charge of enforcing *appellation contrôlée* laws) must be forewarned, so that it can send a commission to the vineyard to see whether the grapes are healthy and ripe enough. Once the go-ahead has been given, the grower puts the grapes in a small wooden vat and crushes them by foot.

Fermentation lasts for between three and six days. 'You tell when the wine is ready to be taken out of the vat,' says Serge Bonnet, the leading producer, 'by tasting it. You take it out when it starts to bite – to taste astringent. The colour varies, but the taste does not. If you wait too long, you start to get the perfumes of a red wine. You have to get your timing right within a margin of half an hour.' After fermentation the wine is aged for several months in old oak casks, and is ready to drink as soon as it is bottled.

Bonnet's Rosé de Riceys is an extraordinary, light yet very complex wine, which tastes of oranges and cloves. It is the finest pink wine I have tasted. Other leading producers include Gallimard and Horiot.

*

Jura

Pinot Noir was brought to the Jura from Burgundy in the early Middle Ages. It has never succeeded, however, in ousting the local grapes Poulsard and Trousseau. Often, the three grapes are blended together. A wine made purely from Poulsard has quite nice sweet fruit but will tend to smell of drains; one made from Trousseau will have more colour and extract but not a great deal of taste. Yet a blend of these two with Pinot Noir can be superb. I have tasted a ten-year-old Côtes de Jura from Jean Bourdy which resembled a mature, gamey red burgundy.

The leading producer of pure Pinot Noir wines is Château d'Arlay, owned by the Comte and Comtesse de Laguiche, who are related to the Marquis de Laguiche in Chassagne-Montrachet and the de Vogüé family in Chambolle-Musigny. They make a lean, dry Pinot Noir, with a taste of bitter oranges. It is slightly maderized ('cooked', like Madeira), and tastes much as I imagine many red burgundies tasted in the nineteenth century.

Loire Valley

Menetou-Salon

The red wines made from Pinot Noir grown in the vineyards around Menetou-Salon, a small town twenty miles south-west of Sancerre, are often said to be a little less elegant than those of Sancerre (see below). What this often means in practice is that they have more flavour. The best producers include: (for red wines) Bernard Clément at the Domaine de Chatenoy; (for pink wines) Georges Chavet at Les Brangers.

Orléanais

In the Middle Ages the wines made from Pinot Noir grapes grown around the city of Orléans on the Loire, like those grown around the town of St-Pourçain (see below), competed with those of Burgundy. In the sixteenth century they competed with the wines of Champagne, which were then still and red. At the beginning of the seventeenth century, however, Nicolas Brûlart, the Chancellor of France and a major vineyard-owner in Champagne, enlisted the help of the doctors of the Court in a major propaganda campaign directed against the wines of Orléans. He succeeded. The reputation of the wines of Orléans was destroyed and never recovered.

Today they are not even entitled to *appellation contrôlée* but only to the humbler V.D.Q.S. (Vin de Qualité Supérieure) status. The only Pinot Noir I have tasted from the Orléanais is made by Daniel Montigny at Clos St-Fiacre. It is decent but herbaceous. It does not justify the resurrection of the region.

St-Pourçain

Strictly speaking, St-Pourçain is not in the Loire Valley as it lies on the Sioule, a tributary of the Allier, which is itself a tributary of the Loire.

In the fourteenth century the wine of St-Pourçain fought with the wine of Beaune for precedence on the table of the King in Paris and the Pope in exile in Avignon. It was a battle by proxy between the Duke of Bourbon (whose domaine included St-Pourçain) and the Duke of Burgundy. One of the reasons why, by the end of the century, the wines of Beaune had won this particular battle, is that it was simply too complicated to send wine from St-Pourçain to Avignon. The other reason is that the Dukes of Burgundy became much more powerful, not merely than their rivals the Dukes of Bourbon but also than the King himself.

Today the wines of St-Pourçain are so obscure that, like those of Orléans, they are entitled only to V.D.Q.S. status. In the Middle Ages St-Pourçain was better-known for its pale red wines. These days its white ones enjoy a better reputation. Most of the red wines are made from a blend of Pinot Noir and Gamay (the grape of the Beaujolais), although separate bottlings of Pinot Noir are made by the co-operative and by Gérard and Jean-Louis Pétillat.

Sancerre

Pinot Noir has grown all over eastern France for centuries. Sancerre, however, is in western France. The reason why Pinot Noir was planted here was that it used to be part of the Duchy of Burgundy.

Pinot Noir was the dominant grape variety in Sancerre until the late nineteenth century, when the vineyards were devastated by the phylloxera louse. The vines that were replanted afterwards had to be grafted on to American vine rootstock, which was resistant to phylloxera. It was found that the white-grape variety Sauvignon took better to grafting than the black-grape variety Pinot Noir. This was fortunate for vine-growers in Sancerre, because at the turn of the century white wine was easier to sell than red. Even producers of *grand cru* red burgundies had such great problems selling their wines that they tried turning them into sparkling ones. So Sancerre producers concentrated on white wines.

Appellation contrôlée status for white Sancerre made from Sauvignon was granted in 1936, with the requirement that it was to be grown on the best slopes. This requirement was not revoked until 1982. The *appellation* for red and pink wines was not granted until 1959. Pinot Noir was consequently planted either on north-facing slopes or on unsuitable soils, or both. This was ridiculous because the climate is cool: although Sancerre is on the same latitude as the Côte d'Or, the average temperature during the summer is lower.

Because, in many vintages, the Pinot Noir grapes failed to ripen fully, growers took to making them into pink wines. According to one of the growers, Pascal Gitton, it used to be the habit to make red wines only in good years and pink wines in lesser vintages. This is no longer the case. 'I'm against making red wines systematically each year,' he says, 'but people insist.' In the 1980s Parisian restaurateurs decreed that red Sancerres were the fashionable wines to drink. This has put great pressure on supply, and encouraged people to plant more black grapes. Today Pinot Noir accounts for more than 20 per cent of the production whereas fifteen years ago it was less than 10 per cent.

Demand from restaurateurs for red wines to drink young has led people to ferment the juice in contact with the grape skins for too short a period, and even to add oak chips rather than age the wine in barrel. The wines may be drinkable young, but they do not have much flavour. The principal exception to this rule is the late Jean Vacheron, who planted Pinot Noir on the best slopes and matured his wine in barrels bought second-hand from the Domaine de la Romanée-Conti. 'People who like good wine make red; people who want to make money concentrate on white,' he used to say. Other good producers of red Sancerre include: Jean-François Bailly at Bué-en-Sancerrois, Roger Champeau at Crésancy, Pierre and Étienne Riffault at Verdigny and Georges Robin at Sury-en-Vaux.

GERMANY

Why Does Germany Not Produce Better Pinot Noir?

Pinot Noir has been cultivated in Germany for centuries. Cuttings are supposed to have been brought to Ingelheim in the Rheinhessen in 1040 by the Duke of Burgundy, who was attending the *Reichstag* of the Emperor Henry III. Known locally as Spätburgunder (the late-ripening Burgundy grape), it has therefore been cultivated in Germany for more than 800 years longer than in California, Australia or New Zealand, and for more than 900 years longer than in Oregon.

The climate of many parts of Germany is ideal – comparable to that of Burgundy. Admittedly, a lot of Pinot Noir is grown in the Ahr Valley, the most northerly vine-growing region in the country. It lies just south of Bonn, between 50 and 51°N – on the same latitude as Cornwall – and is far too cool to ripen Pinot Noir properly. On the other hand, suitable areas, apart from Ingelheim, include Assmannshausen in the Rheingau, the Mittel-Haardt district of the Rheinpfalz and the Kaiserstuhl in Baden.

So why is German Pinot Noir not better? The reason is that, for most of this century, the wines that have been made from it have been sweet. Sweet red wines were invented – like inexpensive sweet white ones – after the Second World War. A special fermentation method was developed, which involved heating the mash of skins and grapes to 65–70°C, holding it there for a couple of hours, and then pressing. This produced wines with a lot of colour but hardly any tannin or flavour, which could only be described as white wines coloured red.

This fermentation method is still taught by the oenological

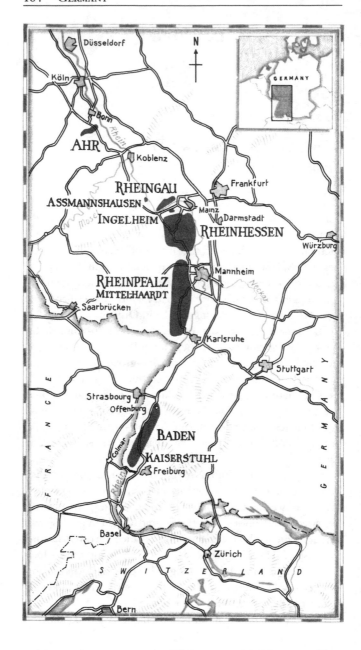

schools of Geisenheim and Freiburg. It is a response to the problem of grey rot – which itself is the fault of the Geisenheim and Freiburg schools, who have developed high-yielding clones of Pinot Noir which are susceptible to rot. There are too many grapes on the bunches: they press each other so hard that they break, the juice runs over them and they start to rot. By fermenting at a high temperature the oxidative enzymes contained in the rot are rendered inactive and the short fermentation ensures that the wines avoid a rotten taste or colour.

A better course would be to plant a lower-yielding clone, or at least a rot-resistant one, such as Maria Feld from Wädenswil in Switzerland. This yields almost as many grapes as the Geisenheim and Freiburg clones but in much more loosely packed bunches. According to Rainer Lingenfelder in Gross-karlbach in the Rheinpfalz, one of the leading producers of German Pinot Noir, 'If there had not been a Maria Feld, we would not have planted Pinot Noir.' At the beginning of the 1980s he approached the problems of German Pinot Noir in a methodically Germanic manner. 'I wondered why Germany couldn't make good red wines,' he said. 'I concluded that it was a question of mentality. Germans have white-wine procedure in the back of their head. You have to make red wine in a completely different way.'

Lingenfelder's predecessors made red wine, like white wine, without putting it through a malolactic fermentation. If they wanted to reduce the acidity, they added calcium carbonate – as indeed is still done at the traditionally minded Neus estate in Ingelheim. Calcium carbonate certainly reduces the acidity, but the point about malolactic fermentation is that it produces a fuller, rounder taste.

Lingenfelder started putting his Pinot Noir through its malolactic fermentation in 1984, his second vintage. At the same time he was experimenting with maturing his wines in small oak casks (which, even in Germany, are called by their French name, *barriques*). In 1983 and 1984 he matured part of his production in *barriques* and part in much larger casks – because his father would not allow him to age the entire crop in *barriques*. Visitors to the estate who compared the 1984 aged in *barriques* with that stored in traditional large casks did not believe that the two were the same wine – and halfway through the ageing process his father was convinced.

Lingenfelder came of age as a producer of Pinot Noir with his fully *barrique*-aged 1985 vintage. He became a *cause célèbre* when the official testing (Amtliche Prüfung, or A.P.) board refused to give the wine a certificate, which meant that it could not be sold as a quality wine, bearing the name of its village and vineyard, but simply as *Tafelwein* (table wine). This is not a unique incident. *Barrique*-aged Pinot Noirs produced by other pioneers have also been refused their A.P. certificates on the grounds that they are 'untraditional' – that is to say, made in a manner that fell out of fashion after the Second World War. This has produced a result that the authorities cannot have foreseen. The designation of *Tafelwein* is beginning to acquire an 'underground' status similar to that of *vino da tavola* in Italy. It has come to be understood that the best wines enjoy the humblest status.

The best producers include:

in the Rheingau: Weingut J. B. Becker* in Walluf and August Kesseler* in Assmannshausen

in the Rheinhessen: Weingut J. Neus* in Ingelheim

in the Rheinpfalz: Fritz Christmann in Gimmeldingen, Werner Knipser in Laumersheim, Rainer Lingenfelder* in Grosskarlbach, Weingut Rappenhof in Alseim and Thomas Siegrist in Leinsweiler

in Baden: Weingut Dr Heger* in Ihringen, Karl-Heinz Johner* in Bischoffingen, Weingut Franz Keller* in Oberbergen, Weingut Salwey* in Oberrotweil and the Winzergenossenschaft Sasbachwalden* in Sasbachwalden

STAATSWEINGUT ASSMANNSHAUSEN

Auhauserstrasse 19, 6220 Rüdesheim

Vineyard: 60 acres

Production: 100,000 bottles

Quality: 🍇–🍇🍇🍇   Price: ★—★★★★★

This is the temple of sweet red wines made from Pinot Noir. In his book on German wine, published in 1976, Fritz Hallgarten described the 1934, 1938 and 1950 nobly rotten Pinot Noir Beerenauslesen as 'the most exceptional wines I have ever met' (noble rot is a fungus which shrivels the grapes, concentrating their juice without spoiling them).

In fact, the estate produces a whole range of wines, from nearly dry to very sweet. Herr Dries, the estate manager, explains that they want to do as little as possible to the wines in the cellar. The degree of sweetness of the finished wines therefore depends on the ripeness of the grapes and changes from one vintage to the next.

I have not tasted a Beerenauslese but I did try a 1976 Pinot Noir Auslese, which had some noble rot. It was certainly different. The red wines I tasted from other vintages were not quite so sweet but they all suffered from the fact that any fruit they may have had was masked by residual sugar.

WEINGUT J. B. BECKER

Rheinstrasse 6, 6220 Walluf

Vineyard: 5 acres

Production: 10–15,000 bottles

Quality: 🍇🍇–🍇🍇🍇   Price: ★★★

Hans-Josef Becker, who carries himself with the air of a First World War cavalry officer, produces the finest interpretation of 'traditional' German Pinot Noir. It is a dry but intense wine, with a taste of bitter cherries. The 1985 vintage made so little sense to the jury in the 1988 Gault-Millau Wine Olympiad that they placed it bottom of the Pinot Noir class, describing it as 'an unhealthy wine, with too much carbon dioxide gas'.

The carbon dioxide is a product of Becker's horror of oxidation. He ferments his grapes in pressure tanks, in which carbon dioxide builds up during fermentation and protects the wine from oxidation. He also conserves the carbon dioxide gas that is produced by the malolactic fermentation in cask. Becker matures his Pinot Noir in large old casks rather than new *barriques*. 'I don't want to do fresh barrels,' he says. 'That's something we never did in our region. That's only following a trend. It gives other countries an opening in our market.'

German producers of Pinot Noir, he explains, will only succeed in establishing a market if they do their own thing. 'That is the way to make good friends in the wine business. We are not comparable to Burgundy: we are much lighter. We would never be able to compete.' Because of its lightness his 1985, although a disaster in France (because the Gault-Millau jury placed it last), was a success in Germany. It was ripe, but only had 10.5 per cent alcohol. 'That's why,' Becker said, 'we have sold so much of it in the famous restaurants here – they can serve it for lunch.'

WEINGUT DR HEGER

Bachenstrasse 19–21, 7817 Ihringen

Vineyard: 5 acres

Production: 5–10,000 bottles

Quality: 🍇–🍇🍇   Price: ★★★

Ever since it started using *barriques* in 1982 this estate has won all sorts of prizes for its Pinot Noir. It certainly has great potential – but it has not yet established a consistent style.

The wines used to be fermented in open vats for only two or three days, and lacked substance. Now they are fermented in closed tanks and have no lack of fruit. In 1991 a 1989 made from grapes from old vines in the Winklerberg vineyard showed remarkable concentration for a German Pinot Noir. Joachim Heger said that it was the best wine he had made so far. Unfortunately, he had matured it entirely in new oak – which was what it tasted of.

KARL-HEINZ JOHNER

Gartenstrasse 20, 7818 Bischoffingen
Production: 1,000 bottles
Quality: 🍇🍇🍇   Price: ★★★

Previously the wine-maker at Lamberhurst in England, Johner is the only producer of Pinot Noir in Germany who has committed himself to maturing his entire production of wine in small oak *barriques*. He claims that he does not know how red burgundy is made. 'I do things by feel,' he says. 'You have to create your own identity.'

In fact, Johner's wines taste more like burgundies than any other German Pinot Noirs – with the exception of those made by Fritz Keller, also in the Kaiserstuhl area of Baden.

WEINGUT FRANZ KELLER

Badbergstrasse 23, 7818 Oberbergen
Quality: 🍇🍇🍇   Price: ★★★

Franz Keller, who owns the Michelin two-star restaurant Schwartzer Adler, imports fine French wines and appears as a pundit on television as well as producing wine, is an important (and self-important) man.

To him went the honour of being the first producer of *barrique*-aged Pinot Noir to have his wine rejected by the official tasting board, when they refused to give his 1978 vintage an A.P. certificate. Since then he has always sold his *barrique* wines as *Tafelwein*.

The wine is now made by his son Fritz and is really good, soft and concentrated.

WEINGUT AUGUST KESSELER

Lorcherstrasse 16, 6220 Assmannshausen

Vineyard: 17 acres

Production: 25,000 bottles

Quality: 🍇🍇–🍇🍇🍇🍇   Price: ★★★–★★★★

August Kesseler is the acknowledged star of German red-wine production. Although, since the mid-1980s, he has matured a portion of his production in *barriques*, his methods more closely resemble those of Hans-Josef Becker (who does not use *barriques*) than those of Rainer Lingenfelder (who does). Whereas Lingenfelder matures his wine in *barriques* in order to deepen the colour of the wine through slow oxidation, Kesseler shares Becker's obsession with avoiding oxidation. His cellar is naturally very damp, yet he still sprays it with water every day – in order to close up the staves of the oak casks so that there is less oxidation. He tops up the wine in the casks every two days, whereas Lingenfelder does so once a month.

Kesseler's horror of oxidation means that the wines that he matures in *barrique* are difficult to taste in their youth: they are austere, with dry tannins, but piercingly long and pure. They are the quintessential German Pinot Noirs.

WEINGUT LINGENFELDER

Hauptstrasse 27, 6711 Grosskarlbach

Vineyard: 5 acres

Production: 18,000 bottles

Quality: 🍇🍇–🍇🍇🍇   Price: ★★★

The history of Rainer Lingenfelder's Pinot Noir – his planting of the rot-resistant Maria Feld clone in 1981, his introduction of malolactic fermentation in 1984 and of *barrique*-ageing for the entire crop in 1985, and the creation of his reputation by the refusal of the official tasting board to grant an A.P. certificate to his 1985 – is described in the introduction to this section on Germany (see pp. 183–6).

The result is a light and elegant but slightly herbaceous Pinot Noir from vines which yield 70 hectolitres per hectare – twice the level achieved by the most conscientious producers in Burgundy.

WEINGUT J. NEUS

Postfach 1520, 6507 Ingelheim

Vineyard: 15 acres

Production: 40,000 bottles

Quality: 🍇🍇–🍇🍇🍇   Price: ★★

This estate was founded last century by Josef Neus, a travelling oenologist from the Mosel. Wine-making methods have not changed since.

The wines exist as a relic of how German Pinot Noir tasted before it became a slightly sweet, quasi-white wine after the Second World War. They are lighter than red burgundies, and earthy rather than fruity. They have complex, secondary aromas, but are slightly spoilt by sulphurous smells.

WEINGUT SALWEY

Hauptstrasse 2, 7818 Oberrotweil

Vineyard: 12 acres

Production: 25,000 bottles

Quality: 🍇🍇–🍇🍇🍇   Price: ★★–★★★

Wolf-Dietrich Salwey started maturing his Pinot Noir in *barriques* in 1985, but his is one wine which is neither transformed nor dominated by the oak. He makes a very elegant, lean, clean

Pinot Noir, which does not undergo a malolactic fermentation. 'I like fresh wines with a pronounced level of acidity,' he explains. 'I think people should be able to drink them young.'

WINZERGENOSSENSCHAFT SASBACHWALDEN

Tal 2, 7592 Sasbachwalden

Vineyard: 275 acres

Production: 400,000 bottles

Quality: 🍇–🍇🍇🍇   Price: ★★–★★★

The Sasbachwalden co-operative is situated in pretty rolling countryside in the Ortenau district of Baden. It sells a lot of its wine direct to tourists. In 1985 it started ageing a portion of its Pinot Noir in *barriques*. The purpose, explains its director Bruno Spinner, was 'to get into a different market segment. Our main customers for the *barrique* wine are top restaurants. We have also attracted consumers who had never drunk German wine before.'

The co-operative's *barrique*-aged Pinot Noir is a good, oaky wine in its youth, although it does not last well. It is hard to believe that it bears some relation to its non-*barrique*-aged Pinot Noir, which is light and earthy and has little fruit. According to Spinner, 'The *barriques* change the wine dramatically and one has to admit that it is not any longer recognizable as wine from Sasbachwalden – or even from Germany.'

ITALY

Surprisingly few good Pinot Noirs are produced in Italy, considering that it has no lack of suitable climates. The Oltrepò Pavese – in the foothills of the Apennines – in Lombardy is sometimes described as 'the Burgundy of Italy', but actually its main rôle is to supply plonk to supermarkets in Milan. The Pinot Noir it does grow is almost all turned into sparkling wine.

In general the production of serious red wine from Pinot Noir in Italy remains in an experimental stage. The principal exceptions are:

in Alto Adige/South Tyrol: Höfstatter
in Lombardy: Beppe Bassi (Pinot Nero di Doria) and Tenuta Mazzolino ('Nero') in the Oltrepò Pavese; Ca' del Bosco ('Pinero') in Brescia
in Emilia-Romagna: La Stoppa ('Alfeo') in the Colli Piacentini

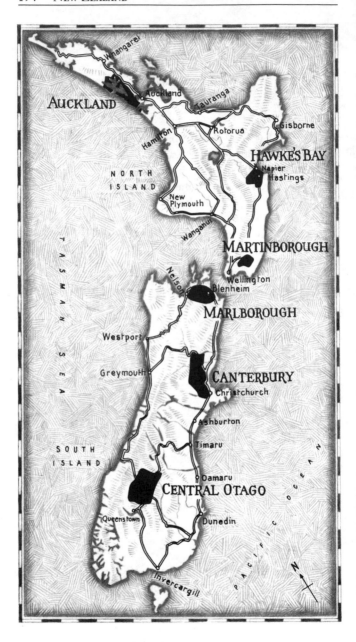

AUCKLAND

Whangarei

Auckland

Tauranga

Hamilton

Rotorua

Gisborne

HAWKE'S BAY

Napier
Hastings

NORTH
ISLAND

New
Plymouth

Wanganui

MARTINBOROUGH

Wellington
Blenheim

Nelson

MARLBOROUGH

Westport

Greymouth

CANTERBURY

Christchurch

Ashburton

Timaru

SOUTH
ISLAND

Oamaru

CENTRAL OTAGO

Queenstown

Dunedin

Invercargill

TASMAN SEA

PACIFIC OCEAN

N

NEW ZEALAND

The Potential to Make Great Pinot Noirs

It is evident from looking at an atlas that New Zealand is the best place in the Southern Hemisphere to grow Pinot Noir. The southernmost vineyard in South Africa is Hamilton Russell, at 34.5°S. The southernmost vineyards on the mainland of Australia – the principal Pinot Noir-producing region around Melbourne – are at 38°S. Only on Tasmania do vineyards extend as far as 43°S. In New Zealand the most successful regions so far for Pinot Noir are Martinborough at 41.5°S and Canterbury at 43.5°S, with the up-and-coming Central Otago at 45°S – the same latitude as that of the Willamette Valley in Oregon in the Northern Hemisphere, and not too far from that of Burgundy (47°N).

New Zealand's vineyards therefore enjoy a longer growing season than others in the Southern Hemisphere, with more hours of daylight in summer. They also have a cool climate suited to Pinot Noir. The central Canterbury coast and Central Otago are as cool as Burgundy; Waipara in North Canterbury and Martinborough are a little warmer. There is also limestone subsoil in Waipara, the same type as in Burgundy, if that is significant. Clearly, New Zealand has the potential to make great Pinot Noir. This potential has taken a long time to be realized. Pinot Noir was introduced into New Zealand in the early nineteenth century, but until consumers started to become interested in fine wines in the 1970s most vine-growers preferred to cultivate high-yielding, rot-resistant hybrid varieties.

The first decent Pinot Noir was produced in 1976 by Nobilo at Auckland on the North Island. This was followed by good wines from Babich and Matua Valley, two other large wineries nearby. Auckland, which lies on a similar latitude to Melbourne, is really both too warm and too wet for Pinot Noir. Moreover, the wines were made from Bachtobel, a sparkling-wine clone which produces red wines with little colour or body. It was not in Auckland that the future for Pinot Noir in New Zealand was to be found.

In 1974 Lincoln College – an agricultural university in Canterbury on the South Island – received the clone 10/5. Like Bachtobel, this had been selected (in Switzerland) for the production of sparkling wine, but Lincoln College carried out trials which showed that it produced much better red wines. On the recommendation of researchers from the College 10/5 was planted at St Helena, a few miles away, in 1978. This was a potato farm which had been struck by potato blight, so its owners were looking for a new crop to plant. It was the first commercial vineyard to be planted in Canterbury. In its second vintage, 1982, it won a gold medal at the 1983 National Wine Show. Suddenly, New Zealand Pinot Noir was on the map.

St Helena repeated this success in 1984 and 1985. But then the wine-maker, Danny Schuster, left to spend four years travelling in Europe and America. He was replaced by Mark Rattray, who had learnt his wine-making in Germany and who took until the 1988 vintage to find his feet. The 1988 St Helena Pinot Noir was a very good, ripe wine in its youth but it was low in acidity and was already looking tired by 1991. The 1989 vintage was too low in acidity and was sold off locally under a second label at a discounted price. The 1990 appeared light when in barrel and was not expected to last long. The wines have declined rather than improved as the vines have matured; the reason seems to be that the vines have tapped a subterranean water supply and grow too vigorously, or it may simply be the result of bad vineyard management. (See 'The Importance of Soil', on pp. 6–10.)

Rattray has now left St Helena and, like Schuster, is making wine in Waipara in North Canterbury from less vigorous vines growing on limestone subsoil. In 1989 they produced the first vintages at two new vineyards, Waipara Springs (Rattray) and

Omihi Hills (Schuster). The 1990 Pinot Noir from Waipara Springs is a lovely, fragrant wine, but with only short-term potential; greater things have been promised (but not yet provided) by Omihi Hills. It may be that the brightest future for Pinot Noir in New Zealand lies in Waipara. For the moment, however, it is Martinborough, at the southern end of the North Island, that is king. Although no Pinot Noir was planted here before 1980, ever since the 1986 vintage from Martinborough Vineyard this has been the most successful region for Pinot Noir in New Zealand.

Danny Schuster attributes the success of Pinot Noir from Martinborough in New Zealand wine competitions to the preference of judges for light-flavoured, aromatic, early-drinking wines. Neil McCallum, the owner of Dry River Vineyard in Martinborough, admits that the region is not unique. He points out that Marlborough has had very little success so far although climatically it is similar. The difference is that in Marlborough a lot of people still use Bachtobel and, with irrigation, they achieve yields which can go up to 100 hectolitres per hectare. 'We are currently more successful,' says McCallum, 'because we only use appropriate clones and limit yields to 50 hectolitres per hectare or less.' The reason why Martinborough is producing the best Pinot Noirs in New Zealand is the attitude of the producers. 'No other district has taken Pinot Noir as its own and marketed it as that,' explains Larry McKenna, the winemaker at Martinborough Vineyard. 'A real gap existed in New Zealand for quality Pinot Noir and Martinborough has filled it.'

It is as yet too soon to say which region has the greatest long-term potential. It may well be neither Martinborough nor Waipara but Central Otago, the most southerly vineyard area in the world. This is quite different from the other regions. Whereas they have mild maritime climates, with a rather limited range of temperatures, Central Otago has a continental climate. The vineyards are the best part of 100 miles from the sea; they are 1,000 feet above sea level, in valleys surrounded by mountains. It is cold in winter, cool at night and not particularly warm during the day in summer.

The potential of the area had long been talked about but no one planted vines, even on an experimental basis, until 1976. The area is now receiving serious attention because of a good, ripe Pinot Noir made by Rippon Vineyard in 1989 and a beautiful, elegant, fruity one made by Gibbston Valley Wines in 1990. The vines at Gibbston Valley grow on slopes where miners dug for gold last century. They were originally planted as a hobby by Alan Brady, who was born in Northern Ireland and worked for years as a journalist and broadcaster. The hobby became an obsession and in 1987 he hired a wine-maker, Rob Hay, and started producing wine on a commercial basis. He sensibly recognizes that 'it would be presumptuous to assume that one good wine is going to launch [him] on the road to greatness.' One need only think of what has happened to St Helena.

The Pinot Noir industry in New Zealand is so young that all it can really offer is promise. This is as true of Martinborough as of Central Otago. The vines are still young and only a small range of clones is cultivated: most of the successful vineyards make their wines principally from 10/5. Several new clones have recently been introduced from America, including Pommard, the principal clone grown in Oregon. Wine-makers hope that this will enable them to produce more concentrated wines with a better ageing potential. Time will tell.

The best producers are:

on the North Island: C. J. Pask in Hawkes Bay and Ata Rangi, Martinborough Vineyard* and Palliser Estate in Martinborough

on the South Island: Omihi Hills, St Helena and Waipara Springs in Canterbury and Gibbston Valley Wines and Rippon Vineyard in Central Otago

MARTINBOROUGH VINEYARD

Princess Street, Martinborough
Vineyard: 16 acres

Production: 20–30,000 bottles

Quality: 🍇🍇🍇   Price: ★★★

In 1978 Derek Milne, a New Zealand government soil scientist, wrote a report on alternative land use in the Wairarapa region at the southern end of the North Island. He identified the area round the town of Martinborough as being ideal for grape-growing, and the climate as being suited to Pinot Noir and other cool-climate varieties. In 1980 he decided to put his money where his mouth was and, in partnership with Russell Schultz, a pharmacist and home wine-maker, planted the first Pinot Noir vines in Martinborough. The first two vintages were made by Schultz in 1984 and 1985. In 1986 they took on a professional wine-maker, Larry McKenna, an Australian who had previously made the wine for Delegats in Auckland. With his first vintage McKenna established for the Martinborough region the reputation which it holds today of producing the finest Pinot Noirs in New Zealand.

McKenna makes the wines according to Burgundian principles. Because he feels that the 10/5 clone, which pre-dominates in their vineyard, naturally produces a rather soft style of wine, he tries to create structure by his wine-making technique. He ferments between 25 and 50 per cent of the grapes uncrushed as whole bunches – so that he has a certain proportion of stalks in the vat – and leaves the wine in contact with the skins and stalks for a week or two after the end of fermentation. This produces wine with a sufficiently good backbone for it to take, in a top vintage such as 1989, five or six years to reach its peak.

The wine is undoubtedly good but it could do with more depth and complexity. McKenna believes that with the in-troduction of the Pommard clone he will be able to produce a fuller-bodied wine with good natural structure which will not require him to include stalks in the fermentation vat. Only then, he believes, will New Zealand be able to produce truly world-class Pinot Noir.

*

SOUTH AFRICA

South Africa is the last of the New World countries to have come to terms with Pinot Noir. At the end of the 1980s South African Pinot Noir was described by Michel Fridjhon, one of the country's leading wine-writers, as 'almost the same kind of contradiction as Army intelligence'. The problem lay with the clone that was imported in the 1970s to replace the existing virus-infected clone, whose difficulty in setting its crop had discouraged producers from planting it. The new clone (BK 5 from Wädenswil in Switzerland) was certainly virus-free but it was not suitable for making red wines. It had been developed for producing sparkling ones. It readily produces a large crop of grapes (low yields are not necessary for sparkling wines). If it is forced to produce still red wines, they turn out very light in colour (colour is undesirable in sparkling-wine grapes).

It is amazing that any good Pinot Noirs have been made from BK 5. Hamilton Russell* has made a remarkably good wine by severely reducing the crop. Throughout the 1980s it was acknowledged by everyone that Hamilton Russell produced the best Pinot Noir in South Africa. But Hamilton Russell's reputation is now beginning to be contested by vine-growers who have planted the new Burgundy clones, which were finally released for planting in 1987. Walter Finlayson at Glen Carlou in Paarl beginning in 1990 and Philip Constandius at Delheim in Stellenbosch beginning in 1991 have made delicious ripe wines in climates which are theoretically much too warm for Pinot Noir.

The best Pinot Noir so far produced in South Africa was made from Burgundy clones in 1991 by Peter Finlayson, the man responsible for the Hamilton Russell wines in the 1980s. Finlayson was enabled to set up on his own by finance from Paul Bouchard, one of the directors of the Burgundy merchant firm Bouchard Aîné. The vines were imported from Burgundy in 1982 on an experimental basis – the K.W.V. (Koöperatieve Wijnbouwers Verenining, which means vine-growers co-operative society but is in fact the authority that controls vine plantings and wine sales) wanted to test them out before authorizing a general importation. The Bouchard-Finlayson vineyard is situated in Elgin, an uplands plateau close to the sea, to the west of Hermanus, where Hamilton Russell has his vines. It is the coolest vine-growing region in South Africa – cooler than Hermanus, although slightly warmer than Burgundy. The reason why it has only just begun to be planted with vines is that farmers have been able to make more money out of growing apples and pears.

It could be argued that South Africa will never become famous for its Pinot Noirs, because it does not extend far enough south from the equator. On the other hand, wines produced from Burgundy clones in cool climates such as Elgin will ensure at least that it becomes worthy of international consideration.

HAMILTON RUSSELL

P.O. Box 158, Hermanus 7200, Cape Province

Vineyard: 42 acres

Production: 40–50,000 bottles

Quality: 🍇🍇🍇   Price: ★★★

Tim Hamilton Russell says that he started searching for the perfect site to grow Chardonnay and Pinot Noir in the early 1960s and that it took him ten years to find it. Surprisingly, he ended up at Hermanus in the Hemel-en-Aarde Valley, where his family already owned some property. Hamilton Russell used to work in advertising, so he knows how to promote his wares.

The vineyard is three miles from the Atlantic Ocean. It is not quite perfect, he admits. It is situated at 34.5°S, so it does not enjoy nearly such long hours of daylight in the summer as

Burgundy, which is at 47°N. 'I would have preferred it,' he says, 'if South Africa could have stretched another 150 miles into the Atlantic.'

The main problem for Hamilton Russell, as for every other producer of Pinot Noir in South Africa, lies in the clone (BK 5) that was made available to him. Hamilton Russell tries to compensate for its natural lack of colour and body by close-planting, short-pruning and thinning the grapes in summer. This keeps the yield down to only about 25 hectolitres per hectare – much less than the norm even in Burgundy. Even so, the wine is not particularly concentrated. But it is serious, and it is built to age. The 1989, in particular, disproves the theory that it is not possible to make fine wine from BK 5.

In 1989 Hamilton Russell was one of only four vine-growers to sign the Winelands Commitment, which committed its signatories to the removal of all apartheid policies among their vineyard workers.

SPAIN

Most of Spain is much too warm for Pinot Noir, but three New World-style producers in Catalonia have had a go. Jean León in Penedès tried it but gave up; Raimat makes an unexpectedly good wine from irrigated vines in the hot climate of Costers del Segre; only Torres* has found a suitable climate by going up into the hills, and looks to have a future.

TORRES

22 Commercio, 08720 Vilafranca del Penedès

Vineyard: 25 acres

Production: 20,000 bottles

Quality: 🍇🍇–🍇🍇🍇   Price: ★★★

For Miguel Torres, who enjoys an international reputation for the wines he makes from a number of grape varieties, Pinot Noir is the final frontier. This may seem surprising, given that he learnt his wine-making in Dijon in Burgundy thirty years ago, but he has been experimenting ever since.

In the 1970s he grew Pinot Noir in a relatively warm climate, and made it into a wine called Santa Digna. It was not wholly successful as a straight varietal, so he tried adding Tempranillo. This wine is now called Magdala and is a blend of half Pinot Noir and half Tempranillo. In the 1980s Torres tried again, this time in a cooler climate. He planted Pinot Noir at the Mas Borrás vineyard in the High Penedès, 1,700 feet above sea level. The subsoil is limestone, as in Burgundy. Torres chose limestone not because it drains well but because it acts 'like a sponge', holding on to water and releasing it slowly. It is dry in the summer in the High Penedès, so it is important to maximize the effect of any rainfall.

The first commercial vintage was the 1985. It came third in the Pinot Noir class in the 1988 Gault-Millau Wine Olympiad. The 1986 was spoilt by rot and the 1987 by too much oak, so they were blended into Viña Magdala. The 1988 was therefore the second vintage to be released. It is a well-made wine in a fresh style but without the backbone that might enable it to improve in bottle. This is to be expected, as it was fermented at a relatively low temperature in closed stainless-steel tanks, matured in oak for only two months, and has only 11.5 per cent alcohol. The 1989 and 1990 have been made in the same way. Torres explains that as long as the vines are still young, the wine will be made in a style which emphasizes the fruit.

SWITZERLAND

Switzerland is more famous for its research institute at Wädenswil on the shores of Lake Zurich, which has developed cool-climate clones of Pinot Noir that have been grown successfully in Oregon and New Zealand, than for the Pinot Noirs which it itself produces.

Much of the Pinot Noir produced in German-speaking eastern Switzerland comes from Wädenswil clones – although, in fact, the variety was brought here by the Duke of Rohan during the Thirty Years War. The canton of Graubünden enjoys the best reputation, but the wines tend to be light and of no more than local interest. They are generally labelled *Blauburgunder* ('the blue-skinned grape from Burgundy').

The main wine-producing area of the country is the Valais, the valley above the upper reaches of the Rhône, in French-speaking western Switzerland. Its best-known red wine is Dôle, a blend of at least half Pinot Noir and no more than half Gamay. This is named after the town of Dôle, 100 miles to the west in the Jura, from which the vines were originally imported. It can be compared to Passe-Tout-Grains in Burgundy except that it is lighter and usually contains a higher proportion of Pinot Noir.

The other distinctly local version of Pinot Noir is Oeil de Perdrix, which is an invention of Neuchâtel, just across the border from the Jura lakes. It is a pale and delicate but sometimes intense wine. (The name refers to the pale pink colour of a partridge's eye – which is how both red burgundies and champagnes were described in the eighteenth century.)

A number of serious varietal Pinot Noirs are now being produced from Burgundy clones in French-speaking Switzerland. The problem is that the vines are often young and the yields are generally high. The wines are sold locally, so meet local rather than international taste. They tend to be soft and fruity – similar to the better German Pinot Noirs. They are also expensive – in part because the steeply terraced vineyards (particularly in the Valais) are difficult to cultivate. Since they are not generally exported, they do not have to compete with other Pinot Noirs abroad and the Swiss themselves are quite used to the prices. But when in Switzerland it makes sense to drink burgundy.

USA

California

The Fall and Rise of California Pinot Noir

Pinot Noir has been grown in California much longer than it has in Oregon. The most famous Pinot Noir vineyard in California, Mount Eden in the Santa Cruz Mountains, is the direct descendant of a vineyard planted in Santa Cruz at the end of the nineteenth century by Paul Masson, who had brought vine-cuttings over in a suitcase from Louis Latour's vineyards in Burgundy. Mount Eden was planted by Martin Ray in the 1940s up the hill from Masson's vineyard with cuttings taken from it. By the 1950s Martin Ray was making Pinot Noir along Burgundian lines. By the 1960s he was selling bottles of his Pinot Noir for $50 each. No Pinot Noir vines were planted in Oregon until 1966. But, following the success of the 1975 Reserve from the Eyrie Vineyards in two tastings in Paris in 1979 and 1980, it was Oregon that came to be regarded as 'the promised land for Pinot Noir'.

In 1986 the International Wine Center in New York held a triangular tasting of Pinot Noirs from California, Oregon and Burgundy. This was divided into two parts. In the morning the participants knew which wines they were tasting. They tried seven burgundies and four Oregon and eight California Pinot Noirs. They discussed the wines. They put, as a group, the burgundies top, the Oregon wines second and the California Pinot Noirs third. In the afternoon they tasted a similar number of wines – not the same ones – without knowing what they were. This time, California came top, Burgundy second and Oregon third – but only because the tasters thought the

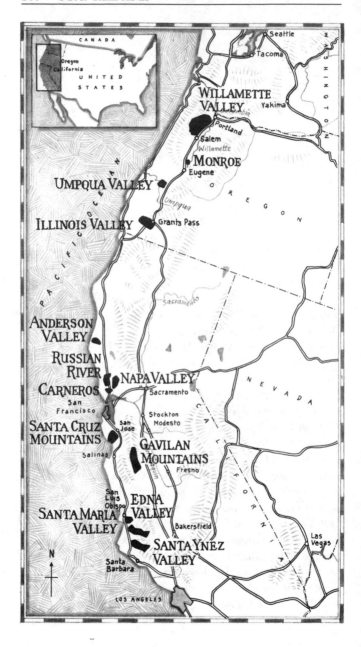

California wines came from Burgundy, the burgundies from Oregon and the Oregon wines from California.

A century after the first Pinot Noir vines were planted in California but only a generation after they were taken to Oregon, wine-trade professionals expected good Pinot Noirs to come from Oregon and not from California. It was said that California had too warm a climate to grow Pinot Noir successfully. This was substantially true. There are plenty of areas of California cool enough for Pinot Noir, but these are not the places in which it has traditionally been grown.

The manufacture of Pinot Noir in California along Burgundian lines was pioneered in the 1950s by Martin Ray and by Brad Webb, the wine-maker at Hanzell. Martin Ray's vineyard was not that cool. Hanzell's was not cool at all. Tom Dehlinger, who worked there in the 1970s, describes the climate as 'Algerian' and points out that a typical summer day peaks at 40°C. It is probably too warm for Cabernet Sauvignon, let alone Pinot Noir.

In the California of the 1950s and 1960s, however, most vine-growers did not care if the climate was right or not. They believed that Man was more powerful than God and that the good Pinot Noirs made in California at that time demonstrated the triumph of technology over viticulture, as they were made in spite of, not because of, where they were grown. Most of them nevertheless produced very bad Pinot Noirs. 'Twenty years ago,' says Francis Mahoney, the owner of Carneros Creek, 'California Pinot Noirs were light-bodied, coloured orange and tasted of raisins.'

In the 1970s California Pinot Noir lost the little reputation it had once enjoyed. The price of Pinot Noir grapes fell by 75 per cent between 1971 and 1974. By the end of the decade Gregory Graziano (now at La Crema) was making a Pinot Noir at the Milano winery in Mendocino County which he sold as Gamay Beaujolais – because at the time Gamay had a better reputation than Pinot Noir. A few vine-growers did seek out the cooler areas of California, among them Richard Sanford and Michael Benedict, who planted a vineyard in the Santa Maria Valley in Santa Barbara County, a few miles from the Pacific coast. They produced their first Pinot Noir in 1976; it sold at very high prices and encouraged other wine-makers to believe that it was possible to find the right place to grow Pinot Noir in California after all. A major change of attitude was necessary, however, before wine-makers in California could repeat their success with Cabernet Sauvignon and Chardonnay, and surpass the Pinot Noirs coming out of Oregon.

In the 1950s and 1960s the professors of the University of California at Davis had been so obsessed with trying to make great Cabernet Sauvignon in the Californian conditions of the Napa Valley that they taught that the techniques for making Cabernet Sauvignon could be applied to all red wines. They were wrong. Pinot Noir is not like Cabernet Sauvignon. It must not be handled aggressively. It is spoilt if it is filtered before being put into cask or in bottle, or if it is racked too frequently from one cask to another. Nevertheless, it was not until the 1980s that Californian wine-makers were persuaded to adopt a more sensitive approach to Pinot Noir – partly influenced by the success of their counterparts in Oregon and partly by the example of wine-makers in Burgundy.

This transformation is exemplified by the changes in the methods of the giant Mondavi company. In the first half of the decade they cleaned up Pinot Noir before putting it in barrel – because, they said, it was unstable – and they filtered it before bottling. In the second half of the decade they changed their minds. Their Pinot Noirs used to be distinctly inferior to the wines they made from other grape varieties. They are now quite delicious. Today the overall quality of Pinot Noir in California is better than that of Pinot Noir in Oregon. Even Oregonian vine-growers admit it. According to Craig Broadley of Broadley Vineyards, 'California makes better Pinot Noir than Oregon because it has more experienced wine-makers with more money.'

The most impressive Pinot Noirs in the United States are produced in California by Williams Selyem, Calera and Au Bon Climat. But the most exciting Pinot Noirs – the ones that make your knees go weak – are made in Oregon by the three remaining pioneers, David Lett, Dick Erath and Dick Ponzi. The majority of Californian wine-makers are simply not psychologically equipped to make great Pinot Noir. Bill Dyer, the wine-maker at Sterling, tried to learn how to make Pinot Noir in 1986 by visiting Burgundy to see how it was done there. He spent some time with Henri Jayer, the most famous small grower in the region. 'Jayer,' says Dyer, 'was amazed by my asking technical questions. He said that what mattered was to have good grapes.'

Anderson Valley

The Anderson Valley is isolated between two coastal mountain ranges in Mendocino County, sixty miles north-west of the Napa Valley. It used to attract those in search of an alternative lifestyle. For many years the major cash crop was marijuana. Psychedelic music is still the mainstay of the local FM radio station. The valley is perfect for cool-climate grapes. The Pacific Ocean is only twenty-five miles away. Winds and summer fogs ensure that the temperature rarely exceeds 30°C during the day. Moreover, it is cold at night.

Vines were introduced in the early 1970s. One of the pioneers, Ted Bennett of Navarro Vineyards, was told by local farmers that wine-grapes would not ripen on the valley floor. But the grapes that these farmers had failed to ripen were the robust red grapes that their cousins grew in Napa and Sonoma. In fact, the Anderson Valley is not that cool. In Bennett's opinion the best vintages for Pinot Noir are the colder ones.

Nevertheless, the cold night-time temperatures – which ensure good levels of acidity – have encouraged several sparkling-wine producers to establish themselves in the Anderson Valley. The decision in 1985 by Louis Roederer, who had looked all over the United States (including New York State and Oregon), to site its American sparkling-wine facility in the Anderson Valley seems to have ensured that the future of the region will lie in sparkling- rather than still-wine production.

The best producers of still wine include: Husch, Lazy Creek Vineyards,* Navarro.

Carneros

A generation ago Los Carneros, the point at which the Napa Valley touches San Francisco Bay, was considered too cool to make fine wines. People said it was good only for grazing sheep (in Spanish, *los carneros*). Although there had been a number of vineyards in Carneros in the late nineteenth century, the region then lay barren until the 1960s, when René de Rosa, a former journalist, planted the now-celebrated Winery Lake vineyard. The reason why he settled in Los Carneros is that he was single and wanted to be within easy reach of the nightlife of San Francisco. Francis Mahoney, who owns Carneros Creek, came to the region in the early 1970s in order to make Pinot Noir. 'It was too hot elsewhere,' he says. 'Carneros fruit had a freshness I had not seen in other areas.'

This region is certainly cooler than the rest of the Napa Valley. Kent Rasmussen says that since he arrived in the late 1970s he has been able to sit and eat dinner with his wife out of doors only three times. Carneros is cooled by a tidal wind blowing from San Pablo Bay. The temperature does not go much over 30°C during the day. However, Carneros is not as cool as other regions which enjoy a reputation for good Pinot Noir. John Paul, now settled at Cameron in Oregon, made the wine at Carneros Creek in the late 1970s. 'The line in California is that Carneros is cool – but it's not that cool. In Oregon every year we pick the fruit 100 days after bloom. In Carneros it is ten days less.'

The growing season in Carneros is shorter not just than in Burgundy or Oregon but also than in the Santa Maria Valley in Santa Barbara, 200 miles to the south. Now that land in Carneros has become very expensive it is to Santa Barbara that the attention of both wine-makers and wine-writers has turned.

The best producers include: Acacia Winery,* Carneros Creek Winery,* Kent Rasmussen,* Saintsbury* and Sterling Vineyards.*

*

Edna Valley

Situated just north of the Santa Maria and Santa Ynez Valleys in Santa Barbara County, the Edna Valley in San Louis Obispo County shares many of their climatic characteristics. It is cooled by ocean breezes in summer: it is shrouded in fog until mid-morning and the maximum daytime temperature rarely exceeds 27°C. It is often warmer in the spring. Despite the theoretical appropriateness of the climate for Pinot Noir, however, no vine-grower in the region made consistently successful wines from the variety before Edna Valley Vineyards* started doing so in 1988.

Gavilan Mountains

California's two most committed *terroiristes*, Dick Graff of Chalone and Josh Jensen of Calera, have established their vineyards in remote locations in this mountain range a hundred miles south of San Francisco, between Monterey and San Benito Counties, because that is where limestone is to be found. In theory, it is too hot to grow Pinot Noir successfully but both Chalone Vineyards* and Calera Vineyards* produce outstanding wines. The rôle played by the limestone in making this possible will remain a matter of controversy for the foreseeable future.

Napa Valley

Although it is the most famous vine-growing region of California, the Napa Valley is mostly too warm for the successful cultivation of Pinot Noir. The principal exception is its southern extremity where it touches San Francisco Bay (for which see 'Carneros'). Of Napa Valley wineries which make good Pinot Noir, Robert Mondavi Winery* does use some fruit from the heart of the Napa Valley but its major source is Carneros; the Étude, El Molino, Sinskey and Sterling Vineyards* Pinot Noirs are made exclusively from grapes grown in Carneros.

Santa Barbara County

Attention has recently been focused on Santa Barbara County by the purchase by the giant Mondavi company first of the Tepusquet vineyard and then of the Byron vineyard and winery in the Santa Maria Valley. 'Santa Maria is the Burgundy of America,' says Michael Mondavi. 'It is cooler than Oregon and has more fossil shells [more limestone] than Burgundy.'

One would expect Santa Barbara County, which is closer to Los Angeles than to San Francisco, to be too hot for Cabernet Sauvignon, let alone Pinot Noir. But near the coast the climate is perfect. The coast runs from east to west, as do the coastal mountains. A westerly wind blows up the Santa Maria and Santa Ynez Valleys, cooling them but itself warming up as it goes. Only a narrow band of land – between fifteen and thirty miles from the coast – is ideal for vine-growing. Any closer to the coast and it is too cool; any further away and it is too warm.

Richard Sanford, a geographer by training, says that he looked all over the West Coast for the right place to grow Pinot Noir before settling in Santa Barbara in 1970. The vineyard he planted – the Benedict vineyard in Santa Ynez Valley – has been described by Jim Clendenen of Au Bon Climat, who makes outstanding wines from its fruit, as 'the coolest vineyard in California' and 'the best vineyard in California for Pinot Noir'.

Benedict, however, stands alone. Rick Longoria, the wine-maker at Gainey, has made wonderful Pinot Noirs from Benedict fruit but only mediocre wines from fruit brought in from elsewhere. Benedict produces outstanding fruit because it has been de-vigorized by the refusal of Michael Benedict, Sanford's former partner, to irrigate. The yields may have been uneconomically low, but at least wine made from it does not taste vegetal or herbaceous.

Elsewhere in Santa Barbara herbaceousness is a problem: the vines are too vigorous, they have too many leaves and not enough sunshine gets to the grapes. But this problem can easily be solved. All that is necessary is canopy management (one of the buzz words of the 1990s), which means training the canopy of grapes so that the fruit is better exposed to the sun. This may not, however, make Santa Barbara more deserving than Oregon of the title 'the Burgundy of America'. A visitor to the region cannot help but notice that the air is thick with the scent of aromatic plant oils and that this characteristic is present in the wines. Whether it should be regarded as a positive feature in a Pinot Noir is a moot point. Furthermore Santa Barbara is situated at 35°N, compared with Oregon at 45°N and Burgundy at 47°N. There are fewer hours of daylight in the summer, so the growing season is not as long.

The best producers include: Au Bon Climat,* Byron, Foxen, Gainey, Sanford Winery* and Wild Horse.*

Santa Cruz Mountains

As we have seen above, the first authenticated Pinot Noir vineyard in the United States was planted in Santa Cruz in the late nineteenth century by Paul Masson. In 1936 Masson sold his vineyard to Martin Ray, a stockbroker. In 1943 Ray sold it on to Seagram – who ploughed it up and turned Paul Masson into a brand name for blended wines – and planted vineyards higher up in the Santa Cruz Mountains with cuttings taken from Masson's vines. It was the wines made by Ray in the 1950s and 1960s that attracted other vine-growers, including David Bruce and Ken Burnap, to the Santa Cruz Mountains. Ken Burnap wanted to find a suitable climate for growing Pinot Noir. 'After three long periods of research in Burgundy in the late 1970s and early 1980s I came up with a set of eleven criteria for a Pinot Noir vineyard. The Santa Cruz Mountains had all of these.' He bought the Santa Cruz Mountain Vineyards in 1974.

The Santa Cruz Mountain Vineyards are on the westward side of the Santa Cruz Mountains, exposed to the sea. The microclimate is cooler and wetter than at the vineyard established by Ray, now called Mount Eden, which is on the eastward side of the mountains, facing the land. But it is still much more extreme than that of Burgundy. In the summer it is hot in the day – it may reach 35°C – but it cools down to 5–6°C at night. The hot days produce grapes with high sugar and tannin contents; the cool nights mean that they retain a high level of acidity.

Santa Cruz is not the promised land for Pinot Noir. Randall Grahm entered the wine business in the early 1980s because he wanted to make great Californian Pinot Noir. On the strength of one bottle of Santa Cruz Mountain Vineyards 1975 he chose a site in Santa Cruz, which he called Bonny Doon. That bottle, he now recognizes, 'sent me off on a wild goose chase. When I made a better wine from Oregon grapes than I could make from my own vineyard, I gave up on Pinot Noir.' After the 1985 vintage he budded over his vineyard to Rhône Valley varieties.

The best producers include: Mount Eden Vineyards* and Santa Cruz Mountain Vineyards.*

Sonoma County: Russian River

It was at Hanzell in Sonoma County that one of California's first burgundy-style Pinot Noirs was produced in the 1950s, but that is not the reason why so much attention has been focused on the area recently. Hanzell Vineyards are in eastern Sonoma, where the climate is better suited to Cabernet Sauvignon. Pinot Noir grows more successfully in the Russian River Valley in western Sonoma, which is cooled by sea breezes and fog.

'I know that this area is as cool as any in California,' says Burt Williams of Williams Selyem, who buys fruit from seven vineyards in the valley. 'This is apparent from the amount of sparkling wine produced. I can make as good a wine from Russian River fruit as from anywhere in the world.' In 1987 Williams proved his point with the release of his first separate bottling of Pinot Noir made from the Rochiolis' vineyard. It has become one of the most sought-after wines in California. The area is not that cool, however. The Rochiolis also have a small patch of Cabernet Sauvignon which produces a very dark, concentrated wine.

The best producers include: Dehlinger Winery,* Gary Farrell,* Hanzell Vineyards,* La Crema,* Rochioli Vineyard and Winery,* Joseph Swan Vineyards,* Williams Selyem.*

ACACIA WINERY

2750 Los Amigos Road, Napa, California 94559
Production: 100,000 bottles
Quality: 🍇🍇🍇🍇   Price: ★★★

'I started as a wine-lover who did not know how to make wine,' says Larry Brooks, who has made the wine for Acacia since its foundation in 1979. 'I learnt by trial and error. I still feel that we don't have a clue.'

Brooks is being disingenuous. He makes the most elegant, most complex and classiest wines in Carneros. He is helped by access to fruit from some of the best vineyards in the region, which he bottles separately: Madonna, which Brooks says is inconsistent because its character is based more on fruit flavours than on tannin; St Clair, which is more reliable; and Iund, which Brooks says does best in poor years, partly because it has 'wild microbial flavours' which make it interesting when fruit flavours are lacking.

AU BON CLIMAT

Box 113, Los Olivos, California 93441
Production: 20,000 bottles
Quality: 🍇🍇🍇–🍇🍇🍇🍇   Price: ★★★–★★★★

Jim Clendenen and Adam Tolmach, the owners of Au Bon Climat, do not hide their light under a bushel. They met whilst working at Zaca Mesa (also in Santa Barbara County) in the late 1970s, only to leave to set up on their own because they had become 'disenchanted with the artistic direction' of the winery. They now apply Burgundian techniques – such as hot fermentation in open-top vats – to West Coast fruit. The resulting wines are concentrated and complex but sometimes rather tough.

Clendenen and Tolmach have bought fruit from all over the place, including Oregon. They have made their best wines since 1987 from the Benedict vineyard (see Sanford Winery entry). Their other Santa Barbara County Pinot Noirs are sometimes a bit vegetal. Overall, their Pinot Noirs are good but not as wonderful as their Chardonnays.

CALERA VINEYARDS

11300 Cienega Road, Hollister, California 950237

Vineyard: 37 acres

Production: 26,000 bottles

Quality: ୨୨୨୨୨   Price: ★★★

Josh Jensen, the owner of Calera, and Dick Graff, the owner of Chalone, constitute their own particular society of *terroiristes* – that is, Americans who believe that the greatness of red burgundy should be attributed to its limestone soil, rather than to its climate. Most of their compatriots think the opposite. Like Graff at Chalone, Josh Jensen chose a remote site high in the Gavilan Mountains because that was one of the very few places in California where limestone bedrock could be found. It used to be a lime-kiln, so he called it *calera*, which means lime-kiln in Spanish. He planted the vineyard in 1975.

The climate is much warmer than in Burgundy, but this does not pose a major problem. The style of the wines simply reflects the climate. Jensen's wine-maker Steve Doerner makes luscious Pinot Noirs from very ripe grapes – picked at more than 13 per cent potential alcohol, compared with the 11–11.5 per cent that is normal in Burgundy. 'We think that in Burgundy they make good wines in spite of rather than because of their climate,' Doerner says. 'They would like it to be warmer. We tried picking earlier and chaptalizing once but I wasn't that impressed by the wine. It had a green taste.'

Jensen sells the produce of his four vineyards separately. (The straight Calera Pinot Noir is made from bought-in fruit, and until the 1988 vintage was not remotely in the same class.) The most flattering is the Jensen vineyard, whose gorgeous 1987 has been described (I do not know by whom) as 'a wine you can go to bed with'. Doerner, however, believes that the Selleck vineyard produces a finer wine, given time. Both are among the best Pinot Noirs produced in the United States.

CARNEROS CREEK WINERY

1285 Dealy Lane, Napa, California 94558
Vineyard: 25 acres
Production: 175,000 bottles
Quality: 🍇   Price: ★★–★★★

Francis Mahoney, an importer of burgundies, came to Carneros Creek to plant Pinot Noir in the early 1970s, before its potential was generally appreciated. He has spent twenty years on important research, selecting the best clones for the region. It is a great pity that he has not been able to carry the dedication he has shown in his vineyard over to his wine-making. Carneros Creek Pinot Noirs are elegant and understated but they lack fruit.

CHALONE VINEYARDS

Box 855, Soledad, California 93960
Vineyard: 32 acres
Production: 55,000 bottles
Quality: 🍇–🍇🍇🍇🍇   Price: ★★★–★★★★

Dick Graff, the owner of Chalone, is the most fanatical of the Californian *terroiristes*. He has a tendency, in interviews, to wax lyrical about 'what we call the *goût de terroir* of the Chalone vineyards'.

His vineyards are virtually impossible to find, as they are hidden in the Gavilan Mountains. The site was discovered in the late nineteenth century by a Frenchman who decided that the soil was the closest he could find to that of Burgundy – in other words limestone, which is rare in California. Graff, a music graduate, took over the estate in the late 1960s. Not only does the soil resemble that of Burgundy, but so does the wine-making style – and not just Burgundy, but the Domaine de la Romanée-Conti itself.

Graff visited the Domaine in 1976 and soon afterwards converted Chalone entirely to its practice of whole-bunch fermentation. This enables his wine-maker Michael Michaud to extend the vatting time to between two and three weeks. The wines, like those of the Domaine de la Romanée-Conti, take quite some time to become drinkable. The 1981 and 1982 are not yet fully mature. The 1986 is unapproachable, but Michaud says that it is the best Pinot Noir they have ever made.

Chalone does produce a Pinot Noir from young vines which can be drunk young. Called Gavilan, it is a simple, fresh wine which does not taste like the other Chalone Pinot Noirs. The quintessential Chalone Pinot Noir, however, is the Reserve bottling, made from the oldest vines, planted in 1919 and the 1940s, and matured entirely in new oak. It is sold only to shareholders and through a private mailing list. But not even the Reserve bottling tastes like the wines of the Domaine de la Romanée-Conti. The Chalone wines are intense and quite full-bodied, because the climate of the Gavilan Mountains is much warmer, not just than Burgundy, but also than elsewhere in California where Pinot Noir is grown successfully.

Chalone Pinot Noirs are sometimes described as having a 'dusty' character when they are young. This may have less to do with the *terroir* than with the contamination of the barrels with the same compound which is responsible for the taste of bad corks. When mature, the wines can be astonishing. In 1990 the 1978 – which included wine from the oldest vines, since a separate Reserve bottling was not introduced until 1980 – had a delicious taste of burnt toffee.

LA CREMA

4940 Ross Rd, Sebastopol, California 95472
Production: 250,000 bottles
Quality: 🍇   Price: ★★–★★★
Other label: Barrow Green

Gregory Graziano, the wine-maker at La Crema, makes so much Pinot Noir that he has to buy fruit from the whole length of the California coast, make it into a load of different wines and then blend them all together.

He contends that the blends are better than the original wines. This is probably true. For reasons on which it is possible only to speculate, La Crema's sources of grapes change from one year to the next. By blending together wines that are unbalanced in different respects, Graziano produces a wine that has decent weight and balance – if not exactly purity of fruit.

DEHLINGER WINERY

6300 Guernville Road, Sebastopol, California 95472
Vineyard: 8 acres
Production: 25,000 bottles
Quality: 🍇🍇   Price: ★★★

'I planted a vineyard,' says Tom Dehlinger, 'because I couldn't get people to grow grapes the way I wanted them to. It is a completely different mentality. I don't think most growers could understand, believe or afford what I want to do.' Tom Dehlinger planted his vineyard north of Sebastopol, in south-west Sonoma, in 1975. The site had been a Zinfandel vineyard in the nineteenth century, and an apple orchard in the first half of the twentieth. 'It had the reputation of being the earliest orchard in the area – because of the soil. We are the southernmost grape-growing point of Sonoma. We have cool air but warm soil. Climate is important but soil is more so.'

The vines are planted on rolling terrain, on a variety of different soils. Dehlinger prunes, harvests and vinifies grapes from his fifteen different plots in fifteen different ways. Then he blends them to make three different wines. They are rich, complex and attractive. They resemble those of Williams Selyem – which are also made from very ripe grapes. 'I like the flavours of ripe grapes,' says Dehlinger. 'The best Pinot Noirs have 13.5 or 14 per cent alcohol.'

EDNA VALLEY VINEYARDS

2585 Biddle Ranch Road, San Luis Obispo, California 93401

Production: 6,000 bottles

Quality: 🍇🍇🍇   Price: ★★★

Edna Valley ought to have made much better Pinot Noir than it has. The vineyard was planted in the early 1970s by the Nivens family, who had seen a study recommending the Los Osos Valley (which is cooled by winds from the Pacific Ocean) for cool-climate grapes.

The Nivenses entered into an arrangement with the Chalone group whereby they supplied the grapes and Chalone made the wine. Unfortunately, the wine-making practices used at Chalone were followed much too slavishly, including whole-cluster fermentation. The grape stems – ripe at Chalone, unripe at Edna Valley – gave the Edna Valley Pinot Noirs a herbaceous character.

In 1988 a new, inexperienced wine-maker, Steve Dooley, took over and he has turned the estate around. The wine-making now incorporates fewer of the methods used at Chalone and more of those practised at Acacia (which was bought by Chalone in 1986). Fewer stems are included in the fermentation vat, and the wine is bottled earlier. It is a ripe, clean, accessible, mid-weight Pinot Noir.

GARY FARRELL

| c/o Davis Bynum, 8075 Westside Road, Healdsburg, California 95448
| Production: 35,000 bottles
| Quality: 🍇🍇🍇–🍇🍇🍇🍇   Price: ★★–★★★

Gary Farrell, the wine-maker for Davis Bynum, started selling wines under his own name in 1982. They are better than the Davis Bynum wines. Farrell says that this is partly because he has access to fruit from the famous Rochioli vineyard, and partly because he does not have the limitations that he has at Davis Bynum. For example, Bynum cannot afford new oak, which Farrell thinks is vital for Pinot Noir.

Farrell's Pinot Noirs are long, clean, balanced and obviously built to age. His best wine does not, in fact, come from the Rochioli vineyard but from the Howard Allen vineyard next to it – which was planted in the mid-1970s with cuttings from Rochioli and is farmed by the Rochiolis on behalf of its absentee owner.

HANZELL VINEYARDS

| 18596 Lomita Avenue, Sonoma, California 95476
| Vineyard: 10 acres
| Production: 12,000 bottles
| Quality: 🍇🍇   Price: ★★★–★★★★

It is a matter of dispute whether it was at Hanzell in Sonoma County or at Mount Eden in the Santa Cruz Mountains that the first Burgundy-style Pinot Noir was produced in America after the Second World War. Hanzell was founded in 1948 by the former United States ambassador to Italy, James D. Zellerbach. He tried to copy burgundy so closely that he modelled his winery on the Château du Clos de Vougeot.

The most Burgundian feature of the wine-making was that the wines were matured in French oak barrels. Other aspects of the method were established by Brad Webb, the original wine-maker, by a process of trial and error. He picked the grapes very ripe and fermented them on their skins for only five days. Zellerbach died in 1961 and in 1973 Webb was replaced as wine-maker by Bob Sessions.

At first Sessions tried picking the grapes less ripe than Webb had. He reasoned that the microclimate was, in fact, much too warm for Pinot Noir – on a summer afternoon it reaches 40°C – and that, if he wanted to produce a Burgundian style of wine, he would have to pick the grapes very early. After a few years, however, he came to the conclusion that they would do better to take what their warm climate gave them rather than try to fight against it. He now picks the grapes as ripe as Webb did, but he does leave the wine for longer than in the past in contact with the grape skins in the fermentation vat. As a result, the wine has a lot of tannin in its youth and needs to be kept for ten years before drinking.

Mature Hanzell Pinot Noir is long and complex, but it shows no great evidence of fruit. It is spoilt by a bitter taste – which Sessions recognizes, and thinks may be the result of ageing the wine for too long in wood. Nevertheless, given the wholly inappropriate microclimate, it is remarkable that Sessions is able to produce serious Pinot Noirs at all.

KALIN CELLARS

61 Galli Drive, Novato, California 94947

Production: 12,000 bottles

Quality: 🍇🍇🍇   Price: ★★★

'We make rich, heavy, meaty wines,' says Terry Leighton, a microbiologist who makes the wine at Kalin at weekends. 'Wines made in this style were made in Burgundy in the 1950s but were abandoned by a lot of people because they demand three to five years of bottle-age before they can be released in tasteable condition.'

In his wine-making techniques Leighton is more Burgundian than the Burgundians. He ferments the wine at a very high temperature – he has made his own selection of thermo-tolerant yeast – for three to four weeks in open wooden vats. He then matures the wine in oak for eighteen months, during which time he does not rack it at all. When bottling, he neither fines (removes particles in suspension with egg-whites, or some other binding substance) nor filters.

The resulting wines – made from grapes bought in from all over California, from Santa Barbara County in the south to Mendocino County in the north – are undoubtedly interesting, but they are too earthy, tannic and glycerous for my taste. They are made with a heavy hand. However, Robert Parker rates them alongside Calera as the best Pinot Noirs produced in California.

LAZY CREEK VINEYARDS

4610 Highway 128, Philo, California 95466

Vineyard: 6 acres

Production: 10,000 bottles

Quality: 🍇🍇🍇   Price: ★★

Hans Kobler, who came to the United States from Switzerland, used to work in the restaurant business. In the late 1960s he noticed that people were starting to drink wine, so he decided to grow grapes for sale to wine-makers. He chose the Anderson Valley because land was cheap. Unfortunately, grape prices fell, so he had to start turning the grapes into wine himself. 'I had no idea how to make wine,' he says, 'I just had to jump in the water.'

Today Kobler makes the best Pinot Noir in the Anderson Valley. It has more depth than the wines made by his neigh-bours, whilst remaining fresh and lively. Kobler modestly attributes the quality of his wine to his range of old, low-yielding clones. His Pinot Noir offers remarkably good value for money. 'Californians would find it much easier to sell their wines in Europe,' he says, 'if they were not so expensive.'

ROBERT MONDAVI WINERY

7801 St Helena Highway, Oakville, California 94562

Production: 600,000 bottles

Quality: 🍇🍇🍇🍇   Price: ★★★

Mondavi is not the sort of winery one would expect to make great Pinot Noir. Although it seeks to cultivate as far as possible the image of a small boutique winery, it is actually the seventh largest winery in the Napa Valley, producing 10 million bottles of wine a year. It used to make old-fashioned, heavy-handed, orangey Pinot Noirs lacking in fruit, but these have been transformed since the 1985 vintage into rich, ripe, concentrated wines bursting with fruit.

Mondavi have learnt to make great Pinot Noir through assiduous attention to detail. They have instructed the growers from whom they buy Pinot Noir to harvest the grapes less ripe – less over-ripe – than they used to; they have reduced the time the wine spends in barrel; they have abandoned their old practice of cleaning up Pinot Noir before putting it in barrel; they have stopped filtering their red wines.

Now they are switching their focus from the Napa Valley and Carneros to the cooler climate of the Santa Maria Valley in Santa Barbara County, where in 1987 they bought the 300-hectare Tepusquet vineyard and in 1989 the Byron vineyard and winery. Now that Mondavi are interested in the Santa Maria Valley, so is everybody else.

MOUNT EDEN VINEYARDS

22020 Mount Eden Road, Saratoga, California 95070
Vineyard: 7 acres
Production: 2,500 bottles
Quality: 🍇🍇🍇🍇   Price: ★★★★

Mount Eden is the descendant of the first authenticated Pinot Noir vineyard in California, planted in the late nineteenth century by Paul Masson with cuttings from the vineyards of Louis Latour in Burgundy. It was first planted in the 1940s by Martin Ray with cuttings taken from the Paul Masson vineyard. Seven acres of these vines remain today.

In the 1950s and 1960s Martin Ray made Pinot Noir by Burgundian methods but more than this is not known. The wines were variable, and suffered from high levels of volatile acidity. Today the estate is owned by a group of investors and the wine is made by Jeffrey Patterson, a beautiful blond, who worked in restaurants before coming to Mount Eden in 1982. Patterson has developed his own method of wine-making. 'There are so many ordinary Pinot Noirs,' he explains. 'You have to go against the grain: ferment hot, rack only once, and never filter.' He matures his Pinot Noir in 75 per cent new oak. This is quite appropriate for such a concentrated wine, produced from a crop which from the dry-farmed, frequently drought-affected and largely ancient vines averages a ridiculous 5 hectolitres per hectare.

Given the small crop and the relatively warm climate, it is surprising that the Mount Eden Pinot Noir turns out beautifully pure and balanced – not a hair out of place.

KENT RASMUSSEN

2125 Cuttings Wharf Road, Napa, California 94558
Vineyard: 10 acres

Production: 13,000 bottles

Quality: 🍇🍇🍇🍇   Price: ★★★

Kent Rasmussen used to be a librarian. 'It was not,' he says, 'my idea of fun. You were indoors too much.' He was also a home wine-maker and decided to turn his hobby into his profession. In 1978 he bought a seven-year-old vineyard whose owner had defaulted on his loan payments. He sold the grapes to, and worked at, Mondavi until 1986, when he started making his own wine.

Rasmussen still sells most of his grapes to Mondavi. The wines are similar. Both are ripe and long on the palate. Perhaps Rasmussen's Pinot Noir is not quite as clean as Mondavi's. But it is big, more individual and exciting, which is what Pinot Noir is all about.

ROCHIOLI VINEYARD AND WINERY

6192 Westside Road, Healdsburg, California 95448

Vineyard: 22 acres

Production: 15,000 bottles

Quality: 🍇🍇🍇   Price: ★★★

The Rochiolis are grape-farmers who planted a vineyard in the early 1970s which made them, fifteen years later, into super-stars. The reputation of the Rochioli vineyard has been created by Williams Selyem, who first produced a separate Rochioli vineyard bottling in 1985. In the same year the Rochiolis started commercial production of their own wine. Today they keep 60 per cent of the production of the vineyard for themselves and sell 25 per cent to Williams Selyem and 15 per cent to Gary Farrell.

Rochioli Pinot Noir is deep and soft, but a bit blunt. It could do with some more new oak to round it out. It is not in the same class as the Williams Selyem bottling – but then neither is the price.

SAINTSBURY

> 1500 Los Carneros Avenue, Napa, California 94559
>
> Production: 200,000 bottles
>
> Quality: 🍇🍇🍇–🍇🍇🍇🍇   Price: ★★–★★★

Dick Ward and David Graves came to Carneros in 1981 because the region had an established reputation. 'We had no money,' says Ward, 'and we had to convince people to lend us some.' Ward describes their wine-making practices as 'very straightforward'. They ferment the wine for five days in closed stainless-steel vats, then macerate it for ten days more. He gets very angry, however, when people accuse him of making wines that are too simple. 'We may do safe things,' he says, 'but we do them in an unsafe way. The wines are absolutely delicious.'

He is right. Although Saintsbury was the first winery in California to produce a nursery-slopes version of its Pinot Noir – a light, easy-drinking wine called Garnet – it was the winery which least needed to do so. The Saintsbury Pinot Noirs can be drunk as soon as they are released; they are also capable of improving in bottle. They have become more profound since the 1988 vintage, but without sacrificing their accessibility.

SANFORD WINERY

> 7250 Santa Rosa Road, Buellton, California 93427
>
> Production: 50,000 bottles
>
> Quality: 🍇🍇🍇   Price: ★★★

Richard Sanford, a geographer by training, says that he looked all over the West Coast for the right place to grow Pinot Noir before settling in Santa Barbara in 1970. This may well be true. But the first grape he planted was Cabernet Sauvignon. Nevertheless, it was Sanford's first vintage of Pinot Noir, in 1976, which made his reputation. A succulent, if rather herbaceous, wine, it suggested that someone had at last found the right place in California to grow the variety.

Sanford soon fell out with his partner, Michael Benedict, and left to start up his own winery. During the 1980s he made wines from bought-in fruit. By reducing the proportion of stems included in the fermentation vat he eliminated some of the excessively herbaceous taste which had been present in the wines he had made in partnership with Benedict. He developed a ripe, accessible style of Pinot Noir with plenty of new oak.

In the meantime, Benedict was having problems with his vineyard. The yield fell uneconomically low because he was not prepared to irrigate. In 1986 the whole crop was ruined by disease. Sanford had on several occasions offered to buy back the vineyard but Benedict had rejected his offer. In 1990 Benedict sold it to an English industrialist, Ronald Atkin. He did not know that Atkin was Sanford's new partner.

Between 1987 and 1989 both Au Bon Climat and Gainey made quite stunning wines from Benedict vineyard fruit. From the 1990 vintage most of the fruit goes to Sanford. The Sanford Pinot Noir is likely to become one of the finest on the West Coast.

SANTA CRUZ MOUNTAIN VINEYARDS

2300 Jarvis Road, Santa Cruz, California 95065

Vineyard: 13 acres

Production: 10,000 bottles

Quality: 🍇🍇🍇🍇   Price: ★★★

'I used to be a wine-groupie,' says Ken Burnap, who purchased Santa Cruz Mountain Vineyards in 1974. 'I hung out with Californian wine-makers, from whom I learnt primarily how not to make wine. I try,' he adds, 'to make wines the way they used to in Burgundy.'

This is not easy, because the climate of the Santa Cruz Mountains is hardly comparable to that of Burgundy. It is so hot and dry in the summer that the vines stop growing. They produce an absurdly low crop, between 5 and 15 hectolitres per hectare. The very high ratio of skin to juice means that there is a great deal of tannin in the grapes. Whatever methods Burnap tries, he cannot avoid making remarkably tannic Pinot Noirs. It may be hot in the day in the mountains but it is cold at night. The grapes have a high level of acidity as well as of tannin, and as a result the wines take years to mature. In 1990 the 1975, Burnap's first vintage, was still not fully developed.

Because of the high tannin and acid contents, Burnap's wines cannot be regarded as typical Pinot Noirs, but within their own frame of reference they are perfectly balanced and should be regarded as a complete success.

STERLING VINEYARDS

1111 Dunweal Lane, Calistoga, California 94515

Vineyard: 62 acres

Production: 70–90,000 bottles

Quality: 🍇🍇🍇   Price: ★★★

Sterling planted their vineyards in 1965 at the warm northern end of Napa. By the 1980s they had realized that it was too warm for Chardonnay. In 1986 they bought Winery Lake, the most famous vineyard in Carneros, in order to have access to cool-climate Chardonnay grapes. 'We had no intention of ever making Pinot Noir again,' says Bill Dyer, the wine-maker. 'But our purchase of Winery Lake brought us the responsibility to make Pinot Noir. I had trained on other varieties, but I was fascinated by the challenge. I had to learn how to make Pinot Noir between April and September 1986.'

The 1986 Pinot Noir is dark, extracted and high in alcohol. 'It is a Pinot Noir from a Cabernet producer,' Dyer admits. Since 1988 his Pinot Noirs have been decent, clean wines, but they do not yet live up to the reputation of the vineyard.

JOSEPH SWAN VINEYARDS

| 2916 Laguna Road, Forestville, California 95436
| Vineyard: 5 acres
| Production: 3–7,000 bottles
| Quality: 🍇🍇🍇   Price: ★★★

Joseph Swan was an airline pilot who, when faced with mandatory retirement in 1967, bought a run-down old Zinfandel vineyard, pulled out the vines and planted Chardonnay and Pinot Noir. He was greatly influenced in his wine-making by Jacques Seysses of Domaine Dujac in Burgundy. Like Seysses, he made his wine by fermenting whole clusters of grapes. Like Seysses's, his wines are austere in their youth. Only after some years in bottle does the fruit begin to emerge.

Swan Pinot Noirs have an unusual mint or eucalyptus character which becomes increasingly strong as the wines mature. This may have something to do with the soil. (It cannot be connected with the presence of stems in the fermentation vat, as the taste has become a little less pronounced since Swan converted to whole-cluster fermentation.)

Swan died at the start of 1989 and his inheritance is now in the hands of his protégé Rod Berglund, who had previously worked at La Crema.

WILD HORSE

| 85b Templeton Road, Templeton, California 93465
| Production: 80,000 bottles
| Quality: 🍇🍇🍇   Price: ★★★

Wild Horse enjoys a good reputation for its pleasant, up-front Pinot Noirs made from fruit bought mostly from the Santa Maria Valley in Santa Barbara County. They lack backbone – but this does not seem to matter. 'Our style is to produce wine that is drinkable soon,' explains Scott Welcher, the winery manager. 'Most people in California drink wine that is less than five years old.'

WILLIAMS SELYEM

6575 Westside Road, Healdsburg, California 95448

Production: 25,000 bottles

Quality: 🍇🍇🍇🍇   Price: ★★★★–★★★★★

Burt Williams was a newspaper printer who started home wine-making in 1962. He did not start making wine for money until 1981. 'It makes no difference that I haven't worked commercially,' he insists; 'if you make wine, it's wine. We had eleven burgundy producers at the winery two years ago. Alain Burguet said, "You make wine exactly as I do. How did you learn to do that?" I replied that I had learnt from old Italians.'

The wines do not taste like those of Alain Burguet or of old Italians. They are concentrated but soft, and can be drunk as soon as they are released. Burt Williams's best wine is a separate bottling of the Rochioli vineyard, which he matures entirely in new oak. This wine had acquired such a cult status by 1990 that he released the 1988 vintage at $50 a bottle – and still had to allocate it among his customers according to their purchases of his other wines.

Oregon

Do Oregon Wine-makers Try Too Hard to Copy Burgundy?

Most of the producers of Pinot Noir in Oregon are emigrants from California. Ever since the first four pioneers – David Lett of the Eyrie Vineyards, Chuck Coury (since gone bankrupt and returned to California), Dick Erath of Knudsen Erath and Dick Ponzi – made the 500-mile journey north in the late 1960s, wine-makers in search of an alternative lifestyle have migrated to the Willamette Valley in north-west Oregon, south-west of the principal city, Portland. Even in the 1960s, it was known that there were climates cool enough for Pinot Noir in California. Before emigrating to Oregon, Ponzi looked in Mendocino County (where the cool Anderson Valley is situated) but simply could not afford the land prices.

Some people went to Oregon because California Pinot Noirs offered such a bad example that they wanted to make a clean break and start afresh. Bill Blosser, who settled in Oregon in 1970 and set up Sokol Blosser Winery, says that he, like Ponzi, looked in California first. 'But almost no one was making Pinot Noir in California. Oregon seemed like the obvious place.' The Californian wine-industry is technology-oriented. Its members believe in stainless-steel tanks, pumps, centrifuges and filters. They are ideal for Cabernet Sauvignon but they are disastrous for Pinot Noir. Pinot Noir needs to be fermented in small quantities, then left alone to resolve itself.

The journey to Oregon is, above all, a flight from the guiding principles of wine-making in California. Craig and Claudia Broadley made the trip in 1982. Craig's main job, he says, is one of selling poetry books; with Claudia's help, he makes the wine at weekends. 'We're typical of a lot of operations in this state,' he declares. 'We are a Mom-and-Pop operation. We are 1960s back-to-the-country people.'

It is logical, says Broadley, that a Mom-and-Pop operation

should have chosen to grow Pinot Noir. 'We aren't the right type of people to make Cabernet Sauvignon. We are little people.' The problem with Mom-and-Pop wine-makers, however, is that they tend not to know how to make wine. They need to learn from someone and, having rejected the attitudes of the Californian wine-industry, the obvious choice is for them to copy Burgundy. They have been encouraged to do so by two major events.

The first Pinot Noir celebration was held in McMinnville in Oregon in 1987. Ostensibly, its purpose was to gain publicity for Oregon Pinot Noir. But another, underlying motive was more important. The money paid by people to attend went towards paying the air fares of Burgundian wine-makers to come over and participate in another Pinot Noir conference, at Steamboat, which was not open to the public (nor indeed to journalists). The Steamboat conference had already been going on for seven years when the McMinnville celebration started. Its original purpose had been to establish a relationship between producers in Oregon and those in California. The first participation of Burgundy producers in the conference marked, says David Adelsheim, 'the turning point of Burgundian influence in Oregon'.

One of the Burgundian wine-makers to attend the 1989 conference was Philippe Senard, who macerates the grapes in their juice before fermentation on the instructions of the oenologist Guy Accad. He spoke about this method. Two months later, most Oregon wine-makers were trying it out – although they had no reason to do so. It can be useful in Burgundy, because it extracts more colour from the grapes, but Oregon Pinot Noirs naturally have quite a good colour. (See 'Colour – A Red Herring', on pp. 20–22.)

The other turning point of Burgundian influence in Oregon occurred in the same year, 1987, when the Burgundy merchant Robert Drouhin bought land next to Eyrie Vineyards in the Dundee Hills. Drouhin made his first vintage in 1988, from bought-in grapes. In 1990 the first six bottles of this wine were sold at auction for $5,300 to the Fred Meyer discount chain.

The arrival of Robert Drouhin has stirred up so much excitement in Oregon that Bill Hatcher, the manager of his estate, has been forced into the deepest secrecy. No one was allowed to taste the 1988 before it was officially released in 1991. Many other details have also been kept secret. For example, Drouhin has grafted his vines on to several types of rootstock. Hatcher refuses to say which ones – on the grounds that this would cause other people to buy them and the supply to run out. Hatcher is terrified that if Oregonian vine-growers and wine-makers knew exactly what Drouhin was doing, they would try and copy him.

Drouhin is applying basically Burgundian methods, since they are what he knows best. However, it is not necessarily clear that Burgundian methods are the ideal ones for Oregon, given that the Pinot Noir is made from different clones grown on a different training system in a different climate. Oregonian wine-makers have so far devoted twenty years to trial and error. They will have to spend another fifty years before they know what methods work best. For the moment, says one Oregonian producer of Pinot Noir, 'people follow Burgundy. They don't know any better. Americans have no cultural heritage, so they have to have someone to imitate.'

The Hyping of Oregon Pinot Noir

In the Gault-Millau 1979 Wine Olympiad French Pinot Noirs did not do as well as expected. The 1975 Eyrie Reserve from Oregon came third. The Burgundy merchant Robert Drouhin said that the tasting had been unbalanced because the best burgundies had not been chosen. So he organized a rematch in 1980, with wines selected from his cellars. This time, the Eyrie 1975 came second, behind Drouhin's Chambolle-Musigny 1959 but ahead of Drouhin's Chambertin-Clos de Bèze 1961.

This tasting is supposed to have put Oregon on the map – but its main effect was to encourage a new wave of producers to set up ventures to make Pinot Noir. Many wine-drinkers still did not know where Oregon was. What put it on the map was a tasting of seven red burgundies and ten Oregon Pinot Noirs from the 1983 vintage, held at the International Wine Center in New York in 1985. The top three wines all came from Oregon: Yamhill Valley Vineyards and Sokol Blosser (both of them made by Bob McRitchie at Sokol Blosser), and Adelsheim.

The tasting was carried out by twenty-six wine-writers and merchants. They were asked to identify each wine as coming either from Burgundy or Oregon, but none of them got more than half of the wines right. It aroused so much interest that another one was organized at the beginning of 1986. This time Eyrie and Knudsen Erath tied for first place. The same year the Californian wine magazine the *Wine Spectator* asked the question, 'Is this the promised land for Pinot Noir?' In 1987 Robert Parker described it as 'the world's only viticultural region that appears capable of challenging the quality of the best French red burgundies'.

However, what the world hypes today, it knocks down tomorrow. At the end of 1989 Parker published his report on the well-regarded 1987 vintage in Oregon. 'I was astonished,' he wrote, 'by the number of wines that were out of balance because of excessively high acidity and insufficient flavour, depth and concentration.' In 1990 the *Wine Spectator* tasted ninety-one Oregon Pinot Noirs, mostly from the much-hyped 1983, 1985 and 1987 vintages. It described a number of them as 'dry, earthy and tannic', and concluded that Oregon Pinot Noir had 'failed the test of time'. Following these comments Bill Blosser of Sokol Blosser Winery wrote to the magazine to point out that, although it expressed disappointment with the 1985s, it in fact gave them higher marks than it had done two years earlier, when it said that American Pinot Noirs were 'better than ever'. 'I've seen this happen in every new region,' says Ken Wright, who worked in California before setting up Panther Creek Cellars in Oregon. 'First you have the discovery articles; then the newness is no longer newsworthy so the articles take a critical tack; finally you get balance. In order to mature you have to go through these stages.'

It was not just the wine-writers who had to mature. It was also the wine-makers. Before their successes at the wine-tastings in 1985 and 1986, before they were hyped by the press in 1986 and 1987, wine-makers in Oregon had a chip on their shoulder. Californian vine-growers had told them that they would have problems ripening their grapes. They sought to prove themselves by making wines that were as big and extracted as possible – the sort of wines that win wine-tasting competitions but are not ultimately enjoyable to drink. This is certainly true of the 1983 Pinot Noir from Yamhill Valley which came top in the first International Wine Center tasting in 1985. By 1990 it had turned positively unpleasant.

One reason why so many 1983s and 1985s had such aggressive tannins is that most wine-makers used an over-efficient destemmer-crusher made by the Italian firm of Zambelli. This crushed not only the skins of the grapes but also the pips, extracting very bitter tannins. It took until 1988 for wine-makers to realize that this was a problem and buy more expensive and more gentle machines.

The 1987 vintage was initially hyped in a press release sent out by the Oregon Wine Advisory Board. In some cases, the hyping was justified. Knudsen Erath and Ponzi both made staggeringly good Reserve bottlings. But 1987 was a difficult year. The grapes were analytically ripe (high in sugar and low in acidity) long before they tasted ripe. A number of people made thin, hard wines because they had picked too early. It was therefore necessary to be able to taste when the grapes were ripe. This was a talent which many Oregon wine-makers had yet to acquire.

All that they lacked was two thousand years of collective experience. When Robert Drouhin went out to Oregon for the first time in February 1988 to arrange to buy grapes people asked him, 'What sugar do you want to pick at?' He answered, 'How do you expect me to know that in February?' When he returned at the end of September 1988 Drouhin asked his manager, Bill Hatcher, 'When do we start harvesting?' Hatcher said that he did not know and needed to check with various vine-growers who had told him that the numbers were not yet right. Drouhin went into vineyards, looked around and tasted a few grapes. Five minutes later he said, 'We pick tomorrow.'

Vintage Guide

The summaries below could equally well be applied to the same years in Burgundy. Although no one can explain why, vintages in Oregon almost exactly parallel ones in Burgundy.

1982   Nice, soft wines. Now over the hill.

1983   Big wines, with too much tannin.

1984   Pretty useless. Too much rain.

1985   A top vintage. Ripe and concentrated.

1986   Variable; good if picked late. Generally lean and tannic.

1987   Variable. Some very good, supple wines.

1988   Classic, balanced wines. Consistently good.

1989   Variable. Some lovely, rich, supple wines. But it was a hot year and some people picked the grapes too late.

1990   At the time of writing (1991) I have not tasted any, but they are supposed to be excellent, combining the ripeness of the 1989s with the elegance of the 1988s.

Illinois Valley

The Illinois Valley lies 200 miles south of the Willamette Valley (see below) and only a few miles north of the Californian border. At about 1,500 feet above sea level, the vineyards experience the extremes of a mountain climate. It can get very hot during the day in summer, but the temperature falls dramatically at night. The growing season is two weeks shorter than in the Willamette Valley.

Vines were grown before Prohibition but not again on a commercial scale until 1974, when the Siskyiou Vineyards were planted by Chuck David, an emigrant from southern California. David, who had made his money by inventing computer discs, died of alcoholism in 1983. The winery went bankrupt three years later but it has since been revived by his widow Suzy. A number of other people planted vineyards in the 1980s

– perhaps hoping to benefit from sales to tourists visiting the Oregon Caves National Monument.

The best producers are Bridgeview and Foris Vineyards.*

Monroe

This is a new vine-growing region in the southern Willamette Valley, sixty miles south of the main Pinot Noir producing area. The coastal mountains are higher here, so the climate is warmer and drier, and the wines riper and fuller-bodied than those produced further north. The best producer is Broadley.*

Umpqua Valley

It was not David Lett of the Eyrie Vineyards who reintroduced vine-growing to Oregon but Richard Somner, who planted Riesling at Hillcrest Vineyards in 1961. Hillcrest is situated in the Umpqua Valley, 150 miles south of the Willamette Valley, where Lett settled. No one followed Somner, and everyone followed Lett.

The only important producer of Pinot Noir in Umpqua Valley, Scott Henry, says that other people planted vineyards near David Lett because it was not too far from Portland, the most important city in Oregon. Henry, who has a warehouse in Portland, only chose the Umpqua Valley because it was the site of his family farm.

The Umpqua Valley is warmer and has less rainfall than the Willamette, and the good vintages seldom coincide. The 1984, a disaster in the Willamette Valley, was successful here.

The best producer is Henry Estate.*

Willamette Valley

The first Pinot Noir vines in Oregon were planted by David Lett at the Eyrie Vineyards in 1966. Before leaving for Oregon Lett had studied vine-growing at the University of California at Davis. One of his old professors told him that he would be rained on all summer. Lett was followed by Dick Erath in 1967 and by Dick Ponzi in 1969. 'Originally,' says Ponzi, 'we thought we would have under-ripe grapes with a high level of acidity. We had to prove that we could ripen the grapes. We had an inferiority complex.' Oregon producers got over this particular complex thanks to the 1978 vintage, when they happily watched their grapes over-ripen on the vines.

The Willamette Valley in Oregon may be cooler than the Napa Valley in California – but it is not *that* cool a climate. Don Lange came to Oregon from Santa Barbara County in California in 1987, expecting a cooler climate. The next summer they had eighty-four days of straight sunshine. At the International Pinot Noir celebration in McMinnville in August, the temperature reached 42°C.

The climate has been compared to that of Burgundy, because the mean temperature during the growing season is very similar. But this similarity hides a much larger diurnal range. Oregon is warmer than Burgundy during the day and colder at night. Looking at their geographical locations, one would have expected it to be the other way round. Oregon has coastal summers whereas Burgundy has continental ones. Most of the principal Pinot Noir vineyards are planted on the hills above the Willamette Valley, which runs for 170 miles from Portland on the northern border of Oregon down to Eugene in its centre. It is about forty miles from the sea.

The vineyards are not cooled directly by sea breezes, because there is a small coastal range of mountains. But cool air does come in from the coast along the Van Duzer Corridor following Highway 18, which connects Lincoln City on the Pacific with McMinnville in the Dundee Hills. As the valley floor heats up and the hot air rises it pulls cool air from the coast. This cools the Dundee Hills in the afternoons. Because of this effect, the Dundee Hills are usually regarded as being cooler than the Eola Hills, where the broader valley floor warms the air more.

This difference is supposedly reflected in the taste of the wines. Dave Anderson of Knudsen Erath says that wines from the Dundee Hills have a spicy taste; he distinguishes clove, allspice, cinnamon and thyme. It is sometimes suggested that wines made from Eola Hills fruit taste of black cherries. In fact, it is impossible to generalize about mesoclimates within Oregon. There are too many exceptions to establish any rule. The

Dundee Hills may be considered to be relatively cool but Pat Campbell at Elk Cove manages to make a rich, tannic Cabernet Sauvignon from a pocket in the Dundee Hills Vineyard where heat tends to settle.

Certainly, wineries in the Dundee Hills have sought to make capital out of their reputation. After all, it was here that David Lett planted the first Pinot Noir vineyard in Oregon, after two years of looking for the right site. They talk about the Red Hills of Dundee – a reference to the red-coloured volcanic clay loam soil known as Jory which is supposed to produce particularly robust, full-flavoured wines. Nevertheless, Dick Ponzi, who makes perhaps the finest Pinot Noir in Oregon today, decided not to settle in the Dundee Hills when he emigrated from California in 1969. 'I am amused by the image of the Red Hills of Dundee,' he says. 'People with wineries there buy in grapes from elsewhere.'

The best producers include: Adams,* Adelsheim Vineyard,* Amity Vineyards,* Bethel Heights,* Cameron,* Domaine Drouhin,* Elk Cove,* Evesham Wood,* the Eyrie Vineyards,* Knudsen Erath,* Lange Winery,* McKinlay, Panther Creek Cellars,* Ponzi Vineyards,* Redhawk, Rex Hill Vineyards,* St Innocent, Sokol Blosser Winery,* Veritas Vineyard* Witness Tree, and Yamhill Valley Vineyards.*

ADAMS

1922 N.W. Pettygrove Street, Portland, Oregon 97209
Production: 20,000 bottles
Quality: 🍇🍇🍇–🍇🍇🍇🍇   Price: ★★★

Most Oregon wine-makers are immigrants from California, but Carol and Peter Adams grew up in the Willamette Valley. 'We had always liked wine,' says Carol. 'Then we found that you could make it – so you didn't have to buy it.'

When the Adams planted their vineyard in Newberg in 1976, Carol was working as a professional cook. 'I taught myself how to cook – and I taught myself how to make wine. It isn't that difficult. I've already done my experimenting with my cookery. I learnt an awful lot from making jam. Men don't like me saying this – because they don't make jam. If you grind up raspberries too much, they are very bitter.'

Adams makes very correct, long, clean wines which mature nicely but never become exciting. She needs to introduce some faults into her wine-making.

ADELSHEIM VINEYARD

22150 Quarter Mile Lane, Newberg, Oregon 97132

Production: 50–60,000 bottles

Quality: 🍇🍇🍇   Price: ★★★

David Adelsheim was one of the second wave of pioneers who planted vineyards in the early 1970s. He has now handed over the wine-making to his assistant Don Kantzner and is most concerned with promoting wine in Oregon generally. He is involved in setting up the annual Pinot Noir conference at Steamboat and the celebration at McMinnville.

Adelsheim's best Pinot Noirs come from the Seven Springs vineyard in the Eola Hills, of which he shares the fruit with Domaine Drouhin. The 1989 was rich and spicy from cask. The 1988, bottled as Eola Hills, was very tannic in 1990. The other wines are good but not great. They have fruit but lack elegance.

AMITY VINEYARDS

18150 Amity Vineyards Road, Amity, Oregon 97101

Production: 50,000 bottles

Quality: 🍇🍇–🍇🍇🍇   Price: ★★★

'We have a reputation for producing tannic wines,' says Peter Higby, the cellar-master of Amity. The reason, he explains, is that most of their grapes come from Sunnyside vineyard in Salem, which is situated in a warm microclimate.

They sell their best wine under the label of Wine-maker's Reserve. It is an excellent dark, rich wine, which is clearly made from Pinot Noir, but it resembles Châteauneuf-du-Pape more closely than it does burgundy.

BETHEL HEIGHTS VINEYARD

6060 Bethel Heights Road, Salem, Oregon 97304

Production: 20–25,000 bottles

Quality: 🍇🍇–🍇🍇🍇🍇   Price: ★★★

Bethel Heights is one of many estates in Oregon whose Pinot Noirs have become less aggressive since the 1988 vintage because it has given up using the cheap, over-efficient Zambelli destemmer-crusher which grinds up the pips, leaving a bitter taste in the wine.

The wines are made by Terry Casteel, who in his previous life was a psychologist in Seattle. In general, his Reserve bottlings are a quantum leap ahead of his ordinary ones. The 1987 Reserve would be wonderful – if it were not for an aggressive aspect to its tannins. There is no such problem with the deep, concentrated 1988 Reserve.

BROADLEY VINEYARDS

265 S. 5th Street, Monroe, Oregon 97456

Vineyard: 15 acres

Production: 15,000 bottles

Quality: 🍇🍇🍇   Price: ★★★

Craig and Claudia Broadley emigrated from California to Oregon in 1982, after seeing an article in the *San Francisco Chronicle* which told people to move to the country, plant five acres of vines and live off that. They settled in Monroe, in the southern Willamette Valley, near the university town of Eugene. This is sixty miles south of the main vine-growing area. 'We originally wanted to move to the Dundee Hills but we didn't like Portland,' Craig explains. 'It is a big boring town. We had friends in Eugene, which is a hipper place.' The climate is slightly warmer and drier than in the Dundee or Eola Hills and the Broadleys pick the grapes earlier.

The wines are dark and strong and perhaps a bit too aggressive. 'We try to extract a lot,' Craig says. 'I think making elegant wines is pretty easy to do. Our 1987 was too elegant. That is not appropriate for an area that is warm in the fall.'

CAMERON

8200 Worden Hill Road, Dundee, Oregon 97115

Production: 15–20,000 bottles

Quality: 🍇🍇🍇🍇   Price: ★★★

John Paul is a former marine microbiologist who set up the Cameron winery in the Dundee Hills in 1984 after working at Carneros Creek in California and looking at the possibility of planting a vineyard in New Zealand. 'I came to the Dundee Hills because of the track record of the area,' he explains. 'I came here because of the wines David Lett had made at Eyrie.'

Paul has accepted established Oregonian viticultural geography, but not established Oregonian wine-making methods. Ever since David Lett made the first vintage of Oregon Pinot Noir in 1970, most wine-makers have fermented their grapes in small boxes called totes. Paul, however, carried out tests which showed that because of their small size fermentation in totes does not get hot enough and does not extract enough colour. So he had stainless-steel fermenters built, based on the size of the vats used in Burgundy. He had measured these on a visit there by lying down in an empty one and stretching out to touch the sides with the tips of his fingers and his toes.

Paul is the rising star of Oregon wine-making, and the heir to the mantle of David Lett. He makes lean, tight, long Pinot Noirs from low-yielding vines. They should age splendidly.

DOMAINE DROUHIN

P.O. Box 700, Dundee, Oregon 97115

Production: 30,000 bottles

Price: ★★★★

No rating is given for this estate because when I visited it in the spring of 1990 the manager, Bill Hatcher, refused to allow me to taste the wines. 'We are protective of some of the things we do in the vineyard and the winery,' he explained. 'I know that people meet for weekly discussion at Nick's in McMinnville and at the annual conference at Steamboat. But in other industries people don't share secrets.' It is not surprising that Hatcher is so cagey, as the whole of Oregon, as well as other potential outside investors, is waiting for the result of Drouhin's venture.

Robert Drouhin first visited Oregon in 1961. He believed it would be an ideal place to grow Pinot Noir, but thought no more about it. In 1980, in a much-publicized Pinot Noir tasting in Paris, Drouhin's Chambertin-Clos de Bèze 1961 was defeated by the 1975 from the Eyrie Vineyards. This may have encouraged him to start thinking of Oregon again.

In 1986 his daughter Véronique went to Oregon to gain some practical experience of wine-making. She chose Oregon, she says, because the wineries there were smaller than in California. Her father came to visit, tasted the wines and said that it would be nice to make wine there. In 1987, out of the blue, David Adelsheim rang him to say that there was suitable land for sale. 'Why not?' thought Drouhin, and bought it. 'America is a new country free from many regulations,' he later explained to a journalist from the *Wine Spectator*. 'In Burgundy it's not intellectually very exciting. I don't ask myself many questions. Here I am constantly challenged. You feel like a pioneer.'

The Drouhins have invested $10 million in their property.
They started planting vines in 1988. Véronique makes the
wines – in the first few vintages from bought-in grapes. People
who have been given a sneak preview say that the wines are
both elegant and easy to drink – the same style as Drouhin
make in Burgundy.

ELK COVE VINEYARDS

27751 N.W. Olson Road, Gaston, Oregon 97119

Vineyard: 18 acres

Production: 30,000 bottles

Quality: 🍇   Price: ★★★

Pat Campbell, the wine-maker at Elk Cove, freely admits that
she 'tried to learn by copying Burgundy techniques'. She visited
Burgundy in 1976 during the harvest and made her first wine
the next year. She is thus among the most experienced of Oregon wine-makers and she enjoys a good reputation for her
Pinot Noirs. At the estate in 1990 I tasted the wines she had
made in 1986 and 1987. I thought they were rather earthy and
unlikely to give anyone much pleasure.

Before the 1988 harvest Campbell, like many other wine-
makers in Oregon, got rid of her over-efficient Zambelli
destemmer-crusher. In London in 1991 I tasted two wines she
had made in 1988 and 1989. They were not so earthy, and had
plenty of fruit, but they were over-extracted and lacked
elegance.

EVESHAM WOOD

4035 Wallace Road, West Salem, Oregon 97304

Production: 10,000 bottles

Quality: 🍇🍇   Price: ★★★

Russ Raney set up Evesham Wood in 1986 after corresponding with Henri Jayer in Burgundy. 'I'm not ashamed to admit that we would like to emulate Burgundy,' he says. Raney, who used to work at Adams, does not make wines that are funky enough to be compared to burgundies. He makes clean, firm Pinot Noirs which resemble the Adams wines, only without quite the same degree of finesse.

THE EYRIE VINEYARDS

935 E. 10th Street, McMinnville, Oregon 97128

Vineyard: 16 acres

Production: 15–30,000 bottles

Quality: 🍇🍇🍇🍇   Price: ★★★–★★★★

Today David Lett is revered as the pioneer who ventured into the wilderness and found a new home in Oregon for Pinot Noir. His former colleague, Chuck Coury, has been forgotten. But, in the early 1960s, when they were studying viticulture together at the University of California at Davis it was Coury who, according to Lett, got him interested in Oregon in the first place. 'He was a wonderful theoretician,' says Lett.

Lett and Coury came to Oregon together in 1965. Both planted vineyards. Lett survived but Coury did not. He went broke and now sells bicycles in Calistoga in California. So it was Lett, not Coury, who put Oregon Pinot Noir on the map. Lett says that the turning point for Oregon came in 1980, when in a tasting in Paris his 1975 Pinot Noir came out ahead of a 1961 Chambertin-Clos de Bèze from Drouhin. A number of subsequent arrivals in Oregon have planted their vineyards as close to Lett as possible; others have copied his wine-making methods.

Lett has always fermented his grapes in small bins intended for collecting cherries. Originally he used them for reasons of convenience. 'I had very little room,' he explains. 'I used cherry bins because it was easy to get them out of the way afterwards.'

These bins have become the standard fermentation vessels for Pinot Noir in Oregon. The drawback in using them is that the fermentation temperature never gets very high and the resulting wines are quite light. Lett's wines, however, have great intensity and by Oregon standards they are supremely elegant. The Reserve bottling is made from the original vines, planted in 1966. The 1985 was fabulous, but quite unready, in 1990. Lett described it as 'the most perfect Pinot Noir I have made', and said that it would need twenty years in bottle.

FORIS VINEYARDS

654 Kendall Road, Cave Junction, Oregon 97523

Vineyard: 10 acres

Production: 3,500 bottles

Quality: 🍇   Price: ★★

Ted Gerber used to live in California. He made wine from grapes he bought from a grower in Gilroy in Santa Clara County. 'I liked his life. This guy said that if he was a young man he would go to Oregon.' In 1974 he went to Oregon. For some years he grew grapes rather than made wine. Then he made wine to be sold by other people. Eighty per cent of his Pinot Noir still goes to Staton Hills in Washington, to be sold as Staton Hills Oregon Pinot Noir. 'It was,' he says, 'only after the good press for the 1983 and 1985 vintages that we started bottling wine ourselves. You couldn't sell Pinot Noir here before that.'

Today Gerber makes a crisp, quite green Pinot Noir. Back in California, he says, it would be described as 'a simple quaffer'.

HENRY ESTATE

687 Hubbard Creek Road, Umpqua, Oregon 97486

Vineyard: 6 acres

Production: 30,000 bottles

Quality: 🍇–🍇🍇🍇   Price: ★★–★★★

When he was working in the aerospace industry in California, Scott Henry became friends with Gino Zepponi, the founder of ZD Winery. In 1972 Henry had a 'mid-life itch' and went back to his family farm in the Umpqua Valley to grow grapes.

He planted vines on fertile soil on the valley floor. The yield is very high indeed – 100 hectolitres per hectare – but, thanks to the training system he developed and which bears his name (see 'Quality versus Quantity', on pp. 14–16), the wines do not taste particularly over-cropped.

Some of them do suffer, however, from his insistence on maturing them in American oak – a method which he learnt from Gino Zepponi and which is still practised at ZD. Henry says that he uses American oak because it gives less of an oak taste. In fact, his Barrel Select 1986 tastes like Rioja. His 1987s are much better balanced.

KNUDSEN ERATH

17000 Knudsen Lane, Dundee, Oregon 97115

Vineyard: 30 acres

Production: 100–150,000 bottles

Quality: 🍇🍇–🍇🍇🍇🍇   Price: ★★–★★★

Dick Erath, one of the pioneers of Oregon viticulture, arrived in 1967, a year after David Lett. An electronics engineer by training, Erath has pioneered a number of wine-making methods – including the now-standard method of macerating the grape skins in the wine for a week or more after the end of fermentation. Erath first did this in 1976. 'I backed into it,' he explains, 'because it was handier to get the wine through its malolactic fermentation before it went into barrel.' In 1977 he went to Burgundy. 'I'd read about hot fermentation but I didn't realize how hot it was till I went.' He abandoned the small cherry boxes which were then standard in Oregon and took to fermenting his Pinot Noir in large stainless-steel tanks. These got the temperature up another 4–5°C and extracted more colour and tannin as a result.

Erath makes four levels of wine – Dundee-Villages, Vintage, Vintage Select and (in top vintages) a Reserve bottling – and at each level his Pinot Noir offers outstanding value for money. The Vintage Select can be very good but it is sometimes spoilt by a pronounced bitter cherry-stone character. The 1987 Reserve was made with fruit from Leland Vineyard, away from the main vine-growing area on the east side of the Willamette Valley. When I tasted it in 1990 it exploded in my mouth. It is a truly great wine.

LANGE WINERY

18380 N.E. Buena Vista Road, Dundee, Oregon 97115

Production: 8,500 bottles

Quality: 🍇🍇–🍇🍇🍇   Price: ★★★

Don Lange came to Oregon from California in 1987 in order to make Pinot Noir. He chose Oregon because, after tasting wines from all over the West Coast, he found that the style of Pinot Noir he wanted to make came from Oregon. What appealed to him was the elegant style developed by David Lett at the Eyrie Vineyards. He does not approve of the general run of Oregon Pinot Noirs, however. 'Why are we looking to make immensely tannic wines here in Oregon? It's senseless. It contradicts all that David Lett has been doing for the last twenty years.'

Lange makes a lean Pinot Noir, which tastes of bitter cherries. It is so light, he says, that many people cannot taste it.

PANTHER CREEK CELLARS

1501 E. 14th Street, McMinnville, Oregon 97128

Production: 20,000 bottles

Quality: 🍇🍇🍇   Price: ★★★

Compared with most Oregon wine-makers, Ken Wright is very sure of himself. He started Panther Creek in 1986 after working in the restaurant trade in the Great Lakes and in wineries in California. 'I spent years experimenting in California,' he explains. 'I kept my mouth shut and my ears open.' He extends the fermentation to two weeks by climbing into the vats naked to disperse the hot spots where the solids have packed and where it is about 15°C warmer. As Wright points out, 'The body is the best instrument. Punching down doesn't deal with the hot spots and it shortens the fermentation.'

The resulting wine is soft, dark and extracted. It is impressive but hardly Burgundian. 'I don't care what the Burgundians do,' he says. 'The only thing that matters is attention to detail. Most wine-makers in America,' he adds, 'think only of efficiency, when their whole effort should be directed at getting better wine into the glass.'

PONZI VINEYARDS

Vandermost Road, Beaverton, Oregon 97007

Production: 35,000 bottles

Quality: 🍇🍇🍇🍇   Price: ★★★–★★★★

In the late 1960s Dick Ponzi was living in San Francisco, designing rides for Disneyland. He wanted out. 'It was,' he says, 'a period of unrest in the United States. People were looking for alternatives. They wanted to go back to the land.' In 1969 he emigrated to Oregon. He was the fourth of the pioneers after David Lett, Chuck Coury and Dick Erath. He chose a site in the Tualatin Valley, to the north of the others: it was nearer Portland, so he thought he could enjoy a better lifestyle.

The site was a relatively warm one. In his early years, however, Ponzi enjoyed a reputation for making wines that were tightly structured and relatively closed in their youth. He changed his style after the 1983 vintage. 'I tasted burgundies and found that they were more approachable,' he explains. 'I recognized that people wanted more accessible wines. The beauty of Pinot Noir – which people have not discovered – is that you can drink it young.'

His 1987 and 1988 Reserve Pinot Noirs are truly wonderful wines, with intense, soft crushed fruit. By 1990 they were already perfect to drink. His ordinary Pinot Noir takes longer to develop. Ponzi makes not only great wine but great beer at the Bridgeport brewery in Portland.

REX HILL VINEYARDS

30835 N. Highway 99W, Newberg, Oregon 97132

Production: 80,000 bottles

Quality: 🍇-🍇🍇🍇   Price: ★★★–★★★★

This winery enjoys a good, but until recently unjustified, reputation. It was set up in 1983 by Paul Hart, an insurance actuary in Portland. The first five vintages were made by David Wirtz from bought-in grapes. The 1983 from the Maresh vineyard caused a shock because of its release price of $20. This, like all of Wirtz's wines I have tasted, suffers from excessive tannins – which may or may not be blamed on his use of the over-efficient Zambelli destemmer-crusher, which grinds up the pips.

In 1988 Wirtz was replaced by Lynn Penner-Ash, who had worked for ten years in the Napa Valley, mostly at Domaine Chandon and Stag's Leap. She had no experience of making Pinot Noir. But, she points out, 'If you understand wine you can work with any variety.' Penner-Ash has turned the estate around. She is producing wines which are clean, balanced and in the context of Oregon wine-making, very Californian.

SOKOL BLOSSER WINERY

5000 Sokol Blosser Lane, Dundee, Oregon 97115

Vineyard: 40 acres

Production: 80,000 bottles

Quality: 🍇🍇   Price: ★★★

Bill and Susan Blosser emigrated from California to Oregon in 1970. 'It was,' they say, 'an intuitive decision – a crazy pioneering spirit.' Until 1987 they employed a wine-maker, Bob McRitchie. McRitchie's greatest success came when not one but two of his 1983 Pinot Noirs (Sokol Blosser and Yamhill Valley Vineyards, which he had made on contract) came top in a tasting of Pinot Noirs from Oregon and Burgundy in New York in 1985. Since 1987 Bill Blosser has made the wines himself. His Pinot Noirs have plenty of fruit but not the right balance, and they lack elegance. In 1990 he admitted, 'I still don't know how to make Pinot Noir.'

VERITAS VINEYARD

31190 N.E. Veritas Lane, Newberg, Oregon 97132

Production: 40,000 bottles

Quality: 🍇🍇   Price: ★★★

Veritas was started in 1983 as a retirement project by John Howieson, a doctor. He explained that after thirty years of treating pain he wanted to be associated with a source of pleasure. The wines enjoy a good reputation. They have quite nice fruit but are spoilt by harsh tannins.

YAMHILL VALLEY VINEYARDS

16250 Oldsville Road, McMinnville, Oregon 97128
Vineyard: 62 acres
Production: 35,000 bottles
Quality: 🍇🍇🍇   Price: ★★★

Yamhill Valley shot to fame when the 1983 Pinot Noir came top in an Oregon-versus-Burgundy tasting held at the International Wine Center in New York in 1985. This wine had actually been made by Bob McRitchie, the wine-maker at Sokol Blosser. Yamhill's own vines had only just been planted.

In 1990 I found the famous 1983 and also the 1985 and 1987 to be tough, earthy and tannic. The wines have changed significantly for the better with the 1988 vintage, the first to be made entirely with Yamhill's own fruit. They got rid of their old, over-efficient Zambelli destemmer-crusher and as a result they can macerate the skins in the juice for much longer yet end up with wines that seem to have much lower levels of tannin. The wines now taste more of fruit and are much more enjoyable. 'We no longer go for tannin and extract,' says David Rice, the marketing manager. 'We have modelled our style on Saintsbury in California.'

Washington State

The climate of Washington's principal vine-growing area, the Yakima Valley, is too extreme for the successful cultivation of Pinot Noir. The Staton Hills winery does bottle a decent Pinot Noir, but it buys the wine from Foris in Oregon. Salishan* is politically in Washington but geographically in Oregon, at the top of the Willamette Valley.

SALISHAN VINEYARD

Route 2, La Center, Washington 98629

Vineyard: 5 acres

Production: 5–10,000 bottles

Quality: 🍇🍇🍇   Price: ★★–★★★

Salishan is situated in the Willamette Valley, the main vine-growing region of Oregon, but it is just over the border in Washington.

Lincoln Wolverton, a consultant economist, compared the temperatures of Oregon and Burgundy and concluded that Oregon was much warmer, with summer daytime temperatures 3–4°C higher. So, in 1971, he established a vineyard at the northern, cooler end of the Willamette Valley, where the charts showed that the climate was much closer to that of Burgundy.

The wine is made by Lincoln's wife Joan, a former journalist. Because of the cooler climate, it is lighter than Oregon Pinot Noirs. It is elegant, smoky and good value for money.

BIBLIOGRAPHY

Burton Anderson, *The Wine Atlas of Italy*, Mitchell Beazley, 1990

Bob Campbell, *New Zealand Wine*, Cuisine Publications (annual)

Clive Coates, *The Wines of France*, Century, 1990

Rolande Gadille, *Le Vignoble de la Côte bourguignonne*, Les Belles Lettres, 1967

Rosemary George, *The Wines of Chablis and the Yonne*, Sotheby's, 1984

French Country Wines, Faber & Faber, 1990

James Halliday, *Australian Wine Compendium*, Angus & Robertson, 1985

Australian Wine Guide, Angus & Robertson (annual)

Anthony Hanson, *Burgundy*, Faber & Faber, 1982

Matt Kramer, *Making Sense of Burgundy*, William Morrow, 1990

Robert M. Parker Jnr, *Burgundy*, Simon & Schuster, 1990

The Vine, Clive Coates M.W., Lamerton House, 27 High St, Ealing, London W5 5DF, England

Wine, Evro Publishing, 60 Waldegrave Road, Teddington, Middlesex TW11 8LG, England

The Wine Advocate, Robert M. Parker Jnr, P.O. Box 311, Monkton, Maryland 21111, United States of America

The Wine Spectator, M. Shanken Communications, 387 Park Avenue South, New York, New York 10016, United States of America

Wine & Spirit, Evro Publishing

GLOSSARY

APPELLATION
CONTRÔLÉE

French laws controlling the origin and style of wines.

BARRIQUE

The term used variously to describe the Bordeaux cask of 225 litres and the Burgundy cask (also called a *pièce*) of 228 litres.

CHAMPAGNE
METHOD
(MÉTHODE
CHAMPENOISE)

The method of making sparkling wines that is used (but was not necessarily invented) by the Champenois. The second fermentation, which produces the bubbles, occurs in the bottle in which the wine will eventually be sold. Sometimes described as 'bottle fermentation'.

CHAPTALIZATION

The addition of sugar to the grape juice before (or during) fermentation in order to increase the alcohol content of the finished wine.

GOÛT DE
TERROIR

The 'taste of the soil' (but see TERROIR, below). Often used by Burgundians in order to try and explain away off-flavours in their wines.

GRAND CRU

One of the best-situated twenty-five red-wine vineyards in Burgundy.

INAO

The Institut National des Appellations d'Origine: the body that administrates *appellation contrôlée* laws.

MACÉRATION
CARBONIQUE

The intercellular fermentation of unbroken grapes. This method has been popularized by wine-makers in the Beaujolais.

MALOLACTIC
FERMENTATION

A second fermentation, occurring either during or (more often) after the alcoholic one, in which harsh malic acid is transformed by the action of bacteria into softer lactic acid. Not to be confused with the secondary fermentation which puts the bubbles into sparkling wines (for which see CHAMPAGNE METHOD).

OENOLOGIST

A wine scientist. Someone who understands the technology of wine-making but does not necessarily know how to make wines taste good.

PINOTTER

To taste of Pinot Noir but nothing more: a pleasant, simple wine.

PREMIER CRU

In Burgundy, the next rank down after *grand cru*.

SAIGNÉE

The 'bleeding' (drawing off) of juice before fermentation in order to concentrate what remains.

TAFELWEIN
(GERMANY)

see VIN DE TABLE (FRANCE)

TERROIR

Literally 'soil', but intended by French vine-growers to apply to all the elements affecting the growing conditions in a particular vineyard: not so much the soil as the 'life of the soil'.

TERROIRISTE

Someone who believes that soil has more effect on the taste of a wine than does the climate or the way in which a wine is made. Nearly all Frenchmen are TERROIRISTES but very few Americans or Australasians are.

VDQS

The category of French wines between *appellation contrôlée* and *vin de table*.

VIEILLES VIGNES

Old vines. There is no legal definition of when a vine is old but it is unlikely to be less than twenty or thirty years of age.

VIN DE TABLE (FRANCE)

The most lowly category of wine; simply 'table wine'.

VINO DA TAVOLA (ITALY)

see VIN DE TABLE (FRANCE)

VINS DE GARDE

Wines made with the intention that they should be allowed to mature in bottle, not drunk young.

VOLATILE ACIDITY

Acetic acid. If present in small quantities, it can enhance a wine's bouquet; in large quantities it turns wine into vinegar.

INDEX